TRAPPED BY A DREAM

WHEN FATES COLLIDE

TRAPPED BY A DREAM

WHEN FATES COLLIDE

A true account taken
from the journals of Boots Butler

As written by
Leola Butler

CITI OF
BOOKS

CITIOFBOOKS, INC.
3736 Eubank NE Suite A1
Albuquerque, NM 87111-3579
www.citiofbooks.com
Hotline: 1 (877) 389-2759
Fax: 1 (505) 930-7244

Ordering Information:

Quantity sales. Special discounts are available on quantity purchases by corporations, associations, and others. For details, contact the publisher at the address above.

Printed in the United States of America.

ISBN-13:   Softcover   979-8-89391-567-9

                  eBook   979-8-89391-569-3

                  Hardback   979-8-89391-568-6

Library of Congress Control Number: _____

Contents

FOREWORD

When Boots originally wrote his journal entries it was not so the stories that were within the pages would be published, or for them to even be read by anyone else, other than possibly his family members. Keeping a journal has been something he has done since he was just a boy. The details which are written in them are not only factual, but intense.

During the many years that I have been married to this man, he has explained to me how writing down his memoirs has given him a vehicle to review certain times and life events. Especially the monumental experiences, which have not been lacking in his life. Beyond the years he spent in military and government service, Boots has dedicated his life to helping those who are unable to help themselves. His journals are filled with documentation of heinous crimes, and heroic acts.

Some of Boots greatest success stories have been while he worked under Somewhere Out There, a non-profit organization that specializes in the recovery of missing, kidnapped, and exploited children. No one who works for this organization receives any pay, but pay is unnecessary for the dedicated men and women who are involved in these recovery missions. They are like Boots. It is not a job, but a labor of love. The object is to make a positive difference in the life of a child through their recovery, and sometimes, final closure for the family. Many child recoveries have been performed not only in the United States, but also around the world. This case, brought to you in this book, was registered with Somewhere Out There, and Boots was head investigator and team leader.

This story is from one of the unique accounts in Boots' journals. It involves the collective abilities of Boots working with an extraordinary group of comrades in arms to extract a prisoner. They do this with complete selflessness and courage, and once engaged they will not quit. Their motto is "failure is not an option." These are the words they live by, and would die by if need be.

There are those who might scoff at the heroic measures that Boots has gone to in saving just one child, but he counts them one soul at a time. More importantly, what he does, he does not do to gain a place in history, but for a high ideal. Quite simply, to help those who are unable to help themselves. His actions are the direct result of not tolerating those unable to follow decent rules of conduct. One of the things he does not tolerate is those who would enslave others, and believes that any means necessary should be used to stop them.

Many names have been changed in chronicling this experience. Particularly the names of the children, because those are the ones that we are bound by law, honor, and duty to protect. The desire in telling this story by me is an attempt to show the goodness of men, rather than just the evil deeds they are capable of. That there are still those who will do battle for the innocent, no matter what the cost. They give the world hope, and as long as there is life there is hope, and hope can prevail.

CHAPTER ONE

It was February 17, 1997. That was the day I received a very important but disturbing phone call. It was from a young woman quite unknown to me, but she would not remain so. Her name was Daria. She explained that she was my friend, Nadia's cousin. She sounded of Russian descent. I had already discovered Nadia's ancestral background was Russian. This young woman either still had a Russian accent, or she lived in a household, and probably a close-knit community of Russian speaking peoples. It was definitely with a Russian accent that she spoke with me. It was 20:15 hours when the phone rang. This phone call was a plea for help.

I was in my new office which had been constructed in my absence in the fall of 1996 by my wife Lee, my son Marshall, daughter Monique and her husband Nathaniel, and grand-daughter Marina. They had built this office onto our large country cabin, situated in Republic, Washington. It was located on our twenty-five acre property. Our sanctuary in the hills. These types of calls were not unusual, rather they were commonplace.

My wife had answered the phone, and was listening to this young lady as she explained she presently lived in Brighton Beach, New York City on the East Coast. She attempted to explain her problem somewhat to my wife, my very own Russian lady with fiery red hair, along with a temper to match, and a love for me that I am sure I don't rate or deserve. What else can be said about the one and only woman in this world I could love? She began to explain to this young woman that I was sitting right here in the office, and that she should be, in fact, explaining all of this to me.

Lee handed me the phone saying, "Honey, this young woman needs your help. Would you please talk to her, okay?"

I reached for the telephone, and in turn my wife reached over to hand it to me. Leaning, she brushed her lips lightly against my cheek. I believe that Russian girls are trained in schools about this kissing cheeks thing. That, and holding onto an arm. It is very pleasant and much appreciated, along with very old-fashioned. This is quite an enjoyable experience.

I said hello and all I heard was a female voice that sounded almost frantic.

"Hello? Hello? You don't know me."

I had to think that this was an understatement!

Again she spoke, "Hello, my name is Daria and I hope you will help me."

I had no idea what she needed help with and as I began to ask, she cut in again saying, "Please help me."

I had to tell her, "Miss, if you will try to explain why you need my help then I could decide if I can, or if I know someone who could help you."

There was that sound in her voice again! "No! I was told you would, or could help."

So I started slowly once more, "Okay, what's the problem?"

At this she retorted with, "I am supposed to ask how much you will charge?"

Not knowing even what she was speaking of, all I could say was, "Well, I don't know. I cannot tell you unless you could possibly tell me what it is that you require of me." I tried to say this in my most tolerant and patient voice.

She said, "Well, I called one man. He told me he would charge four-hundred-fifty-thousand dollars to try to get her, but he didn't. And wouldn't say he would get, only to try, and I call another. They say we crazy and not to try by them. They could not help Daria."

I answered her saying, "Daria."

She said, "Yes."

I continued one more time, "Would you please tell me how I can help you? What service is it that I perform that could possibly help you?" I hoped I would finally get the story.

"My cousin is in Holland working for a very bad man. He has her passport and he tell her if she want it back, she have to work one year for him. He also paid her room and board so she must work longer."

Fearing a labor dispute, I had to wonder how any of this either concerned me, or what I could do about it. I asked, "How much longer does she have to work in order to get her passport and papers back?"

Daria answered, "She has now worked for fifteen months, and he will not return her papers."

I was stunned. I had to wonder if I was hearing things. I had just heard a definite one-hundred-eighty degree turn in the way she spoke and was constructing her sentences. Even her accent was less pronounced! It was an extremely strange thing to have happen in a conversation, but no one, not even if you were deaf and dumb, could not recognize the unmistakable sound of desperation on one hand, and the abject terror in her voice on the other. I was concerned, at the very least. I didn't question the change in her speech, rather I was quite desperate for information. Her fear was palpable. To the point that her voice was cracking and she was choking back the tears.

Slowly, I began to speak. "Daria, slow down. Darlin', please take a deep breath. Calm yourself and try to think. I need you to tell me just exactly what has happened to your cousin."

She answered questioningly, "You mean Svetlana?"

I spoke slowly, "Yes darlin'. Start at the beginning. Please. Slowly and step-by-step. Daria, do this for Svetlana, and me and you."

I could hear panic in her voice, "Oh! You know her name! Who has called you?"

I started to get a little irritated, "Daria, stop. Stop it now! No one has called me but you. It was you yourself who mentioned her name to me. Do you understand that you told me? No one else. Please slow down, Daria. I need to know exactly what is wrong."

Daria almost whispered back, "I do not want to reveal any information on the telephone."

I thought, "Well, this is curious." I had to wonder what was so secretive. What possibly could make this information so sensitive that it could not be spoken of on the telephone? "Why not?" I asked.

She answered quite quickly, "Someone, anyone could be listening to this phone call."

I was getting a little tired of this run around. How could anyone be expected to help if no one would reveal any specific information? It's just not possible. "Daria, this is not the USSR and there aren't any secret police who would even find this conversation worth the time it takes to listen to it!"

She was adamant, "Well, I need to talk to you in person without anyone else around and without the chance of being overheard."

With a sigh of resignation I replied, "Okay. Where are you again?"

Her voice seemed to lift, "I'm in New York City."

I had at least one more question for this young lady. "Who gave you my telephone number, if I might at least ask that question?"

Daria answered lightly, "My cousin Nadia gave me your phone number, and she told my uncle and me that you were one of the best. That you could do anything."

A young Russian woman popped into my head, and I remembered one of my good friends. Richard. Nadia was his girlfriend who had begun business as a bail bondsman and had an incredibly rough time doing it because of its gender-based makeup. She was trying to break into a largely male profession. Her company had posted a one half million dollar bond on a drug dealer, who had no intention of remaining in the area. He had been arrested and was to stand trial. He then conveniently skipped a bail appearance.

This left my buddy Richie's girlfriend to face the judge, and to absorb a loss of great magnitude. Nadia had tried to find a hunter to track this scandalous son of a bitch who had run with her money, and left her business on the brink of devastation. At least, that was until Richie had contacted me to see if I could help.

Knowing Richard for most of my life, I wouldn't turn him down when he asked. He went on to explain Nadia's problem and her pride at being independent, so much so, that she wouldn't beg anyone to help her. As I thought about this, I told Richard to be in her office at 10:00 hours and I would take care of this prideful girlfriend's problem. She was who my buddy loved, and planned to marry very soon.

I walked into Nadia's office. I was in all-black clothes with my black cowboy boots with bells, a black campaign hat, dark sunglasses, and a titanium three-fifty-seven magnum in my shoulder holster. With each step you could hear the distinct "ching, ching" of the bells. It was one of my trademarks.

She was a little shocked when I looked at her and said, "Miss, is the bondsmen in? I'm looking for work." She looked at me and then got up. She walked around me and asked if I had any experience.

"Yes ma'am," I said, "I have worked for Walker Bail Bonding. It's a bonding company out of Los Angeles, California, along with offices in every major city in America."

I gave her the telephone number to check my references. When she realized these telephone numbers were for the owner of Walker's Bail, and they were his home phone number, which is private, and his private car phone number, she didn't have too many more questions. She said I was hired for the job. I did it at one-half of what I'm normally paid for such services. As a footnote, Nadia received her bail money back and I gave them the job for free, as I believe it is customary for the best man at a wedding to give the bride and groom a wedding present. I thought twenty-five-thousand dollars was adequate.

After the mention of the name Nadia, with many fond memories old and new, I began to get a feel for how bad this problem of Daria's must be, and indeed, how desperate her cousin Svetlana had to be. She must really be in a very bad situation. It must be extreme. At least bad, with a four-fifty big boy bid and a flat go away as well. We would have to see. I thought, "Well, this seems to happen a lot to you and the clan," as I fondly called them. In fact, it happened quite often.

"Daria, could you explain to me how you're going to tell me anything that I need to know without my getting on an airplane and flying to New York City to meet you for a day?"

She replied, "Well, it has already been taken care of. I did it at home this morning, right down the street from my house, okay? Couldn't you tell me about how much this will cost or at least give me a hint?"

I could only answer, "Sorry darlin', I couldn't even begin to guess at a cost until I get the information I need. When I've got something figured out, and I'm not sure how I'm going to do that, but then, we will talk Daria. When I do figure this out.

Okay?"

She answered, "Okay, Boots."

Ahhh! Nadia gave her my operational name. It is the name that only my friends use when talking to me. The name when I am with my comrades, the clan, I'm addressed as Boots. It seems Nadia wants me to take this case for her cousin Daria, although it must make Svetlana, Nadia's cousin, or sister, or something! I would consider what to do and say, but I knew Daría definitely wished for me to think of her as a friend and not just a client. Well, so be it! Let's see what Daria gets to me in the way of information. It would only be then that I could make a reasonable decision. So, we will both have to be patient.

"As soon as I see what has been sent Daria, I will call you. Is that in keeping with what you want?"

She agreed with me, "Yes Boots, it's perfect. I will be awaiting your telephone call."

And with that, I said, "Goodbye Daria." "Goodbye Boots," she answered.

As the phone went dead and there was no sound, I had a strange feeling. I just couldn't help but feel a real sense of excitement at the sudden prospect of another rescue mission. Of all the things I do, the most fulfilling is rescue missions and especially rescuing children. It is contrary as well as idealistic. I admit that. However, in my mind, I had already decided to accept this job for many of my own reasons.

I hung up the now dead telephone and my wife turned to look at me. With a slight smile in her voice, she spoke, "When are you leaving babe?"

I turned and looked back at her saying, "Not until I find out some particulars, love. At least, if it's all right with you. I think I would like to do this."

A look of real concern came over her face as she was saying, "It's fine, Boots. I can feel it too. She needs your help, and no one else's. After all, Nadia gave her your name, because she is right. Nadia, I mean. You can do anything. I've watched you do it, but more importantly, Nadia's cousin needs your help and from the sounds of the situation, or maybe it was her voice, she needs your help desperately, babe. But please try to do it without getting dead."

I had to laugh at that! "Okay, I'll do my best, beauty, believe me, and if I can't I will be the first one to admit I can't."

Lee laughed back, "Oh yeah! You bet! That'll be the day! A fine day when my husband Boots doesn't take risks with his life to save someone! Boots, I'm not a stranger. I've heard the clan talk about you."

I had to turn away. "Well, they exaggerate an awful lot."

Lee knew better. "No they don't, and I'm proud Boots. Damn proud. I wouldn't want it any other way."

I had to tell her thank you, but we both had to laugh at the thought that I wouldn't go.

In truth, I was already working on ideas for getting to Holland and the fact that if I was successful at rescuing Svetlana and her papers from this man, whoever he was, would that be the hardest part, or would it grow progressively harder? It could start out hard and get easier. However, I doubted this. If it followed true to form for me, it would be hard from the startup to the finish.

As the days passed, I became frustrated at not having the information I so desperately needed. Intel. How could I even think about evolutions. Information becomes imperative. I needed Daria's information now. I contemplated a phone call addressing this to Daria. However, I decided it would be unadvisable due to how she felt about phone lines and transmitted information being overheard.

With knowledge comes power. The power to plan. To overcome. To accomplish anything, and if nothing else, I had already figured out that for some reason this job would just take more knowledge. I was almost positive that it would take an extraordinary amount of all things, including knowledge and bravado. At least everything I had done in this field up to date had taken just that, knowledge and bravado. God help us all!

Three days had expired and the fourth was beginning, when I finally received a phone call from my friend, Nadia. She explained to me that Daria had sent the information package to Richie's office, just in case someone tried to intercept it. I had to wonder what was so important that it was necessary to hide information like that. I decided not to express my opinion on the subject. At least not now. When she asked me when I was coming over, I replied, "If I can pack and clear it with Lee, I will leave around 12:00 hours and I should easily arrive at your

house by 19:00 hours. Is that okay?"

Nadia just said, "You bet, babe."

Because of the kind of friends we are, I just told her, "Cool, sweetheart. I will be there as soon as possible. Kiss Richie for you, but hug him for me, okay?"

I heard her light laugh and then she said, "Okay boots, bye-bye."

It was a short time later, while I was talking to my wife and busy gathering my gear, when I said, "It's that time, babe." Lee walked towards me, and by just looking at her, I could tell she knew I had to find out what this story was all about, and would be leaving soon. She asked me if I knew how long I would be gone. Not even knowing exactly what I was getting into I had to say, "I have no clear timeline on this one. If I engage, or decide to, I will call, honey."

With that she laughed, and said with a sweet voice and a glint in her eye, "I would like that! You know it's nice to keep a girl informed!"

I answered with, "Are you sure it's okay? I could get one of the clan to do this, you know."

She put her arms around my neck, smiled, and came back with, "I would love for you to do that, but I know you. I don't think you could live with yourself if you didn't do this, if you could. I married you knowing this, Boots, and I would never ask you not to go on something like this. I just couldn't do that, and I won't. I love you just as you are, and for what you are. Go and get this girl and when you're done, come home to me." Lee held my face with her hands and kissed me gently.

I smiled and told her, "I will babe, at least I will if I can."

As we talked, I explained where I was going and why. She said that she would call Nadia and make all the arrangements.

As I packed, she came in and folded one of my shirts, then stopped and told me, "I love you, babe." Lee looked into my eyes, and I into hers, and we kissed. Lee looked up again and said, "I'll be here when you get done and get back, or on the other side, babe."

I just had to kiss this wonderful woman who was my wife at least one more time. I told her that I loved her and would see her on the flipside. It was a saying I had used to date in government service. It means if for some reason I don't come home, I would see her on the other side when she got there. The next life. To hear this goodbye was something she had grown accustomed to over the long years of comings and goings, along with my long periods away from home. It has never made her happy, but this is a real world with real world problems and in the end, anything could happen. We all hope that it won't happen, but bad things can happen to anyone. It's just a fact of life, and you can choose to live with it, or you can lie to yourself and others.

As I loaded my gear into my car, I turned to survey my "other" life. It was like taking a picture of my wife and family. My loved ones and the house and home I shared with them, one and all. I knew from experience it would be filed away to be brought out when I needed cheering, or inspiration when things got tough.

I drove out of this world of mine and I began to wonder why I went on these operations. With everything I loved and valued far behind me, but deep down in my soul I knew I couldn't turn my back on people who were in trouble and needed help. It wasn't just a habit, it was a way of life that had started long ago before I joined the Marines. The need to help. The desire to be there to defend, or give a hand up to someone who did not stand a chance to win against a bully. Or the disaster. I knew I would be engaged in this work until I went to the other side. It was a calling and it was something I could do and was proficient at. This business that authorities and countries don't always agree about which is the correct and the right course of action, or what should be done. That's why I go. I'm the conscience.

CHAPTER TWO

The trip out of my paradise was beautiful, but it paradoxically was tiring. I grew closer to my objective, Nadia's house, and the tiredness I felt ebbed and waned, then left for a while. It was exhilarating to say the least to be able to visit with my very good friends. Richie and Nadia were true friends of mine. If I needed it, and they had it, whatever it was, or if they could acquire it, it would be mine for the asking. This was a two way street. What I could get or do was indeed theirs.

I pulled into their driveway. From the doorway I saw running towards me, a small, and elfin like figure. It was my Nadia. She was not a large woman. She was all of five feet tall in heels, slender build, and had an hourglass figure. But this in truth was of little consequence to me. What she had in her that I will always need is acceptance and a solid love. Her hair was black as coal and would have drug the ground if it was not put up. Her eyes were honey brown. She was a truly beautiful woman. I have a picture of the both of us. A good close-up of her in her wedding dress with Richie along side, and me in my best man monkey suit.

Richie and I had been friends since Catholic military school. He was quite tall and measured in at six feet, six inches. With his shock of strawberry-blond hair and his blue eyes, and his well muscled and tanned body, he looked somewhat like one of those male-models. Some might say of these two, Mutt and Jeff? But, no, they were a very strikingly attractive couple. But, above all else, Richie was a friend willing to go out on a limb if necessary.

I exited the car while Nadia bounced across four feet of earth and jumped into my arms. She kissed me on the cheek and squealed, "Boots! I'm so glad to see you!"

It was a joy to be here and not alone, at least not just yet. As soon as we went into the house, it was intensely apparent that she had decided to cook. I was inundated with the aromas of fresh, simmering herbs and vegetables, roasting meat, and succulent sauces. Old world smells of my home. And to think Richie told me he didn't think she could cook! Well, she had either learned, or he was mistaken.

Dinner progressed to its conclusion, and afterwards it was clean up time and then into the den. There we could talk and laugh about old times, have a few beers, and laugh some more. Of course, there were the inevitable conflict stories. Some good and some bad, but it was necessary to round out a full day for me. I had no intention of even glancing at Daria's papers until tomorrow. First, I needed a good night's sleep.

I awoke and staggered haggardly into the bathroom to shower and shave. There was a knock on the door. Here was Richie's hand, stuffing a large cup of coffee through the crack in the door. This was a sorely needed wake me up tool! I began to come alive.

I entered the large kitchen with a breakfast bar. "Ahh, yes." It was my favorite place to sit! After more coffee and Danish, it was time. "Nadia, where are the papers that Daria sent for me?" Nadia let me know they were in the study and I told her, "When you're ready, let's go have a look-see at what's in the packet."

She answered, "Boots, I have a quick errand to run. It'll take about an hour. Can we do it when I get back? Is that okay?"

I needed to unpack and I knew once the packet was opened it would take precedent over everything else. I said, "I'll wait for you to get home, kid."

She left and I headed for the spare bedroom that I was staying in. It was a lot more like being home rather than being on the road. It is always nice to be welcomed somewhere other than the Holiday Inn!

I finished unpacking and decided to go down to the kitchen for some more coffee. I poured another cup. I had just sat down and breathed, deeply and fully. It was relaxing. It seemed like moments instead of an hour, but it went by without notice. Suddenly, there was Nadia with arms loaded full of groceries. I jumped up to help and could see on her face, she was relieved. They were heavy and almost bigger than her. I grabbed at the bags and she started to laugh. Of course, I had to follow suit. She had broken the eggs and they were running all over. It was just one of those things. After, getting control of ourselves, and the eggs, it was on to the study.

"Okay, Boots, here it is." Nadia handed me the brown manila envelope.

I sat in the large easy chair and began to read. After a few pages I knew it was my very worst fear. A white slavery gang. I contemplated action against one of my most hated enemies. There was almost a feeling of excitement, but in reality it was a feeling of dread and foreboding. I continued to read and I found myself getting angry, then beyond that into furious. Here was one more assault on humanity, one more time.

This young woman, Svetlana, was not the first to be in this predicament. This type of slavery is far more prevalent than most of America wants to hear about, let alone admit to its existence in this country, and throughout the world. Unfortunately, it is extremely wide spread around our world. It seems every so called "civilized nation" desperately tries to deny its existence, going so far as to turn a blind eye to this crime. They just want to pretend it doesn't happen. Those of us who have witnessed this crime, and have seen its dehumanizing cruelty and brutal applications, can never again reject its factuality. It is real, and it is here to stay unless we stamp it out by any means necessary.

White slavery is a despicable crime that affects hundreds of thousands of victims per year. Victims as young as two years of age, to the ripe old age of twenty-five, or maybe even thirty years old. Most are used as sex toys, or as slaves. When the tormenters are done with these poor creatures, they somehow wind up very dead. Often overdosed on powerful drugs and left to die. When they represent no further monetary value or when they reach an age that they no longer represent "mysterious youth." At that point they are disposed of. This crime is not only part of a female victimization world, but victimizes the male world as well. Young boys are also a prime target. As far as procurement goes? Well, as long as people continue to have children there will always be targets of opportunity for the lowest forms of life who would prey on them. Parents who do not watch their children, or are complacent to their children's whereabouts, all too often end up calling people like me and the clan. Men and women, who not unlike myself, try to rectify this disgusting situation and retrieve their loved ones. Svetlana was a victim of a scheme to ensnare young women and trap them into this terrifying way of life, and death.

When the Soviet Socialist Republics disintegrated there was little thought given to the ramifications. Not only in their fledgling governments, but they had little, or no idea as to the power of organized crime. To date, the most powerful force had been the government.

When it collapsed, a vacuum in authority was created allowing the Russian mafia, one of the most violent and powerful crime syndicates in the history of man, to come into power. If you don't agree with what they are doing, or to what they want, there are no questions. There, remorseless killers do their job. They eliminate anyone with dissension to their authority or power.

They run the governments in the old Soviet bloc countries, for the most part, and crime is a job. It is like being a cop, but with no compunction to help anyone but themselves. The Russian mafia is made up of the worst and most bloodthirsty criminals, and ex-military personnel. Even a majority of KGB and some of the old police forces belong to this group!

There are only a few who are willing to try to stop these heinous people, and I'm one of them. I take it to their level, and let the chips fall where they may. Open opposition is the only course of action. No other enforcement unit in the world should have the privilege to act as if these criminals have rights. What they do is not exercising rights, but violent despicable criminal acts. It does not slow down, at least until a group like mine goes into action. We will oppose these criminals where they live. We have no real concern that they may have rights as victims. They are the victimizers, and will continue to offend until they are defeated.

Svetlana was from a small village in the Ukraine. There were not any good paying jobs to be had for a seventeen-year-old girl. Especially for a young lady with dreams of independence and wealth. She wanted to finally have the ability to acquire nice things, but most of all was her desire to help her mother. They had a dream to follow the rest of their family to the golden shores of America. Pride did not allow for her asking for favors of money to accomplish this. Rather, Svetlana had seen a light at the end of the tunnel, and the opportunity to earn more money in a year than she thought she could earn in a lifetime.

She was planning to get a job as either a nanny, or as a trusted member of a family as a governess. Hopefully, to the children of a rich and influential family in a foreign country. It was her dream to travel to either England, or even France for this type of work. Svetlana had done her research well and was extremely confident and excited. She knew that if she could receive an appointment she would then be in a position to do the things that people who have little or nothing and only live to survive, can never do. She knew in her own heart, she was on her way.

It had been two weeks since Svetlana had decided the right course for her life. It would be a dream come true to be able to send enough money home to her widowed mother in order to begin the process through the myriad of papers and payoffs to get her mother to America. There, she would live with what was left of her family. All she could think of was then following her mother in one year, or even two years. She would still be young, and have a fair amount of money. She would then go into business with her mother.

As Svetlana proceeded to the employment agency that had advertised for applicants for just the job she wanted, she was extremely excited. She looked at the building. There was the sign. Executive Placement Services. "Wow," she thought, "it's not a dream." If she had only known the truth, I would have never met this truly magnificent young woman, but these people played a cruel joke on her dreams.

She approached the front door, opening it slowly and taking in the view of the entire inside. Everyone there was in expensive clothes and looked very professional. She just knew this was a good company. She went in and was approached by a young woman not much older than she. Svetlana explained how she had chosen this company, and she was assured that she would receive the highest recommendation that the interviewer could give, but there were many papers for her to fill out. There were so many official documents, that Svetlana could no longer keep track of all the papers she had signed. There were papers for her passport, so she could travel to the country she would be employed in. She would need contracts to Executive Employment Services. There were visa papers, and of course, there were the inevitable health records that would be needed. Her file was growing to one-hundred-twenty pages. She couldn't believe what was involved. Then it was time for her to have her physical. Of course, being a healthy young woman would be of paramount concern to the wealthy people who she would eventually be working for. She knew that of course there would be very close personal contact with not only her employers, but the children she would have charge of.

It was growing late, and there was no way that she, or anyone else could complete this daunting task in one day. The lady who had done the first interview returned with a very large smile and told Svetlana that she was extremely qualified and could, or would it be possible for her to return tomorrow to continue the process. She wanted to know when Svetlana had planned to go to work. With the exuberance of youth, Svetlana intimated to this woman that as soon as possible would be the best. As girls of her age are very enthusiastic about most everything they could dream of.

The interviewer was pleased and confidentially told Svetlana that an opening was being created. Evidently, a girl had decided to leave her employer for a different job opportunity. Svetlana was overjoyed by this, but became more excited when this woman explained to her that the bosses had thought that Svetlana would be more than adequate to fill this position. Svetlana was beside herself with hope and happiness. She, of course, promised to return.

Almost running back to her home, she could not contain her joy and rushed in to tell her mother the good news. Patiently, her mother listened and counseled Svetlana not to get her hopes up too high, but nothing could douse the fire that burned inside of this girl. Not even her mother. It was a long night for Svetlana. The excitement only seemed to increase robbing her of sleep, but not of the enthusiasm that was overwhelming her.

Finally, morning came and she was off to return to Executive Placement Services. She could hardly contain her exuberance and was even bouncy. She approached her contact interviewer, so she could get on with the process of finishing her paperwork and application. While Svetlana was working on the papers, the office woman approached her with news of employment. The bosses had asked if Svetlana would be willing to accept employment the day after tomorrow.

They had decided to let her fill the now vacant employment position. They had made it very clear that to be so well thought of by these successful people was indeed a huge compliment. This was an opportunity not to be passed over lightly. Svetlana let them know she would be available when they wished. She was to return for her indoctrination at 17:00 hours tomorrow. Now, she was beside herself with gratitude and agreed to return as requested.

She returned home to tell her mother. There was a new pride and joy in their home that evening. I think for quite a long time there had been none in this house. They laughed together. They cried the cry of the impending separation for a long period of time. Neither one had been apart from each other since Svetlana's birth seventeen years and four months ago. It became almost unbearable, the interminable night and day, for both of them were excited. Svetlana mother's was excited because her daughter was making her dreams come true, and with Svetlana's success it would make it possible for both of their dreams to become reality.

As the time for Svetlana's indoctrination approached, they realized that in less than thirty hours they would be separated. They told each other how it would be brief, compared with the interminable morose that was their village. There was little hope here, but hope prevails in the people's hearts of this land. And, hope burned and prevailed in Svetlana.

The time arrived and Svetlana left for indoctrination. She entered the building of Executive Placement Services, but as she was to find out, she would have to have the proper immunizations. As she approached the nurse she might have felt something, an inkling maybe, but she couldn't let her mother's hopes die. Nor could she ignore her own dreams. This was the way things were done. It would be okay. The night wore on. That was the last time anyone knew of her whereabouts. Svetlana had disappeared from her homeland not to be heard from again.

It was unknown what had happened to her. For many painful months there was no word from Svetlana. No letters to her mother and none of the promised money. Fear grew in Sasha's heart. It became so powerful that Sasha, Svetlana's mother, went to Executive Placement Services. She was told they had no idea what she was talking about. They told her no such young woman had ever signed a paper with them, nor had she ever been there.

Sasha knew she was being lied to. She had followed Svetlana, and watched unnoticed where her daughter had gone and who she had spoken to. She recognized the woman as Svetlana's interviewer. The interviewer explained that this was a brand-new company, and also stated that they had not been in this area then, and no young woman matching Sasha's daughter's description had been there. Somewhat bewildered, Sasha made waves with the authorities about her daughter's disappearance. Tragically, she was making waves in a no wave country. She could do nothing else but give up.

Setting the report down, I looked up to Nadia and asked, "Have you read this information?"

Nadia had been patiently waiting while I read, "No Boots I haven't, but I do know that Svetlana's disappearance was sudden. I also know that my Uncle Gregor and Daria are handling everything."

I had to wonder to myself if she realized what this could mean. I turned to look at my friend and recognized her depth of understanding. The pain was in her deep eyes. The haunted look was there, and the tears were overflowing from these deep caring and beautiful eyes. Finally, the gut wrenching sobs were too much for me to handle. I cried and screamed in anguish. I felt the hatred I had felt all of my life from the depths of my soul. Rescue. Revenge. Death. All screamed at me.

Hours later, there in the den, I was locked in a battle with myself. The battle I fight every time in order to quench the fires of hatred, and meld it into the quest for rescue and retribution. No matter what the price. This would be done, even if I paid the ultimate price.

I sat there in total distraction with no realization of where I was, or of those friends around me who sat unwavering and waited for what might come. Although I had no memory of this happening, without my knowing it, my friend Nadia, out of concern timidly walked to my side. Her lips touched my cheek. I screamed. It was not the reaction Nadia had expected and she quickly retreated to Richie's arms for protection from a crazed man. It was very soon after that I realized where I was and a comprehension of what had just occurred. Richie reassured Nadia that I wasn't insane, but I wondered if maybe that statement had not been quite correct.

"He is making a breakthrough. I've seen this happen before. Things gripping him, involving him and he broods and worries things out until there is nothing left but him." Richie stared over in my direction, "You've decided, haven't you Boots?"

"Yes." Richie knew me well. I had indeed made the decision to find out what had happened to Svetlana, and return her.

Nadia broke her silence, "Then you're going, aren't you Boots?"

I answered with determination. "Of course I am. I have no choice. It's what I do. It's what drives me." My soul would not allow for any other answer to be possible.

I returned to my black world, staring into the flames of the fire now burning brightly in the fireplace. A fire that should be warm and inviting. Instead, I saw only ice and coldness. Alone in myself, I saw the truth of it. That I was never designed to be a prisoner. No human would remain so as long as I drew a breath of air, or had blood pumping through the veins that were mine. It is not acceptable to me in any form. I would rather be dead, and if that's what it would take to free this girl from her prison, it was a price that I would be willing to pay.

I once again returned to this world, from the world of my thoughts and feelings. I turned to Nadia and she came to my side. She had seen my tears. I had to think that these tears were remnants of my own torturous fight with myself.

I asked Nadia to call my wife, and then the two of them could make the arrangements for my imminent departure from my friends and family, along with the west coast. I had decided what had to be done. What must be done! I was on my way one more time to once again do what I do the best. I struggle against injustice. I struggle against oppression, and against evil people. I was brought into this world for this reason. I believe this with all of my being.

Nadia and Lee would get me booked onto the first available air transport. I was leaving for New York City. Then I would call in the clan. It was time to move, and move now. There was no longer a question. I had decided to engage. To follow this through and to plan an evolution. It should come to light here that an evolution is a practiced plan. Practiced until it becomes automatic. With unknowns planned into the course of action within the scope of the evolution. So began the quest for information to solve this problem. The problem of one mother in anguish, a family that cares, and a young woman whom naïvely had become a participant in the world's oldest trade, by way of the second oldest trade, slavery. A terrible form of ownership that not only happens to black people, but to all people who have no champions, or men to fight for them. Without clearer action to prevent the occurrence of slavery, slavery will always exist.

Nadia had decided that my car would be safer in the confines of her large garage. I must admit, I had to agree. She explained that since my departure was to be a self-styled one, carried out immediately, that Richie and she would make sure it was done.

Morning approached and I found myself single-minded and elusive. I really wasn't into any sort of conversation, but Nadia insisted. I have found that Russian women do not take no for an answer, and will persist until one acquiesces to their wishes. This knowledge was gleaned from my own personal experience. I married one. Lee is a devastatingly beautiful woman, and with her came an entire family of Russian in-laws. It was the day I consider my ultimate blessing.

Once again, I was packing gear when Nadia came over and said, "Boots, I know I don't have to tell you to be careful. I know you won't. I do have to tell you this Boots. I'm so proud of you, and I am so very thankful that you are my friend." With that she hugged me, and kissed my cheek. A very Russian thing to do. Thank God, it is a great thing to have happen!

I had nothing much to say on the way to the airport. My flight left at 05:45 hours. It was an early morning for Richie and Nadia, but not so for me. At 04:00 hours is when my eyes pop open. It's been like that for so long that I believe it started the day I was born!

After we arrived at the boarding gate for my flight, I bid farewell to my friends with handshakes and kisses on the cheek, an inevitability with Nadia, as well as my own wife. The goodbyes related and repeated were not necessary with me. I wanted to be on my way, and did not like the emotional thing, nor did I care for the delay. Of course, I would live with it just the same. I began boarding procedures and turned once again to my friends. I waved at Richie and then blew a kiss, and my love, to a little Russian girl I had befriended some years back, Nadia. I had come not only to love her, but to consider her one of my closest friends in this life.

CHAPTER THREE

I found my seat in the rear of the plane. It was a compulsion not to allow anyone behind me. This action stems from old habits, and I've never felt a need to change it. I sat down and began to think of this problem. Without the knowledge I needed to plan, or who in my band of cutthroats to call for this mission, I was pretty well stuck. I had already begun to think of this mission in a much more important manner. I had a feeling that I would be needing help as usual, and the list of the clan this year was smaller due to attrition.

It must be understood that not all missions are one-hundred percent foolproof nor are they all survivable. That's okay. To those of us who belong to this band of men who try to right the wrongs perpetrated by man, on man, there is always a cost. Sometimes, it can be either personal life or limb, and some even pay the bill with their lives. It's never pleasant to lose a member of the clan, but nothing in this life comes without cost. Sometimes, what we want can have a high price, but we persist in these endeavors. Not only for others, but for ourselves. It gives you the ability to hold your head up high and feel that you have accomplished something important. It is not necessary for anyone to know what you do, or have done, or what you will do. With the grace of God anything is possible, if you only believe.

Plane rides are plane rides. They are riding in an airborne Greyhound bus, you just don't have to ride as long! You also cover more ground, and you of course, do it much faster. The plane ride was uneventful, at least there were no huge air pockets or too big of bumps. Nonetheless, it's an eerie feeling riding six miles high, or higher in a sardine can with wings and little else but larger than normal refuelable sky rockets for power. Actually, it is quite uncanny and a pain in the butt. We approached my next destination, LaGuardia International Airport, New York City and I felt the pilots reduce thrust as we descended into the Big Apple.

I had not been to New York for over a year. It was a little anti-climatic for me. Sometimes you hear visitors bubbling over with enthusiasm. I cannot help but wonder what they will find so interesting in two-thousand-five-hundred square miles, or more of concrete bordered by more concrete. It's unnerving to me at times. That excitement for excitements sake of visiting strange places was washed out of me twenty-five years ago and over one-hundred-seventy-five cities and airports ago.

As the flaps slid out and into place, I could not help but wonder who this Daria was. I wondered what she was like. Judging from Nadia's description and explanation, I wasn't sure if I would like this young woman of affluence and privilege. Nadia thought so, but I think differently than most other people.

The plane touched down on the runway, as all objects large or small are launched into the air, they are returned one way or the other. The reversers kicked in, and a new feeling overcame me. I found a feeling of familiarity at what I was getting ready to plan and then accomplish. It seemed I was once again back in the saddle. Strapped up and ready to begin. We taxied up to the jet way. I wondered, quite aloud, what was I expecting, and looked around with the contempt I have for people. People who in their ignorance could allow things like this to happen. I do realize that it's not common knowledge, but it doesn't feel that way. It is something so personal, it defies explanation.

The plane came to a stop and the foreword hatch was opened. I marveled at the mass of people who stood so they could be bounced and jostled, trying to be the first out of the doorway and up the jet way. I don't think I've ever wanted to be first out of a plane that badly!

I turned on my phone in anticipation of a phone call, and I was not to be denied. As soon as I had turned on my phone, it began to ring. Before I could answer, it stopped. I was watching the traffic jam recede, and I instinctively looked around. "Well, only the stewardess and me now. I guess it's time to grab my gear and get off the bus."

I stood to stretch my tight and kinked muscles and joints from their long disuse. It felt good to stand. When I stood, the bells on my right boot gently reminded me why I was here. The bells musical notes of beauty. My trademark is silver bells. Each bell represented more than one victory in my fight against this terrible creation of mankind. It was something I did to remind me, and others. To me, a soul must ring true, like the bells musical notes of beauty. Each bell, is the sound of a soul returned to its proper place in this orchestra we call life. For each ten souls I had a bell. Right now there are seven bells attached to my boot. When I walked, they played together, a symphony of souls. I grabbed my jacket and briefcase. I reached for my campaign hat and placed it on my head. Outfit complete. I felt good as I reveled in the fact I was here.

The phone resumed its insistent ringing. I answered the call.

"Boots! Boots, is that you? Where are you? I can't find you. Where are you? Did you make the flight? I hope you're here! Please answer me!"

I admit it angered me. Who was this childish young woman? Couldn't she just slow down and let me answer? Well I'll tell her! The damned chatterbox. She must be scatterbrained or what. "Miss? Miss, would you please shut up? This is Boots. Yes, I made the flight. Yes, I'm on the plane, and don't presume anything about what I am doing, damn it!"

I heard a soft, almost hurt, pleasant voice with a fairytale Russian accent to it. I must admit, it sounded very nice. "I'm sorry, Boots, I did not mean to make you mad, or insult you. I'm Daria."

Being a little more controlled, I said, "Well, Daria, I can't talk to you if your mind is all askew with questions and doubts before

I even get off this plane."

Her voice was much calmer now, "Where are you Boots?"

I answered with, "I'm still on the plane. I don't make it a habit to rush off of planes with the people I don't know behind me." She let that go, at least for the moment. "Nadia did not tell me what you looked like."

I could hear the smile in her voice as she said, "That's okay. I know what you look like. Nadia called me this morning and she told me how tall you were, what you are wearing, that you are all in black. Even your cowboy boots! She said they have bells on the right side."

All I could think was, "Well, I'll be damned! Nadia, my love, you know me well!" Speaking back into my cell phone, "I'm coming out of the plane hatch and going up the jet way. I'll be with you in just a few minutes. I'm sorry if I hurt your feelings."

There was no answer, but out of the left corner of my eye I saw a very beautiful young woman with knee length ebony hair moving very fast to intercept me. Before I could get my phone put back into my pocket she had me in a whirlwind. She hugged me, kissed me, and latched onto my arm. It felt like she had a hold of the wrong arm, and in fact she did. It was my right arm that she had. It's my offensive and defensive arm. I am equally good with either arm, but it is a preference that I have.

I dissuaded this impetuous young woman, and transferred her to my left arm. I turned slightly, taking her all in. "My name is Boots, and I'm at your service, miss."

She verily boiled over with smiles of pleasure as she held my arm with a surprising amount of strength. She kissed my cheek and proceeded to tell me, "My name is Daria and it is with great pleasure to meet you, friend Boots. I thank you for myself, and my uncle, my family and Sasha, and most of all for coming to save Svetlana."

This touched a nerve in my soul and I couldn't help but bristle up and tell her that no one would stop me from rescuing her cousin. She began to cry softly. I bundled her into my arms and told her it would be alright. I could only hope I was right, and would be in time to save just one more human.

Daria acted like a small child at Christmas who had secretly wished for a special gift, that she had revealed to no one, and to her utter surprise and joy it had appeared before her very eyes. I must admit, it was very pleasant to have this beautiful girl firmly ensconced and attached to my left arm. She fit under my arm and had it wrapped tightly around her person and grasped by her arms. I remembered the way Nadia fit in that spot, and how my beautiful wife fit just like this woman. I guess it's a Russian thing after all.

As Daria and I began to walk, we talked. I noticed a very unusual scent coming from this young woman. It was a perfume unfamiliar to me, however not unpleasant, but unique. It was one of the strange things I would get used to. She guided me to an extremely well-dressed man, and introduced us. The man was her Uncle Gregor. Reverting to Russian without thinking, I greeted this man in his own native tongue. I explained if one was to understand the plays of Chekov, the language had to be understood.

With this statement I must have rang a bell with him, as he smiled broadly and chuckled at the amazement of his niece. He looked at his niece with a smile and said, "You did not think that a brigand, a pirate, could speak our language and love the Russian masters?" At this, she even laughed at herself and it was apparent that I was going to like Daria very much and would enjoy her company from time to time. That turned out to be an understatement, as I could barely escape her at all.

We had reached the mezzanine, when I noticed an almost imperceptible and subtle movement from Gregor's right-hand. With that movement, all of my senses and instincts came to full combat alert, ready for any possibility. It was a prudent reaction in my world, however it was not necessary and had been an automatic response from my training. It was in truth a reaction from my overcautious mind. To the best of my knowledge, it was a sign to his doorman.

As we began to walk, Gregor's doorman opened the door and raised his right arm. To my amusement, a rather large and sleek, black limousine opened up like a cavern, ready for us to step into and be comfortable in. I made sure Daria went in first. Her uncle had entered from the other side of the limousine. I, in turn entered this extraordinary piece of luxury and the door closed behind me as if it sensed I was sitting. However, this was not the case. There was an assistant driver who took care of the doors. I realized as I seated myself, Daria was as close as two people could be, with a not so unpleasant pressure on my arm.

It was a stressful trip for me, for some unknown reason. I was in this car, on my way to a section of Brighton Beach I hadn't been to since 1967. It was then when a friend in training with me at Camp Lejeune, North Carolina had invited me to a wedding. It had been a culture shock to me, to say the least. A large and festive Jewish wedding. I have to admit, it was an impressive affair for a young man who had looked upon his home as the normal amount of civilization. My remote village had a population of two-hundred humans in ten square miles. There had been that many participants in the wedding party alone.

We had driven quite a ways before anyone spoke, and Daria had remained silent for far longer than it seemed she was used to. She began to explain about how things were going to be. She planned on being my hands when needed, a shoulder when I wanted, and a hostess if I had need of one. In some ways I found myself rather at a loss as to why she would do this, but I wasn't going to burst her bubble if this is what she had planned. After all, she was my employer.

The ride proceeded with small talk about nothing. It was not until we pulled into the parking area did I have any idea at the company I was now keeping. It was apparent from the onset, this man Gregor had money, but it was not until I saw this car and the town house we had come to did I realize he was a far wealthier man than I had anticipated. This was no ordinary home. It was a palatial home with grounds, in a concrete jungle. To me it could not be real, however before my eyes, this oasis had appeared.

The car came to a stop and the door to the town home opened. A man and a helper came to the car and opened Gregor's door first. All that was said was, "Good day, sir," as my door was opened by the helper. I extracted myself from the car with Daria hanging on. My briefcase in one hand, Daria in the other. The helper unknowingly reached for my briefcase, but after the look he got, he withdrew his hand or he would have lost it!

Daria ushered me into the home. Right behind her was Gregor. I was stunned at the interior. It was, I would say opulent at the least, plain ostentatious at the most, however, it was definitely a Russian home. It was not unlike those I had visited before. The furnishings and tapestries, in any case, were far more exquisite than those in my village in Alaska. This was a four-story town home, ornately decorated. What a place! Nadia had not prepared me for this, and Daria had not mentioned any of this before.

We proceeded to the sitting room which had a very exquisite and highly polished, brass samovar. It was the largest and most ornate coffeepot I had ever seen! It made superb coffee and as we sat and drank this delicious brew, I decided it was time for some answers.

There should be no one listening in this home who was not supposed to hear it anyway. "Daria," I said, "You must tell me how I can help you. I think I know, but would you please tell me, so we are all of one thought?"

I found myself in the presence of a gentleman. Gregor looked at me, then excused himself and said, "I'll see you two later at dinner." It seemed I would be getting all of my information from Daria after all.

Daria explained dinner was at 19:00 hours and that I would have to dress.

"Daria," I said, "I did not take time to pack suits."

Smiling slyly she answered, "That's okay. I'll show you later."

Smiling back at her I asked gently, "So little one, shall we talk, or play games?"

Looking very concerned she began, "No. We should talk. We have found out that Svetlana was tricked and drugged, at least we think so. She is in Amsterdam, and the Russian Mafia owns her. They will never let her go. They will use her up and then kill her. Boots, can you return her to us?"

I thought quickly because I had already decided, due to the nature of the beast, I could not let this slavery go on. Looking into Daria's eyes I said, "That's what I thought. Do you know what you're asking of me? It would entail my clan and me to go to a foreign country and possibly have to kill some people in order to get your cousin out of her predicament and bring her home."

I could see the trepidation in her face as she replied, "Yes, I know it would be very difficult and dangerous, but what are we to do? They have Svetlana and we want her safely here."

I had to think for a moment. Could there be an alternative to an assault on Svetlana's captors in Amsterdam? I would have to ask Daria.

"Could I have some more coffee and would you be so kind as to go and get your Uncle Gregor for me? Then I can answer."

Daria jumped to the opportunity and leaving the room answered fleetingly, "My pleasure, Boots."

I sat drinking coffee and awaited the return of Daria and Gregor. I was curious about all of this. Daria soon returned with Gregor. He sat and I stood. It was time for some answers.

"Gregor," I began, "I am pretty sure you have accessibility to many influential friends and plenty of money. In some cases like this, one can usually arrange to purchase the slave. Why don't

you just buy Svetlana and get her back that way?"

Hastily, he replied, "This is not possible."

The answer was much too quick and I needed a better reason than he was giving me. I asked, "Why is it not possible?"

Gregor retorted once again with, "It is not possible."

I started to become slightly perturbed and responded, "Wrong answer Gregor! I want you to think about this for a minute and then answer. But, I need the whole answer. It might change what I say. What I might have to do. I have to know whether or not it is possible."

As he paused, I wondered why it was not possible. Looking away, Gregor spoke, "Because I have publicly denounced the Russian Mafia. Not only in this country, but in the Rodina."

I was sure this was a mouthful for Gregor. He continued with a faraway sound in his voice, "They do not know Svetlana is my niece, or they would kill her immediately."

This statement alone put a different light on the situation. "Well, Gregor, that's a good reason."

With a penetrating look, he probed, "I need to ask you how much you would charge to try and get Svetlana out of there. I will pay whatever I have to. Anything you ask will be yours. Svetlana's return is most important to me and I will comply with what is necessary."

I thought to myself, "Wow, this man would be easy pickings for a dishonest operator!"

I had to say yes, but this rescue will be done on my conditions. "I'll tell you what Gregor. If you pay for all approved expenses, you can consider me hired. I will need my own men. The clan. We will charge you nothing, but you must pay for anything I deem necessary concerning the rescue."

Gregor looked bewildered. "How is this possible? Men always require great financial remuneration for this type of request."

"Maybe it's because I'm not a person who can profit from someone else's misfortune," I said.

He sat shocked and stunned. He was willing to pay anything and make someone very wealthy, but I didn't want his money. All I needed was his support. He sat for approximately five minutes with a dumb look on his face.

Suddenly, the tension broke. Then Gregor spoke, "This will be fine. This is very acceptable."

All of a sudden Gregor had become animated. I am sure he expected an astronomical fee, and from what I could figure out he was willing to pay it and hold no grudge. It was not the money that changed the way he thought of me and my clan, rather it was that money was not the ultimate prize. Svetlana was. In many ways, I am sure a majority of people would feel as though we had received nothing of a personal reward. In truth, they would be very wrong. The reward comes when the mission is accomplished, and the rescued child is at home. Then you can look back and know the job was completed the way it should be.

This was no different to me than other operations the clan had collectively paid for out of their own pockets, for this very reason. When Gregor spoke again it was with respect rather than as if he was just paying a wage to an employee. It was different now. He had opened up and was being as Daria said later, "Almost like he was before Svetlana's mother had called him frantic about her daughter." He had evidently been in a black mood for quite some time.

Daria joined the conversation, "When I talked to Nadia she told me to contact you. She said you and your friends can do anything. That's why I called you. Uncle Gregor commented that he had no idea of what to expect and he didn't even know if you could be discrete enough to be told the whole story."

As I looked at Gregor I began to explain, "If you had not been forthcoming enough to tell me the whole story I would have had to have second thoughts about this mission."

He paled and asked me, "Do you have plans to leave? I would like for you to please stay in my home. My money is yours. Anything you need is yours."

He looked relieved when I said, "No, not anything, Gregor. Only your trust is necessary."

That, I meant with everything that I am. Gregor was telling Daria it was unusual to meet a man of quality. One who was not a mercenary man and did not seek riches or fame for their deeds. That it was a blessing that Nadia had known and suggested me. It made me extraordinarily self-conscious, but it also pleased me greatly. I was growing somewhat fond of both of them, but especially the always gracious Daria, who would become my constant companion. I feel that compliments are for beautiful women, not for men of war. I am a man of war, and will remain a man of war until I meet my comrades on the other side to work together once again.

I later asked Daria why her uncle's feelings had not been included in the packet sent to Nadia's. She explained that her uncle believed no one could judge a man except in person, and only then can you tell if they are men of high standards, or low wants.

Gregor again bid his farewell and Daria suggested that we go for a walk through the garden in the conservatory. We did not turn to go outside, but instead began walking up a flight of stairs to who knows where. We entered an elevator and Daría pushed the button that said observatory. As we rode up I wondered what I should expect. I can tell you, it wouldn't have been enough. This rooftop oasis amidst the desert of the city, was where I would come again and again for quiet and solace. Just to be me. It was beyond beautiful, and as Daria slipped her hand into mine, I found myself reverting into a second childhood that seemed to be available at my beck and call. Here I was in a castle, complete with the fairy princess!

We sat down on a cushioned bench. I could feel the always present pressure on my left side of Daria. I lit a cigarette and began to think about the Russian Mafia, Svetlana's situation, the great difficulties that could be involved, and the mission. I could feel a certain insistence that Daria had something she wanted to say. You could just tell. She sat beside me and held my arm.

The question was there on the tip of her tongue. "Boots, can it be done? Can you do it?" she finally said.

Still considering what direction I would go, I answered, "I will try to Daria. I believe it can be done, it will just be in how, but I can do it. I just have to think about it."

With a smile back on her lips she said, "I also believe you can. I'm glad you're finally here and that you're going to try."

CHAPTER FOUR

It was almost the dinner hour and still had no idea of where my room was. Daria decided it was time that I found my cave in the house. She said all men are like bears, they need their own caves and only visit the girl bears when they want to. I had to laugh and agreed. She guided me down the hall, where we stopped at her room and she explained that this was her cave. Her uncle's was up on the next floor. Mine was right there, next to hers. It was at the end of the hall. Her door faced down the hall and mine was the next door down from hers. She showed me her room.

She opened the next door and said, "This is your room. It has a connecting door, I hope that is okay."

I laughed and said, "Well it doesn't bother me."

As she showed me my room, she stated with pride how she had personally done this room for me. She had obviously prepared for my coming. I had to shake my head when she opened the closet and there were five suits and a tuxedo. "How did you know my sizes?" I asked.

Daria simply stated and said, quite matter of factly, "Nadia called your wife, and then called me with the right sizes."

I was amused. Three Russian girls. One thought. It was not surprising. As Daria left she said she would meet me at my door in forty-five minutes for dinner. I realized I hadn't looked at my watch since my arrival at 13:20 hours this afternoon. I, of course, showered, shaved, and dressed. It all fit like a glove, down to the shoes. What a deal was about all I could think.

Daria, once again took up her position on my left side. There was an amount of strangeness to all of these happenings. I had found myself in a mansion three-thousand odd miles from the land that was my turf being shepherded by a gorgeous young woman with expectations of what, I'm not positive. In my heart, I believe she feels somewhat responsible for my involvement in the struggle for her cousin, in the very near future. In feeling this responsibility, she had thrown herself completely into the fray. I believe, in her own inimitable way it was her wish to be of comfort and share the workload. It is to be said by me many times in the future, that she was by no means a yoke around my neck, or the clans. She was a loyal and stalwart influence to one and all.

When dinner was announced around the house, on all floors and every room, it struck me of the extreme disparity of lifestyles between Daria and Svetlana. Not the things that Daria had or could do, but in the vast separation in circumstance. As dinner progressed, Gregor made it known that he would like me to come with him into the sitting room for coffee or a drink, and of course, the applicable tobacco use. This was one of the two rooms where smoking was allowed. As we began to relax, the conversation inevitably turned to the business of tomorrow.

"Boots," Gregor began, "I have been thinking that it would be difficult for you to stop and discuss every purchase with myself or Daria, so I have decided that tomorrow morning, you, I, and Daria will go to the bank. It is time that I show my trust and faith in you and Daria to be wise, and make the purchases without my input. I would still like to be informed on the purchase of very large items."

Of course, both Daria and I agreed to this without hesitation. As this bit of business was concluded, Daria looked at me with eyes that said, "Let's get out of here." So, before Gregor could disentangle himself from us, Daria and I begged to be excused. We went to the rooftop hideout, or as it was sometimes referred to, Boots Place, which amused me. I never discovered how much the account was worth and I never tried. I would use it as if it was my own, and I do not spend my money foolishly. I know that every penny counts, you just never know when.

This is not to say that the clan did not get the best that money could buy, but there is a difference between needed and wanted equipment.

A short time later, Gregor approached me so we could discuss what he foresaw as a burden on me and my time. He apologized for Daria and the way she had attached herself to me. Indeed at her attempts to dominate my time, and my person. I assured him that all I represented to her was a new experience, and possibly, a new toy albeit, or maybe a trophy. I also told him that new toys get old and trophies tarnish. That is always the fate of trophies. I made sure to tell him that she would become bored with me and find a new interest. He laughed. I had to wonder about this as I could see nothing to laugh about.

Gregor had decided I would need an office of sorts, with a large table for meetings and training. We proceeded to the basement level where Gregor spoke to me about arrangements for the clan. He wanted to know if he could not only bare the expenses, but indeed also open up his home to each and every one of my clan. This very sincere man had deemed it his duty and responsibility for not only supplying all of our needs, but also our housing. All things were within his power. I looked at this man and had to think of the stretch his understanding was reaching. I told him it was not necessary, but he insisted.

He asked if I had an idea of how many gentlemen would be coming. I had already decided on six team members and myself. He went into immediate action. He let Daria know that there would be six more guests. She was overjoyed at the prospect, and began preparations at once. She would have the clan move into the third floor with the both of us, in order for them to be close in case they should need anything. Gregor did his part by hiring extra staff to care for the clan's needs. It was a very generous gesture.

Before I could realize it, Sunday arrived. I awoke to find a note under my door. It said, "Boots, please dress in the gray pinstriped suit. We leave for our church at nine thirty." It escaped me that their faith would not be Roman Catholic, but rather Eastern Orthodox. This would not be my first time observing a religious experience in this faith. It was rather similar to my own. They were both solemn, with a great deal of pomp and circumstance.

I found myself sitting in this house of God, but my mind would not let me commune with my creator. Instead, I could not get past the need for information and intel on the problem at hand. It was disrespectful, I agree, but it was necessary to my mission. The thoughts began to gel in my mind. I had to find a solution to this grave need. What I needed was firsthand knowledge. A singularity. It was a difficult thing to find. Suddenly, out of nowhere, a name popped into my mind, as well as my mouth. At times like this, it was difficult at best to control. Out of my mouth came, "I'll be damned!" I realized immediately where I was, and how many pairs of eyes were staring at me. I felt like crawling into a hole and covering it up!

After the service, I explained to the priest, with Gregor and Daria at my side.

The priest only looked at me, smiled, and stated, "I can forgive you, my son, but can you forgive yourself?"

I couldn't. I had ruined my first visit to this place of God, and vowed to never utter another word inside the doors of this cathedral. Although Daria cheered me significantly by making great sport of my faux pas, in a good-natured way.

After my entrance into Russian religion, we returned to the house and went into the sitting room. I explained to Gregor and Daria that a friend of mine, a black man I had served in the Marines with, would be the first clansman I would call upon. They asked why. I explained that although he had had a very bad upbringing in Chicago, after the Marines, the call to serve God and man had reached his soul. He had become a Baptist preacher, but when I needed him, or he needed me, we had but to make a call. Gregor and Daria were thrilled at the prospect of the first of six clansmen to come.

CHAPTER FIVE

Preacher had been a kid growing up in the Cabrini Green Housing Project. He had no parents, to speak of and had become an astute student of street life. He had been part of the gangs in the very early sixties in Chicago. He freely admits, he had stabbed and slashed his way into this life. He had indeed also, shot some people when he was very young. He ended up, once again, standing before a judge. The judge spoke to him about what would happen to him when Preacher would turn eighteen. He would be tried as an adult and sent to prison. As the judge continued, he explained that if Preacher had any brains he would enlist in the Marines before that happened. The judge promised that Preacher would serve long and hard times in the very worst prison the judge could find. Preacher enlisted that day in 1967. It was the same year that I had enlisted, and somehow, we wound up in boot camp together. This was where we became fast and hard friends.

Our training progressed, and along with other men who would join the clan at a later date, went into recon. This is the toughest training the Marines have to offer. All things happen for a reason that often we cannot hope to decipher. We all wound up shipping to Vietnam in 1967. The war turned bitter in 1968. We were deployed to Khe-San when the Tet offensive became fact. In Khe-San we were constantly on the move in the jungle. We seldom saw Khe-San, which was a large fortified firebase in the middle of nowhere Vietnam. The firebase was located eight miles from the Ho-Chi-Mihn trail. This was the main supply and troop movement avenue that the enemy used for incursions into Vietnam. They began to pound Khe-San with artillery and rockets.

Our base in Hell. There was at least one round hitting the base every forty-five seconds. The shell bursts were about eight-hundred to one-thousand-two-hundred pounds each.

The pounding of Khe-San continued, and bush operations were carried on until the North Vietnamese Army had seized total control of Hue City, the ancient capital. They were a well-trained group of soldiers who were as fanatical as their brethren, the Viet Cong guerrillas. With ten-thousand combined troops, the North Vietnamese Army along with Viet Cong guerrillas, took possession of Hue City. Our very small unit was withdrawn from Khe-San to spearhead a bid to take back the city. With a total of eight-hundred and fifty men, the Marines moved in to take the city back from insurgent forces holding two-thousand-fourhundred South Vietnamese soldiers in a trap. Our job was to defeat the enemy troops, rescue the friendlies, and to take this city back from the enemy. No modern day unit of our size could neutralize this city. It has been proven.

The first eight hundred meters took us twelve days without air support or artillery. It was not to be allowed. The city, in twenty-four hour a day, constant fighting, was taken back in twenty-eight days, with what would be considered very light casualties. I had never met anyone who had been in the fight to take Hue City back who had not been wounded at least once, kept on going, and didn't quit. These are some of the men of the clan, and especially the Preacher, who had been wounded twice and refused to quit or back down. This was my friend, Preacher, then and he is still willing to fight for right. I could expect no less from him, and he would expect no less from me.

It was a strange camaraderie that I had with preacher. I remember how he got his name, in Vietnam. Our team had been deployed, and the mission was a risky one. The Skipper, our commander, had already informed us that with all we were up against, it would not be a cakewalk. The estimated losses on this mission had been figured to be thirty-eight percent killed in action, and seventeen percent wounded. These odds were high, however they were acceptable, even to us. So much depended on our success. The lives of the A.R.V.N. detachment were very much in doubt. They stood to be wiped out. Blotted off the map. The bastards had claimed this on Marine Corps turf. Who the hell did they think they were? They had angered us in a way they could not begin to fathom.

Just before we boarded this plywood coffin was when Preacher got his name. It has stuck by divine intervention. We approached the Perfume River to board the transport assault boats. We were one-half mile above Hue City, as we looked across the river to the place we would soon be going. It was the only place the boats could load. In the two-mile trip down river through the middle of Hue City, we had discovered that the hundreds of heavy weapons the N.V.A. had would be aimed directly at the boats, in which were packed with Marine personnel in a bid to gain a foothold on the North shore of the city. Since two-thirds of the city of Hue lies in that direction, a bridge assault had been tried. However, it was beaten back with massive casualties four times, hence the river assault.

Divine inspiration, plus a grounding in religion from his grandmother, Preacher asked us all to kneel on our left knee. He began to speak like a young Jesse Jackson, which didn't amuse us. Rather, as Preacher said, "God has told me to perform this service." He began, "Brothers, as we once again charge headlong into the jaws of death with the enemy. Lord, we know that in your wisdom, you will take your pick of the warriors knelt here before you."

At that moment, the N.V.A. opened up and it was the sound of the death rattle that I had heard so many times before. Preacher continued, while standing quite erect, "We pray to you, Heavenly Father, to show infinite mercy and love by taking us quickly. Do not let us languish in dumb anguish. Protect us, Almighty Father from all things, and bless your Marines as they prepare to face this ordeal. Amen." It made us aware, once again, of God's inexhaustible love. Preacher started once more, "Oh Lord, Yea thou we walk through the valley of the shadow of death, we shall fear no evil, for after all, you made us the meanest mothers in this valley!"

Somewhere in the background came, "When I get to Heaven, to St. Peter I will tell. One of God's Marines reporting in, Sir. I've served my time in Hell."

This was all, and it was appropriate. I thank Preacher to this day.

I called Preacher at his church in Chicago. The phone began ringing and many fond memories of this man flooded into my brain. When he said hello, I was indeed smiling.

"Hey Preacher," I said when he answered.

I heard his familiar voice say, "Hey Boots! What it be bro? Are you calling to be friendly, or can Preacher give you a hand, or what?"

I proceeded to tell him, "Preacher, I have a situation, my friend."

All he said was, "Okay brother, let's hear it."

I explained the situation, short and to the point, relating what I knew. He told me he was due for an exciting sabbatical. God! I love that word, sabbatical! It meant that the preacher was coming to preach his kind of right and might for God and the world. When I asked him when he wanted to come, he told me to give him forty-eight hours to get his stuff done and cleared, and then he would be on his way. I had to tell him, "Preacher, this is a tough one."

But he just said, "So were the others, Boots, or have you forgotten?"

No, it was not likely that I had forgotten. Never.

He said, "Shoot me the travel arrangements by fax, send my pass and ticket, and I will see you on Wednesday morning, if that is okay."

I told him that would be great and that I hadn't contacted any other players. We would decide together, as usual. I said to him, "Preacher, you know there is only one logistics and supply man who is the best, but we will discuss that when you get here and have time to talk about the whole picture."

He just let that go, and thanked me for the last time. I had to tell him that it had been my pleasure and thanks for this one.

He laughed and returned with, "That is what the clan is, Boots, and you know it."

I said, "Yes, I do, my brother. See you on the flip side Preacher."

He replied, "The other side, Boots."

After he hung up, I knew this would make the operation more capable of being successful because he was of the highest caliber of man and soldier.

When I had finished talking to preacher, Daria let me know that it was her turn for a chunk of my time. We left for the roof. I was a happy man. One of the original clansmen had heeded my herald for assistance in my cause.

Daria and I sat and talked for a while and laughed at a few dumb jokes, when out of nowhere, Daria looked at me and asked, "Do you really think that it can be done?"

One more time in my life, without knowing for sure, I said, "Absolutely." I was committed to this rescue because it was the thing that should be done, and because of my personal hatred for the Mafia.

I realized that and said so, quite out loud, "Well, Daria, we have begun to build a winning team. The personnel I have in my mind are all A list operational men. They are of the first echelon. These friends of mine make me the best and I them. The clan is made up of guys like Preacher and me, as you know."

She looked up at me and said, "I know, Boots, but it gives me comfort to hear these things."

The preparations were in progress for Preacher's trip and arrival. I had turned these arrangements over to the lady of the house. Daria. She rose to every occasion and I felt she was quite remarkable at her commitment. Of course, I should have guessed from her background that she had learned to be capable without even realizing it. Daria was quickly becoming a much needed assistant; however, it was apparent that her true inspiration was her absolute desire to please me in any way possible. I needed her to be my hands when mine were full, and she was accomplishing this far better than she would ever know.

Let it be known, that this rescue mission amounted to taking one or more of the Russian Mafia's prize possessions. Their property. A fact that would not be happily accepted or tolerated. People who take from them, or speak against them have a habit of falling off the face of the earth. They could afford the very best soldiers and would not hesitate to use them if the need arose.

"A tactical planner and advisor will devise a plan in such a way as to achieve the desired results with minimal cost to the antagonists. If it is only a small victory yet achieves its objective, it is a successful and well-devised plan." The preceding statement was written over two-thousand-four-hundred years ago. It is quoted from the book, *"The Art of War,"* written by Sun Tzu and his great-grandson Sun Pin. In fact, it is used by every military service. It must be understood here, that in most countries militaries tactical planning units it is called the bible of war. With that being said and quoted, the plan we had to devise hinged on the lessons in the *Art of War.* We needed a small victory, with little if not any cost to the clan, yet the results we desired. It should be understood that criminal organizations rarely use logic to ensnare people. Rather, it is done by fear, by terror, and by overwhelming force. If you can hold your own against the force, or circumvent it, the other two are not a factor. If this cannot be achieved one of the other conditions must be defeated. Fear destroys hope. Without hope there is no victory. With that said, if you can defeat one of the three conditions of power, you can achieve a victory. This was subscribed to by General George Patton in World War II in the relief of Bastogne.

Daria and I began the transformation of the meeting room in the basement. I had not grasped the enormity of this room, or of the table. The room was twenty-four feet wide and forty feet long. As for the table, it measured five feet wide and sixteen feet long. It was quite impressive. The chairs were very comfortable, high back, leather, executive chairs. It also was equipped with two bathrooms, a shower, and a small kitchenette.

In the acquisition of equipment, we purchased four corkboard easels, four feet by eight feet. They were installed onto movable trolleys. We also purchased four four foot by twelve foot stationary corkboard easels. They were installed on stationary wheelless trolleys. We then purchased one overhead enlargement projector. We looked around and saw there was very little high tech equipment. We had four computers delivered and installed by IBM Corporation. We ordered two fax machines with dedicated communication lines. This was in addition to everything we would need for security for this operation. Such as, one large capacity paper and file shredder that Gregor's contacts had installed.

There were also two four drawer, high security file cabinets, along with all the paper products and supplies we could possibly use. Gregor had brought a high capacity copy machine from one of his offices. We then had a phone system put in with four dedicated lines. This would be everything we could want or should ever need. Standing there surveying all of the changes and new equipment, I concluded, the war room was complete and finished.

CHAPTER SIX

I found, it was then time to sit with Gregor and find out what he might know, and who had supplied the information. I had planned to speak to him alone on this subject, but since Daria had been involved up to her pretty little neck for over a week, she had been hearing things that I am sure she never knew. She, in truth probably could have lived her life without hearing or knowing any of it. The best time to speak to Gregor was after dinner, in the sitting room. It only took the patience to wait until dinner.

One more incredible repast with Daria directing the entire meal. She did this with total ability and panache, smiling like the Cheshire cat. Afterwards, it was time to step into the sitting room. As the nightly ritual began, I asked Gregor how it was that he knew where Svetlana was. Better yet, who told him where she was. Gregor hesitated. Exasperated once again, an obviously continuous situation in dealing with Gregor, I said, "Gregor, I don't want to hear any names. Just the circumstances as to how this information was attained.

"Okay." He replied, "When Sasha called me and explained what had happened and the circumstances as she knew them, I had a few friends look into Executive Placement Services in Russia. It would seem there were quite a few young women disappearing after going to one of their offices. One friend checked deeper and found out it was a front company for the Russian Mafia. Their desire for workers stemmed from their need to recruit or steal young girls to be forced into prostitution. They began looking and checking around carefully and indeed discovered that Svetlana was in Amsterdam. She was in a building that housed women and young girls for the illicit sex trade. My friend became extremely nervous. This friend and his wife went to Amsterdam in hopes of locating the building that housed Svetlana. After locating this building, he instructed his wife to take pictures as if she were a tourist. However, while she was taking the pictures of Svetlana's possible prison, she became so frightened that the pictures she had taken were of poor quality. This was either due to the fear that enveloped her, or just bad film."

I sat there for a moment in shock, and could not believe what I had just heard. A little astonished I said, "Do you have the photos Gregor, and are they available for me to scrutinize?"

He told me that he would have to retrieve them from his den where they had been kept, well protected. I asked him to go and get them for me and explained to him, "I might be able to detect something someone else missed, and maybe we should consider having these photos reprocessed by a professional photo enhancer. Possibly, they might be able to repair some of the quality problems."

Gregor departed to his den without hesitation. I looked at Daria and asked, "Have you seen this set of photos, babe?"

She intimated that she had no knowledge of any photographs, let alone exactly where Svetlana was. She had only inserted into the packet what her uncle had requested. I asked if that was unusual, that Gregor had not shown the photos to her, but she said, "I don't think so, sweetheart, but then my uncle is sometimes a very private man."

I had to consider Gregor. He had not even bothered to put this information on the table to be perused. Let alone to mention it existed. It did seem strange to me. If I needed to save a family member from these people, I would be completely straight forward with any, and all information available. No matter how insignificant it may seem, or how poor of a quality it might be. When Gregor re-entered the room, he had a manila envelope in his hand. I stood to either walk to him, or receive the envelope containing the photos. He appeared to hesitate just before handing it to me.

When I looked at the pictures I realized no one would be able to bring out the building. It was too unclear. What was clear was that just to the left of this hell-hole was another building. It was equally as grainy and foggy, almost like there was a light leak in the camera body, but there was also what looked like a street identification plaque. The majority of this sign could not be read next to this building. The name was not clear enough to read, however, the first seven letters were clear enough, maybe, if we used a magnifying glass. We might be able to at least get the beginning letters. After about twenty minutes of staring and changing the angles, we had gotten the letters onto a piece of paper. I had no idea what it might spell out, but Daria and I both agreed on which letters they were. S-T-R-U-A-S-S. It could be difficult to locate the name. What we needed was a large street map of Amsterdam.

I asked Daria, "Could you arrange to purchase such a map?" She replied, "Yes, Boots. I am at your service."

I told her, "Thanks, beautiful. When we get a map, Daria, we might be able to find this street name and in turn find the one and only, Svetlana." In all actuality, I held little hope, but I wanted to be surprised.

Since Gregor's landmark admission about the photos had come approximately sixteen hours before Preacher landed at La Guardia International Airport, Daria had already made transportation arrangements with the driver. The car was to be in front of the terminal and the assistant driver would hold up a sign that read "This driver for Preacher." Daria had thought maybe she should have been sterner, especially with a man of God coming, but I convinced her it would be just perfect! I was not the only person happy in the morning. The Preacher would be here in two and one half-hours and then everything would begin to move faster. The train had left the station with an engineer, slowing to receive a passenger. I would realize that indeed, it was a train. I only hoped we could keep it on the tracks the entire way to our ultimate destination, home.

Preacher would arrive to be at my side once again. Not to work for me, but to work with me. I would be excited when this black man arrived. To me he was a friend and a godsend. With his brave attitude, along with his indomitable gift of gab, coupled with his ease around people, he would become my intelligence officer. He has that quality, to act in a sincere manner and to say the right things. Not that he would have to be deceitful. With some help, he could gain entry to this building which housed and held our package, Svetlana. His bravery had been proven over and above reproach. This was done in many venues, not just war, but in the work the clan is committed to do. The recovery of human beings.

It would appear that I had been ignoring my fairy princess. I looked at her and she had a pouty look on her face. It made me smile, and the ice was broken. Daria fairly bounced over and grabbed my arm, as usual. We walked towards the elevator. She was helping to maneuver me, to my refuge on the roof.

We came to the glass enclosure and she commented with, "Boots, you were deep in thought for twenty five minutes. I was getting lonely and was curious about what you were thinking of."

I told her, "I was thinking of the Preacher, babe, and what made him my friend. He has earned the right to be held in my highest esteem. I am sorry you felt lonely and forgotten. Nothing could be farther from the truth, Daria."

We had been sitting when Daria arose, stretched, and brought me a cup of coffee. We sat, quietly drinking the coffee, and I could hear her clucking to herself, making sure that nothing had been left amiss in Preacher's room.

The time was growing short and the arrival of Preacher was imminent. I considered going down to meet Preacher personally, but was gently reminded that was what the butler was for. His job was to receive visitors and escort them to where they were supposed to be. This statement made me somewhat apprehensive, however when in Rome, do as the Romans do! I was definitely not used to anything around me, other than Daria.

It surprised me when the manservant announced Preacher. He informed Daria that the gentleman's suitcases were already in his room. Luncheon would be served at 11:45 hours. Daria looked at her watch and informed the butler that the three of us would require that luncheon be served here in the glass garden.

The butler answered respectfully, "Very good, Miss. Will that be all?"

She let him know that we would need more coffee and he disappeared out of the room. And, there was Preacher, just standing there, looking at me, then at Daria, and back at me. Preacher's eyebrow lifted in a quizzical pose. There was no condemnation, but he definitely did not understand what was going on. He knew my wife, and my wife knew his wife. I would have to explain this situation in private and if he did not understand then, he could just call my wife! What he said made me laugh, along with Daria.

"Well, my friend, it appears that the clan will have to remember how to eat in polite company."

With that said, there was an embrace of old friends and comrades, with a lot of backslapping.

"You old war dog! How do you rate being treated like the idle rich?" he quipped.

Daria looked a bit befuddled, but I explained that Preacher was giving us the once over and was teasing both of us. That he really wanted her to be amused.

"Oh," said Daria, "I thought he didn't understand."

I also, had to admit that I had a hard time understanding this world of affluence. We stood there and Preacher turned on the charm like an old world chandelier.

"It is a pleasure to meet you miss, and Boots was right. You are an exquisite gem. I am so glad to make your acquaintance, and to have the chance to be of service to you and your family."

Preacher definitely had not lost his dashing ways! I knew that preacher had more questions than what was on the final exam for a master's degree. Not only about the mission, but the vaunting Miss Daria as well, along with our seeming attachment. We would talk at length later, but just now, Preacher was going to receive a lesson in Russian haute cuisine.

Believe me, when I say it is extraordinarily aromatic and down home good! We would lightly discuss the subject of the mission after lunch. When we had resumed a normal and balanced equilibrium of talking about family and old missions and days gone by, I felt a gulf between us. When I realized this gulf separated our ease of being,

Preacher expressed some reservations about the situation with Daria. He wanted to council me.

When I heard this I had to resort to a cliché, "You dirty old den mother! Lee has already talked to this girl. They discussed my wants and needs. Along the way, Daria needed my clothing sizes, and with Nadia's help, she got all the sizes from my jackets down to my socks. This information was happily shared between Daria, Nadia, and Lee!"

He looked surprised; however, when the full portent of what I had said became sorted out in his moral code, he apologized. I looked at him and it was apparent that he had thought the worst case scenario. He then had to withdraw the thought, and the gulf between us was gone. It had been amusing, as I hadn't really given it a second thought. I knew I would never look back on this incident, and only mention it because he cared enough to want me to explain, as he was worried about me.

Dinner approached and was Preacher in for a surprise! Dinner was the formal production of the day. We entered the dining room and I had to do a double take at his suit. He looked somewhat mystified!

"Ahh, I understand how you feel my friend. Daria made sure that you would be properly dressed for any occasion." Of course, she had called Lee to find out if she could help in procuring proper sizes for Preacher's attire. Lee called Preacher's wife and explained to her what was going on, and the request was happily completed. Daria received what she needed to go shopping for Preacher with his wife's blessings. This same situation would occur five more times. For those men who had no wives or significant others, Daria went to the horse's mouth and asked. She was fearless, and sometimes brash, but Daria would get her way or she would know the reasons why.

After the evening meal I formally introduced Gregor and Preacher. After a brief amount of time it was apparent that they had a mutual respect and admiration for each other. We retired to the sitting room, which had become a nightly ritual. There appeared to be a great rapport building between our benefactor and the Preacher. They discussed many subjects and found themselves in agreement much of the time. As the evening wound down, of course, it was time to escape to my rooftop refuge.

Daria and I excused ourselves, so as not to disturb the present debate. I am not positive, but I believe they did not hear us nor did they pay any particular attention to our departure. It was not long after that Preacher joined us on my rooftop. He sat with us and while I had scotch and Daria had her tea, Preacher drank buttermilk. Daria had not missed anything that would make Preacher more comfortable!

It was obvious that preacher wanted to begin immediately. In fact, to start the arduous process of, one, discussing the mission, its dangers and objectives. Two, the possible ramifications of the intended and impending mission, and three, the personnel that would be needed. Keeping in mind the qualifications by specialty, and most important, where this mission was to take place.

As we began to discuss this mission, Preacher sat and began to digest what I had to say. "Preacher, here is what we are up against. The Russian Mafia has been responsible for more white slavery than most other criminal elements. You know about slavery, Preacher because of your ancestors. It's one of the Mafia's specialties. As you know, anytime you go up against a powerful organization, there are greater risks. They are recalcitrant and violent. Without reason, not because it is what they do, but rather to prevent by example any attempt to stop their operations. You know they will seek immediate and maximum retaliation, without any compunction as to who their victims might be. These bastards, in the name of power and money have killed men, women, and even children. These are not people to be brash with. They are a vicious, unforgiving, and inhumane group." There is nothing to be said that is not negative about them.

Preacher spoke, "Okay, what are our chances Boots?"

"Oh, around little or none. What do you think?" I said.

"Well, either way, I want in on screwing these bastards over. All right, let's go on Boots. We will need several specialties." Preacher sounded adamant.

I told him that I believed I had a tentative plan, however, that would follow later. I asked, "Do you want to discuss the third question, or would you prefer to know where our job will take place?"

Preacher smiled and said, "I think that if you say Russia, I will have to consider your sanity."

I had to assure my friend that it was in the free world and asked why he would have to consider my sanity.

He retorted, "Because you are crazy!"

I had to admit that, but to walk into the lion's mouth to see if he would eat us seemed, oh probably, just a little extreme. I had to ask if he would still back me.

He answered, "I would have to say with unequivocal assurance, I would follow you to Hell, Boots."

I replied, "Well, we don't have to return there Preacher. We have already been there and back." We both agreed.

I began, "The target location will be in Northern Europe, the country is Holland and the name of our host city will be Amsterdam. This place is, I think, a four story building, and I will show you from the photograph why I do not know for sure. We will need to retrieve intel."

Preacher said, "You don't have a choice Boots, I'm the goat, and I do realize what I am getting into."

I answered Preacher back, "So, how do you want to play it, Preacher? There won't be any backup and no safe houses."

Preacher knew what I was talking about, "Like there were any in South East Asia. There wasn't much there either. So, what we have is a young woman who somehow became the property of the Russian Mafia and is now employed as a full-time dolly girl.

She's in a shithole in Amsterdam. Is that about the situation?" I told him, "Yes."

He looked at me and said, "Jesus, Boots. There are extreme problems here. The in is easy, the snatch is almost impossible, and how the hell do you expect that anyone will be able to escape?"

All I could say was, "I'm working on it Preacher. I'm working on it."

Preacher talked to me about how we would need the very best troops we could get. They're all in the clan. I agreed, but do we need shock troops along with a sky out team? We didn't think we would need any shock troops, but we were going to need equipment, and we would most definitely be needing papers. We both thought of only one refined gentleman who could fill that requirement, and in unison we said, "Slick."

CHAPTER SEVEN

Slick is the best of the best in acquisition of material and paperwork. He was born in Marseille, France. Marseille is a port town on the Mediterranean Sea in the Gulf of Lion. It's proximity to Nice, Monaco, and Genoa along with Barcelona, made it an ideal location for black marketeers, smugglers, and people of many facets of the criminal underworld. This was Slick's back yard, so to speak. He was considered by his teachers to be overly bright and ingenious. He spent more time on the streets and around the smoky bars and cafes than he had ever spent in school. When he attended school, you could be sure Slick had something he wanted to sell or trade. However, I do not believe that Slick ever made a fair trade. Knowing him, he either made the lion's share of the money, or to be sure he always came out on top of a trade.

Instead of using his genius for an education of the formal kind, he applied all of his energies and intellect to the streets, and what he could accomplish there. He was a master smuggler and black marketeer par excellence. He learned the trade of forgery along with influence. It was said on the streets "La Faux" was the best. Time passed quickly for Slick as he reached farther and farther into the world of criminal endeavors.

The inevitable happened. He was implicated in a crime without an alibi. He was eighteen years old. The magistrate sentenced him to prison for six months. Upon his release, he had heard there were several officers from the French Foreign Legion in attendance seeking recruits. They approached Slick, and it flashed through his mind that his father had died at Dien-Bein-Phu in the country of Vietnam. He went his own way for a while longer as he pursued his career.

He saw it all of a sudden and it became apparent that the Gendarmes were trying to find a reason to arrest him. Any reason would do. You see, he had risen to the surface of the underworld, and had made quite a name and reputation for himself. He was proud of it, but the Gendarmes had taken a personal interest in procuring him for arrest and trial. Then off to prison, toot sweet, removing a thorn from the police's rump. They wanted him gone. When he discovered this, he needed an out. The policy of the French Foreign Legion is your past remains behind you. It does not come with you. There is no past in the Legion, only legionaries. As was customary for him, Slick excelled in the Legion and became a hero of France.

He was one of the best supply people in the Legion, in his later years. He spent what he called six glorious years in the Legion and upon leaving this prestigious service was asked to become a fellow of the French Secret Service. There was no way Slick was going to make serving his government his life's work. There wasn't enough money in it, or quite enough excitement. But, he used his time well, gaining many influential friends and acquaintances.

He had met many people in his four years in the secret service. Enough, so that he could get favors when he needed them and through those friends. He met more and his reach began to increase throughout the Mediterranean and the North Seas. Also, many countries down the western coast of Africa, from Algeria around, and on down to South Africa. Even the Comoros and Seychelles Islands. He had his network established. He was capable of making deals in Europe, Eastern Europe and ninety percent of Africa. He had carved himself out quite an empire of influence and business dealings, along with partners. With both civilian and governmental officers from immigration to customs, he was one hell of a good man to know if you needed something. If Slick couldn't get it and have it delivered, it did not exist.

We had met in Nice, France and had become friends after I needed machine tools. He had them supplied in a country where machine tools are frowned upon. As we talked he discovered my true nature and mission in life. He decided to throw in his lot, at least part time with the clan.

We continued to talk about Slick, and Daria asked if he could make things much easier. Both Preacher and I replied in the affirmative. We filled Daria in on Slick's abilities and she agreed wholeheartedly. We decided to request his assistance. I asked Preacher if he would reach Slick and ask him to join us. If it was in the affirmative, to please let Daria know and she would make all of the arrangements. With that, we decided it was time to relax for the following reason, 04:30 hours comes mighty early. Preacher yawned and said goodnight to Daria and me and that he would see us in the morning.

Daria was also a little tired. With me, anything over three hours of sleep is a waste. I have not slept over three hours since I was a child under ten years of age. I have slept longer, but only in the situations where it was a major injury and I was hospitalized for an extended stay and drugged beyond comprehension. I did acquiesce to Daria's wish that I escort her to the third floor and walk her to her door. Of course, I would open it for her, and sometimes I would just walk through her room, to my room. We approached the entrance to her room and she just gave me a hug and went into her room. There had been too much going on in her world today.

04:00 hours and I found myself sweating like I was in a shower.

I turned to my right, and there was Daria and Preacher.

"Boots, are you okay?" it was Daria's quavering voice.

I answered with, "I think so. What's going on? Is there a party going on, or what kids?" My eyes focused on Daria and I saw tears in her eyes. I asked her, "What's the matter little one, you're crying."

She was almost sobbing, "Boots, are you okay?"

I assured her I was fine and looked over at preacher saying,

"What's wrong with you Preacher?"

He looked at me and said, "You still have them don't you?"

Then I knew. One of my omnipresent nightmares. They are as regular as clockwork. I looked at Preacher and had to hold back the urge to yell at him, "Preacher! What did you tell her?"

He spoke softly, "Only that it was one of your nightmares."

This time my voice did rise, "What the hell did you tell her!"

Preacher began again, "I told her it was a nightmare from Vietnam. Boots, she wouldn't let it go."

The mother in Daria was showing like a white phosphorous flare. She was sitting on the edge of my bed with a cool face towel trying to cool me down and wipe away my tears. Then, in turn trying to wipe away her own tears. I had been asleep for fifty-eight minutes and now my sleep time was a dead subject.

I remember the nightmare. A blow by blow account of someplace in Vietnam. It had been this nightmare, among many others that rocked my sleep every night. I had not had a pleasant dream since the day I turned seventeen. In my life, good dreams didn't come to me. They hadn't since the aforementioned birthday, or just before. I asked preacher, "How much did you tell her brother?"

Daria spoke up, "How awful for you, Boots. How terrible. No happy time dreams, only sadness."

I asked Daria specifically this time, "Daria, please tell me what Preacher told you."

Her voice started to break again, "Boots, I promised not to tell."

I asked very gently, "Please Daria."

She finally relented, "Preacher told me you had many friends in the regular Marines and that your men, and the Marines had objectives."

I thought, "Oh my God. This is worse than the nightmare."

She continued, "When you attack, most die. Friends. Your men. Preacher said you went crazy and charged the hill. Many times. You were wounded, but you would not quit. You were a

crazy man then, and you suffer now. I am so sorry."

I had to say, "Don't be Daria, it comes with the turf."

At this she burst out in tears again, "Boots, you were screaming and talking while you were nightmaring."

No wonder this beautiful, sensitive creature was crying. I said, "I lived through it and it eats at me all the time Daria."

She relinquished the face towel. I dipped it in the nightstand basin and squeezed it out. I began to gently wipe her face. Gently. The next minute she was crying once again. Finally, after a long time, she calmed down somewhat, and I kissed her on the forehead and then softly on each cheek. I told her, "It's okay, little one, I'm fine. It was a terrible thing to happen but it's okay, hon. Really. It's just sometimes, well, it just happens and there is nothing I can do about my nightmares except take them for what they are. They are bad memories and a soldier lives with them. Even Preacher."

That is when Preacher spoke up, "Yes, but nothing like yours, Boots."

I shot a daggered look at him and he understood to accept some and play down the rest. Daria calmed down more and I asked Preacher to please take her into her room.

"No!" she said very sharply, "No one goes into my room but you, Boots! Period!"

I answered, "Okay, Daria. Would you please do me a big favor and go into the bathroom for a moment? I want to get up."

She smiled and said, "Well, get up then, Boots."

I had to tell her that I couldn't because I had to get dressed.

A little meek, "Okay," came from her lips as she went into the bathroom.

I jumped up and pulled on a pair of sweats, slippers, and put on a robe. I called for Daria to come on out, and she came out in a flurry. She mothered me for approximately fifteen minutes before I reminded her that she needed her sleep. Preacher had already returned to bed. Daria reluctantly agreed and I took her to her room and tucked her in. I kissed her on the forehead and said, "Sweet dreams, my little one, sweet dreams."

She did what I could not, return to sleep. I was too upset. I left my bedroom after all were back asleep and headed to the roof by way of the kitchen. I had hoped to scare up a cup of coffee and ran into the early shift. When I came in they were a little apprehensive by my sudden appearance, but I signaled them to inaction, retrieved a coffee cup, then poured my coffee, then sat down with the help.

For me it felt like home. Not that I miss home, because I don't, but it did remind me of being with a family. To me, this was most enjoyable, seemed comfortable, and normal. It was just what the doctor ordered! I even had the opportunity to hold the head butler Alexi's grandson. It was very gratifying. There was no one else in the house that was awake. It was 04:25 hours and here I was. The captain of a ship without a whole crew, pacing the aft wheel deck, knowing that my first mate, and my Daria was also asleep. I hoped there would be no lasting effects from what I had put her through.

I returned to the kitchen and inquired if they had a hot pot for coffee. They did and I asked if I could use it.

Alexi looked slightly shocked and stated, "Sir, it is not your job to serve yourself."

I said, "Alexi, I do not want to interrupt the time that you have with your family before your duties start, and I am used to fending for myself."

He had a quizzical look on his face, "Sir, I appreciate what you are saying. Just by offering to, as you say, fend for yourself without bothering me, is not the usual attitude. Miss Daria is right. You treat good people with respect, no matter their station in life. For that, sir, I thank you and it would be an honor to serve you, sir."

"Alexi," I began, "if you insist on serving me, when we are alone, and no one will think less of you, do me a great honor and a favor and call me Boots, when it is safe for you to do so. Please. Do this for me. After all it is a name I am proud of and there are many people who are called sir. There are not many being called Boots. Relax with me, just a little." "Yes, Boots," said Alexi.

I was supremely pleased that I had made a bit of headway in unstiffening the headman. It made sense to me.

05:30 hours is a nice time of the morning. I was writing down names and specialties on a tablet for consideration for inclusion in the team going to Holland. The time I spent on the roof contemplating the mission and its location, caused me to think of what a melting pot of many races and cultures there were in Amsterdam. It dawned on me that an all American ninety-nine percent white team could be a problem. It could cause suspicion. The Mafia has many eyes and informants, and I would be willing to bet even money there was a plethora of informants in hostels and hotels in Amsterdam.

We could rent a house, but seven Americans living in the same house, let alone that six out of seven would be white, reeks of the unknown. My conclusion was that we needed a multicultural team. It would even be better if we added differing philosophies and religions. Nobody would think that blacks would live with whites, let alone all of the clan with a Muslim from the middle-east. We definitely would not look like a group of men together. With all of this staring out of the void, it seemed my initial snap decision would be the proper one. Although Preacher was a black Baptist minister and Slick was a Catholic, like I am, we had to decide who else we would need. Not only the total number, but what they could do along with the other considerations.

After the morning meal, I went to Daria and grabbed her for a change. She smiled broadly, and was extremely happy. She asked me if I was all right and I leaned down until I was an inch from her right ear. I said, "Thank you, for being there and for caring, Daria. It was a terrible nightmare and in truth, you helped to ease the pain and the memories. I am sorry you had to hear and see it. It is never an easy thing to be around."

Things began to become more comfortable, and I was also. I was trying not to feel that in some way I had terrified Daria on purpose. I asked Preacher to help call and locate all of the team members. I envisioned using the clan members that had the qualifications that would make it possible for the evolution I had designed in my mind to rescue Svetlana. I hoped my decisions would work like a charm and would give this plan the highest chance of success. Preacher looked over the list of contacts and declared that I had only chosen A list operators.

I told him, "That's for positive. When you are sticking your neck out, you protect it so your head isn't neatly separated from the rest of your body."

I asked him if he had any questions or comments, to which he replied, "Not really Boots. I figured when all of the personnel arrive, that then we will know what you have planned and who will be doing what job."

I retorted back with, "You always were an astute ass, Preacher."

On that note, we both had a good laugh. Daria just looked at the two of us, somewhat bewildered, as two warriors verbally sparred with each other.

"Here is the list, Preacher. This second page has their contact numbers. I have already contacted Slick and he's just waiting down time. He's already in, just playing by the rules and waiting through the cool off period."

Men, who seem to react to injustice, or need without thought, need time to rethink a commitment they might have made in the heat of anger, or for another reason. The object is to let clan members rethink and decide if a mission is a proper course for them to follow. I have only had to rethink once in forty years, and that was due to the imminent birth of a future clan member, and defender of the people. I felt it was a very understandable reason not to be involved at the time.

Preacher asked me, "Who do you want me to contact first, Boots?"

I told him that the list was decided by need, and that the last one was as important as the first. "Sell 'um Preacher, we need these guys in particular. I went over the list carefully, and these guys are on the top."

When he said, "Okay," and asked what to do about tickets, I looked over at Daria. "Well, speak up, babe. His name is Preacher, little one."

She seemed to be a fair bit taken aback by it all, and I smiled at her. "Just say, Preacher, Daria. After all, are you talking to mice or men?"

She smiled back and said, "Men, Boots."

I continued, "You know Preacher, so let him know, along with the rest of the silly sons of bitches. You can't offend them, hon. They are tougher than that."

Daria addressed Preacher saying, "If you need anything, for any reason, like consumables, hard pack travel, anything you need. Just ask me and I know the answers or the procedures. The only one that can say "yes" if I say "no", is Boots, but I do not think there will be much reason to think that you cannot have what you need."

"Preacher," I said, "I have given Daria the job of my assistant. If you need something, talk to her. If you need transport for someone in the clan, she will take care of everything. As long as you give her all of the information she needs. Is that clear enough for you? It's the way I set this up. I want you to contact Braveheart and Banger. Since Slick will be signing on as soon as the cool down period ends, we won't worry about him. Daria, have you sent him his ticket and his packet, along with traveling cash?"

Daria answered, "Yes I did, Boots. I sent everything by D.H.L. same day service, overnight express."

"Thanks, babe," I responded, "Well, let's get to it Preacher."

CHAPTER EIGHT

What can I say about Braveheart, other than he earned his name in Africa and in the Falklands scuffle? He was decorated in both locations for bravery and for service above and beyond the call of duty. He served in the SAS, British Special Forces. He received his name from his comrades. His mode of operation was very quiet. With Braveheart came other specialties. He had raced F-one road race cars and was beyond average in driving. Along with a steadiness that would and could hold men together in the worst of conditions, he was highly intelligent. His resourcefulness was legendary in Scotland and the units he worked with.

Banger was a go to guy. He did not back down, and if you were pinned down or wounded, he was the guy who would come for you. He was a dry character, with little, or no, sense of humor. His specialty was in major explosives. He boasted that he could cut a coke bottle in half, and had indeed made a great deal of money that way. This was in betting that he could, and subsequently cutting the bottle in half lengthwise. He has this bottle. Banger and I worked in Northern Africa on a joint mission. He had proven himself far more capable than most.

Sandman was a quiet man with a deep faith in Allah. A Muslim by birthright. His country of origin was Iraq. For six years he was a member of the Republican Guard military unit, although it should be made clear, Sandman had not fought the struggle in either Desert Shield, or Desert Storm. He gained his combat experience from the Iraq-Iran War. All he would say about it, as most do, was that it was his duty and that it was exceedingly brutal. It was a long endeavor, and he lost many friends.

He had a chance to cut and run from Saddam Hussein's Iraq before the start of the United States desert campaigns. I met Sandman through a mutual friend who had got him involved in our line of work. After he had made his break from Hussein's regime, he managed to flee to England. Here, he settled down in Manchester and married the bride of his choice. They opened a textile and import shop where they sell Persian rugs, not reproductions, and many products and curiosities from the Middle East. Everything from rugs to pipes and beyond. It is quite a remarkable store.

Then there is Bronco. I had met Bronco in Vietnam. His bravery and guts were apparent on Hill 881. Two and one-half companies of men were destroyed in the fight to gain possession of this hill. When he was wounded, he didn't even realize that it had actually happened. He was not unlike some of the other Marines who had become enraged by the death of their friends. He became a one man Marine Corps and he was not the only one. There were many more such men of his caliber in Vietnam. To me, what makes him special is he is my friend and a partner.

Bronco grew up in Cody, Wyoming with his parents, his four older brothers, his one older sister, and his five younger sisters. This was, I think, a dubious honor for him. He flourished with hard work, good food, and self-worth. He worked on ranches until he joined the Marines in 1967. He made his way to Vietnam and Khe-San, where I found him and we hit it off. It was a crazy war, but somehow, some of us returned stateside, God help us. Bronco had earned his ops name for his passion of riding wild bucking broncs, crazy horses, and even worse, on Saturday nights he rode bulls! He thought it was good exercise and a great deal of fun. Well, it takes all kinds I guess!

Daria was busy making arrangements. She was getting tickets and travel instructions sent to the rest of the clan. She needed to talk to me, in no uncertain terms. Much like me, she needed information, in order to take better care of her charges, at least as she saw it. She wanted lists of information of their likes and dislikes and what kind of food they ate. Flashing on Sandman, I had to inform her that he was Muslim and would require different foods than the rest of us. I asked Daria to please have someone figure the direction of true East, towards Mecca, and to please hang a picture of Mecca on that spot to mark it for Sandman. I was amazed at the efficiency of this young woman, Daria. She was a veritable whirlwind of activity in preparation for the imminent arrival of the clan. Daria seemed to come into her own with this endeavor to prepare five more rooms for the men. She called them the brave that were going to rescue her cousin.

Gregor had been very scarce, other than his appearances at the formal meal of the day. That evening at dinner, Daria announced to Gregor that the clan was now in transit for this location. She also informed him of the need for special foods, prepared especially for a Muslim warrior. This seemed to amuse Gregor.

He glanced around the table and then back to Daria. "Daria, I know nothing of the requirements for feeding Muslims, but I am sure Alexi would know something. If you need something, or a cook, please retain one for our guest."

After that there was only small talk. Gregor was a hard man to figure. He seemed to have little or no curiosity about what was happening, or how it was supposed to happen. All he had ever really said was that his field of expertise lay in finance, and not in war or field operations. That is why he had contacted me, and the clan. It would be different if we returned with Svetlana.

At the onset, I had hoped having a total of seven men in this house would keep Daria busy enough to detach herself from me, but this was not to be the case at all. In fact, she seemed to decide that I was who she needed to be with for the majority of her waking hours. I must admit, it was something I had become much accustomed to. I watched as Daria worried over the rest of the clan's rooms that the staff was preparing with her explicit directions.

The morning that my band of brothers was due to begin arriving, I was already quite awake when the clock spoke to me. It made me aware with its plaintiff insistence that I begin my normal daily routine. However, this was not a normal day and if it could go wrong, rest assured it would go wrong. At least I knew that it would not be a lasting permanent disaster. I had learned the day before that Daria had instructed the driver and assistant driver of Gregor's limousine, to hold a sign at the egress point of each flight that the clan was arriving on. When they were found, they received the same treatment I had from Daria.

Upon their appearance at the citadel (as preacher and I had begun to call the house), Daria released the newly arrived clan members to return to my side. In some ways I found this fact to be quite satisfying, yet somehow quite mystifying. I met my friends and fellow clan members with hearty handshakes and the inevitable hugs. This could seem strange to some, but I assure you, for our own reasons, it was quite normal. It was the greeting of a living friend. The clan began filtering in to this normally routine and quiet household, however, you could feel a kind of electric moment as each one of these men approached. These were my kind of people, raw, but a welcomed sight nonetheless.

After the greetings and reunions, Daria swept into the room as if she was among old friends. She became the quintessential lady of the house and hostess to all who were within these walls. She had spent much time in making sure that everything in each clansman's room was exactly as she had decided it should be. She was quite adamant that each accommodation for the individual members of the group would have everything humanly possible, at least within her power, that anyone could even theoretically want or need. At least, within her own moral standards.

Banger was the last to arrive, entering the citadel at 23:20 hours. I was not there to greet him. In fact, many of the clan were already asleep in their rooms. I was in my rooftop fortress with Daria. I had been on the roof for approximately an hour. I was having a drink and Daria was sitting demurely next to me. Just talking. Chit chat, talk like the kind close friends have. Discussing everything, yet nothing.

Daria spoke sweetly, "Boots, do you think the rooms are okay?"

I smiled at her, "Yes Daria, I think you did a great job."

She acknowledged this with, "I wonder what went through their minds as they opened their respective closets and found suits, shirts, and all of the accessories?"

"I would imagine they were surprised and secretly very pleased, just like I was," I said.

Daria smiled back at me and looked up saying, "I hope so Boots. I hope they feel exactly like they are home."

Alexi entered the glass fortress in the sky and announced that a Mr. Banger was here to see me. I thanked him and Banger entered the sanctuary that I had set aside for myself.

Banger was the first to speak, "Hey Boots, this is a bit of alright, man."

I laughed and said, "It's not like in the bush is it Banger?"

Banger shook his head, "I should say not, mate."

I continued, "It's almost like a dream, you know, too good to be true and not wanting to relinquish everything, you're bloody afraid to close your eyes for fear it will all disappear." "So, how goes it, Boots?" asked Banger.

I answered, "As it always goes Banger and how does it go with you?"

He retorted, "Bored out of my gourd, Boots."

I had to laugh at that, "Well, Banger try to get some sleep if you're capable. Other than that, tomorrow we will start with a talking expedition."

This is when Banger looked at me and asked, "Did Braveheart tell you?" I must have looked very quizzical because Banger said, "Damn, Boots! He talked to the Czar and the Czar lives in Amsterdam now!"

"What?" I said, "Well, we can talk about what he does. You don't suppose the Czar is involved in any way in this mess, do you?"

Banger responded, "No way Boots! He hates the Mafia as much as all of us!"

His statement made me think long and hard.

"Hey Boots. I'm fagged out, man. I got to get some sack time."

I understood him being tired, "I'll see you in the morning, bud."

"Okay," responded Banger, "See ya on the flipside."

Watching him leave I replied, "Ditto, my friend, ditto."

I was not quite ready to call it a night, and stood up to stretch. I then found myself face to face with Daria. It was a mutual reaction when we hugged each other with happiness.

Looking sweetly up, Daria whispered, "It's going to happen, isn't it Boots?"

I looked down at this diminutive girl, and I knew what to say, "Yes, Daria, it's going to happen. By my blood oath and the oath of these fine men who have come, I swear that we will do this mission, even if it was to be the last one I ever do."

This seemed to please her and she bid me goodnight and bustled down to her room. I watched her leave and to myself I said, "With my life, Daria, I promise."

Sitting back down, I lit a cigarette and thought about home, my wife, and everything in my life. This would be the last time I could allow those issues to enter my thoughts. There could no longer be time allotted for this. No subject or occurrence enters into my mind once I'm in my world. The world of my wife and family could not interfere or cause any kind of distraction in these endeavors. It could get me dead, and they wouldn't want that. I hoped for Daria's sake she was pleasantly dreaming of how romantic it all seems to be from a distance. If only she knew the truth, but I am not sure she ever would understand.

Morning for the crew was of course early in the A.M. Everyone was expected to be on the bounce and ready. It was time for work, not lollygagging. There would be little time for anything else but planning and preparation for the mission. The only real distraction from planning and training were Daria's dinners. These were put together in such a fashion that they were semi-formal dinner parties. She was lavish in these dinners and in her own inimitable way, she was indeed the grand dame of the house. She had taken the greatest care and pride in serving Sandman authentic foods, cleaned and prepared to Muslim standards, by a trio of Muslim cooks. The only thing that interrupted training was news, if any, meals when needed, and Sandman's prayer schedule.

There was to be an extremely formal dinner that we were all required to wear tuxedos to. It was a truly impressive sight to behold, if you can imagine the clan in tuxedos! Gregor had decided to show off his private army for the express purposes of taking care of some personal business that he had overseas. He, of course, did not introduce us as military men, nor did he state the purpose for which we were training. However, one fellow made a statement that hit closer to home than I felt comfortable with.

This white haired gentleman looked around at us and said, "Gregor, these fine fellows act almost like a security force."

All eyes turned to Gregor for some kind of explanation. To Gregor's credit, he never batted an eye as he said, "Nonsense, these people are the cream of the crop in their specialties and are capable of acting without my consent in all things. They were hired to do just that."

Even though he really said nothing, or gave any information, this seemed to satisfy everyone at the table. I did, however, catch Daria and Preacher smirking.

There were half a dozen notables from Gregor's family, along with his banker, a stockbroker, a judge and several others. I think, that in some ways they were shocked that people from different walks of life other than their own, could have manners. I must say even I was impressed that there weren't any large or even small faux pas committed by the members of the clan. The truth of the matter lies in this. Not all people, who have wealth, have manners, and people who, in comparison have very little money, can have manners. Many times they act as well, if not better than most of the elite.

CHAPTER NINE

It took a good forty-eight hours for the guys to get over their jet-lag and culture shock. It was that long before we could begin to discuss the mission that had now been dubbed, temporarily, "The Amsterdam Project." Day one, we were all seated around our conference table. I was at one end of the table, with Daria at the head of the other end. We began discussing some ideas when Braveheart asked if he could relate some information that he had already gotten. This info it seemed, came from my old friend, the Czar.

Braveheart began, "It seems, Boots, that around fourteen months ago the Czar moved to Amsterdam. This was solely for the purpose of being with his girlfriend. His house is approximately one and a half miles from the city limits of Amsterdam. He wanted me to tell you all, 'Hi,' and he misses us. Anyway, I am sure that if we wire him the picture, he will find the building. Better yet, we have a main street name. No address yet, but I can call him and maybe get some things moving."

The Czar in Amsterdam! This was a great break! "Okay, bud, get moving."

Braveheart went to place the call and Daria asked if she could get me some coffee, which I answered in the affirmative. I asked for half a dozen hot-pots and some cream and sugar. "Make it strong, babe," I said.

She answered, "Okay, hon."

Yes, Daria would be useful, that was for sure. I spoke directly to Preacher, "Preacher, you know we need intel from outside and inside. But, I mainly need to know about the interior of the building. You know what I mean. Stairways, halls, elevator, if there is one. Who's on what floors? We also need to find out exactly where Svetlana is being held. Intel is paramount to the success of this mission, Preacher."

Preacher answered, "I know Boots. When do I leave?"

I replied with the best answer that I could give him. "I haven't decided yet. We have some security precautions to be considered. You sure as hell can't stay at the Hilton or another brand of upper budget hotels. If you are there as a representative of God, trying to minister to the women of the night, preaching redemption and trying to bring God and some hope into their lives, we can't send a fancy pants. We will have to find somewhat more suitable accommodations for a preacher such as you, but still try to keep you out of the worst places. If we can't find out the information we need from here, you might have to locate something yourself when you get there. Maybe we can rent a place for six months and then you would have a place to stay. With that kind of duration on the length of time you had paid for the rental, no one would ever suspect that you were not going to be there that long. A good set of eyes could pick up on the fact that you rented a place short term, and left. It coincides with the operation and the sudden departure tied with it, could mean trouble coming your way. We do not want the Mafia thinking that you are anybody. We will also see what the Czar knows, if anything."

It was time for me to speak with the Czar. I dialed and it rang once and once again. Just when I thought he might have split, you know, gone out, here he was answering the phone with a, "Howdy y'all," that he said in a heavily accented Russian voice.

It was a sound for sore ears! "Hey, Czar! What's doin'?"

He answered in his familiar voice, "Well, well, friend Boots. I was wondering if you would find way and time to call, old friend!"

Of course, I wouldn't have missed the chance for the world. The Czar. Suddenly, a memory flashed into my mind of long ago in a small bar in Greece. Although the Czar and I were actually bitter enemies in Afghanistan, and several other small skirmishes we had found ourselves in, we were both the same. We were both a product of our respective military services.

The Czar was the product of the Soviet Military Machine. He had been decorated time and again in his countries service and was a hero to his own people. But, as he said, all good things must come to an end, and he was much happier to be on the other side now. After all, there was not a lot going on at home that was good.

I had been in Greece working on an operation that was drawing to a close. I had decided to stay and relax for a few days. The operation I had been on had been very demanding, and as always a whirlwind of activities. I had found a quite respectable restaurant/bar with extraordinary food. Whenever I was hungry, I ate there. As the meals came and went, I could not help but noticing this very large man. He seemed as large as the bears I remembered from my childhood in Alaska.

We met when he came over to my table to find out exactly who I was. We began and continued to talk. This is something that I rarely do. It became apparent we had many things in common. He had been involved with the Soviet invasion in Afghanistan. Something that I had been in bitter operations against on the ground in an attempt to prevent the invasion. We helped to eke out a successful win and had handed this man a defeat. It had been reversed rolls in another conflict. We talked, and it became apparent we would call a truce. We agreed on a cease fire, so to speak. After all, those were days gone by.

After we came to our respective understandings, talk was far more pleasant. After the truce we shared quite a few very wonderful meals together and we found ourselves becoming fast friends. The kind of friend a soldier can only be with another soldier, even when they have stood in bitter opposition to each other. We had many good-natured and hotly contested disputes between us, but we always seemed to laugh together and the tension would break like a glass thrown at a wall.

Two different views had become one and I found myself with a very good friend in this bear of a man. The Czar, as his friends call him within the circle. We were no longer in opposition, although in some ways, all people are. I asked him what he did and he was very candid.

"I rescue people now, friend Boots."

This struck me as very strange, but extremely funny! Two opposing soldiers, winding up doing the same exact thing! I could not think of a better use of the talents that our respective governments or our military and war training and service, had instilled in us.

I started to laugh and he was besmirched as he said, "You find this funny, friend Boots?"

I could barely catch my breath. As I gasped and choked out the truth of it all, that we were finally on the same side. He laughed heartily with me, and then we cried together. This bond, between men of war could not, nor would it ever be broken.

Back to the now, I asked him, "Are you sure about getting involved in this Czar? It might get really tricky and maybe we will all end up dead."

He answered how I knew he would. "Is okay, friend Boots. Czar has long memory, pretty long anyway."

I asked him if he could find us a place to stay that was inconspicuous.

He replied excitedly, "Have got place for you. Have townhouse on property, only flowers around. Have one neighbor, she no care, can have lots of friends. We have big party."

I felt a great relief, "Thanks, Czar. Is there maybe something that Slick could send you?"

Again his loud voice boomed, "Have old Russian tools. No need new tools. Is all right. You come do job. We have good time screwing over Mafia. Make Czar very happy. I no like them. They all need to be killed!"

I did not think it would be necessary to kill them all. "Okay Czar. Let's just get our package and go sailing."

This made Czar happy. "Yes, Czar likes sailing. We get package, maybe have some fun, then go sailing. Czar good sailor. Master."

It was time for our conversation to end. "Okay, Czar," I said, "Give me a buzz when you figure out what's what and maybe a look see at who's who in the zoo."

He stated back, "Da Boots. Das ve danya, my brother."

"Das ve danya," I answered. With that exchange we had now become, quite unexpectedly, a strike force of seven. The brotherhood of the clan works like this and we were all proud to be members.

To say I was surprised is an understatement. That was a break for our side. I wonder what it will be that is inevitable. It had been a most fortuitous day to find out we have a friend where we were going, and he wants to help. He also has an answer to our egress problems. I will have a map tomorrow. Thank you Barnes and Noble!

As one by one the clan wandered into the war room, I felt myself getting angry about the willy-nilly procession that was occurring. I would rather be thirty minutes early than to be one minute late. I yelled into the room, "Damn it! If you don't want to be here then why did you come? You guys have been wandering into this room for twenty-three minutes! I hope you fellas don't plan on doing this when we're doing the job!"

This was met with "no," all the way around, and "sorry Boots," and a "jeez," but they all hurried to get into place.

"Alright guys," I said after taking a deep breath, "Just get here when I ask."

I began as soon as everyone was seated, "Preacher, I got you a home in Amsterdam. It's expensive, but it had to happen. Real expensive, as in nothing! You believe that? I got a hold of the Czar and you'll be staying with him. In fact, we're all going to wind up at his house. Just outside Amsterdam. The Czar says it's on a quiet lane without people and he's got plenty of room."

"Wow," exclaimed Preacher, "it must be some kind of house! Hey, maybe it's an old windmill. If it is we might be able to start an observation post, if it's in the right position."

As dinner approached, a halt to the myriad of discussions were curtailed until after our meal. Here was Daria. She had remained steadfastly at my side, with her holding my arm and making like the perfect hostess, of which there was little doubt. With the other five men firmly within her realm of influence, this young woman had become what she had been trained to be since early childhood. She was the hostess of all that she surveyed and touched. Although, it would seem as if the clan was speaking to her, it was usually long-winded and personal. It was not the same however, between the clan itself. If we were talking and discussing the mission, it was short, choppy, and to the point. There were no expenditures of intellect or formal speech, but this was soon to change.

Braveheart remarked at the evening meal that it was fortunate, that a man like the Czar would be a tremendous asset, even if he had not lived in Amsterdam. It was a point that could not be dismissed. As the meal was winding down and Gregor had been so scarce, I asked Daria where on earth he had gone. Just about that time he walked into the dining room. It was about two-thirds the way through dinner and he was profusely apologizing for his absence. He informed us that business had required his undivided attention and every bit of time that he could spare and provide. Since this particular transitional business was finally past the critical juncture, he could now relax for a while. Everyone felt the same thing. A sense of relief at knowing our benefactor had been once again successful.

We had decided to prolong the dinner hour in order to be respectful to Gregor. He appeared to be genuinely pleased with this. As dinner subsided, the clan, I, and Daria, with Gregor in tow, went to the roof, as all eight of us were hard pressed to fit and to be comfortable in the sitting room. We were all seated and Gregor wanted to know if there had been any solid plans.

I steadied myself and said, "Gregor, we have a foreword base in Amsterdam with a friend of ours, known as the Czar. This base is at his house. We have been assured that it has the needed room and facilities for all of us as we filter into Amsterdam. This will be done in stages."

The clan all stared at me like they were asking, "Why didn't you tell us there was a schedule?"

I continued, "When I spoke to the Czar he made me swear to inform you of the deep shame he feels for his countrymen from the Rodina. He also wanted me to explain that until this situation was brought to a satisfactory conclusion, he would remain engaged in the fight for the return of your family member."

Gregor looked up and spoke, "When you talk to your friend, please tell him of my acceptance of this apology and of his commitment in attaining Svetlana's return. I am very grateful." With this said, Gregor asked if there had been any talk of the final plan.

I had to tell him there was very little. I told him how the Czar would be reconnoitering the building in an attempt to acquire as much intelligence as is possible. If he was as successful as most of us were, he will get the needed information to us. Then an evolution will be brought forth immediately.

Gregor looked very thoughtful when he said, "When all of this is done, I do not ever want to lose track of you, my friends. If you ever need me, you know how to contact me. You will always be on my mind and in my heart. I have grown accustomed to all of you and think of you fondly, as do others in my family."

On that note, our friend Gregor bid his adieu and retired to the fourth level of his home. It was where he felt most at home. I was never on the fourth floor and to Daria's recollection, other than Gregor's valet, there has never been a visitor.

The night was wearing down and one by one, my friends took their leave, albeit with much deference to Daria. She indeed had become the one bit of beauty in this ugly world of our reality. I believe it made her feel very special and I found myself pleased and happy for her. That reinforced my feelings of the clan's collective trust and kindness.

CHAPTER TEN

Morning crashed into being with the Czar calling before I was awake. With the International dateline and the amount of time lag, it took us both by surprise. I asked him if he could wait for a moment, as I was still in bed and in the throes of sleep. He acquiesced. When I returned with some paper and a writing instrument, I indicated that I was ready. Something funny. When the Czar gave a verbal report he spoke perfect English. Not the Queen's English, just American English. "Boots, I have found your building. Is a four story, small office type building. It has two, I repeat two, entrances for everything that comes and leaves. Supplies, personnel, and clients. One door opens onto the front main street where the viewing windows are. Directly in back, and to the right looking in from the elevator, is a rear door. Some clients come through this, but it's mostly used for personnel and supplies. As I said, there is a front door, and it is in a direct line to the staircase. The back door can be accessed by the stairwell just as easily. It seems the first lower houses drugs, alcohol, and gambling, along with what we expected, sales of prostitution. I did not get past the first floor. But your package is above the first floor. As you walk in through the main entrance, directly in a straight line is, ah, how you call, customer service. To the right of this point is alcohol bar and gambling. To the left of both of these places is the drug bar. There are many people. Cannot tell who is who."

We could definitely use this information. "Thanks Czar," I said.

He answered, "You're welcome friend Boots. Come soon to go sailing in North Sea."

I told him, "Okay Czar. Czar, I'm going to set a baseline evolution. Do you want me to express you a copy?"

He told me that was not necessary. "Boots, you to show me when you get here and we will fix good like should be."

I retorted, "Well I hope there is not too much to fix. Will you be able to pick up your guests, or should other arrangements be made?"

He was quick to answer, "Arrangements with people, not know here. Very dangerous. Czar will take care of guests. Know two people I too can trust with life. You meet when here, Boots. You for to think good too. Am going now, Boots. If need something or need me, please to call the Czar."

"You've got it brother," I answered.

"See you on flipside, Boots."

I told him, "See you there my brother, ciao."

"Ciao, brother Boots."

As the line went dead, my mind, logged this information into its proper file, another part of my brain, and my logic center was already in full operation.

I visualized this place that Czar had described and saw no inherent traps, only obvious ones. Although, experience told me there had to be one or two. The largest problem remained in intel. Preacher could not leave without a basic evolution. With knowing the plan, he could infinitely react faster to a change in scenario. All plans go through stages, from inception to the final plan. It would take time. I hope not too much. I wanted my package to be with me and free.

By the time I had completed my extended phone call to the Czar, and laying down in my mind the beginning of the plan, it was lunchtime. I knew this because Daria was getting insistent that her tummy was empty and she was hungry. When I looked at her, she seemed a little distant, so I asked her, "Why?"

"You're ignoring me and I kind of dislike it, but I know that you have to plan," she stated.

I told her as kindly as I could, "If you give me just a little time, I will be starting to bounce this idea off of someone just to hear it. Give me a little time. Babe, this is important to us all. It's my plan, and the clans lives could be on the line, or even worse. The clan could cease to exist, at least on this plain of existence, and in this Universe."

The subject of parallel universes has fascinated me most of my life, while trying to discover where we go when we head for the flipside. Could it be possible that we go to an alternate dimension, or to a parallel universe? Only God knows for sure, but it is still fascinating and provocative thinking.

Daria, evidently understanding the complexity of designing a plan to rescue Svetlana, had decided that I hadn't been ignoring her from spite or ignorance. She realized that, thanks to my friend Preacher, and after confiding in Sandman. She began to understand how I felt and what my responsibilities were. She became like a second pair of hands, reaching things and handing them to me, as if she in her own way, had become like me with a heavy burden on her shoulders.

My early morning phone call precluded me from being available for breakfast. After the call was through, and after taking care of my morning duties, my day picked up. I felt the need for desks, map's, paper, facts, and work. I had duties. Duty to the clan, but most importantly duty to Svetlana. It was time to begin the planning stage. Thanks in part to what Czar had discovered, and in turn had related to me, along with photos and a reasonably hand-drawn draft plan of the exterior layout and the first floor. I had been so intent on my mission to plan I had indeed caused some stir as the clan and Daria seated themselves for their breakfast. I had not appeared in my usual place, nor appeared at all, much to the consternation of all those who were there.

It was Daria who found me behind a desk, buried in paperwork, starting to plan. She began to speak and there must have been a moment that she had sensed and realized the imminent detonation of my temper. She spoke very softly and not in a demanding way or tone. She had come to take care of me and get anything I might need. When she said this, I melted and jumped up. I grabbed her hand and we proceeded to my glass fortress on the roof.

She even managed to make me laugh. Jesus, I need some down time when this is over! Knowing the ending of the story makes it so much easier to see the mistakes in something that has been played. Unfortunately, I did not have this luxury and would undoubtedly make mistakes. After an hour of small talk and luxury on the roof, along with a croissant type bread (only it was of Russian origin), along with approximately ten cups of very strong, black coffee, I indeed felt somewhat human once again. It's never easy to be responsible for life, and keeping that life viable.

I felt it was an appropriate time for me to return to my den of papers. When I told this to Daria, she only nodded her head in affirmation and suggested that I could work and eat in the war room. After all, as you know, there were all the necessary facilities within that room, including a shower. It was a striking idea. I would only have to sleep when I needed it on the third floor. I agreed without hesitation. I would not have to depart from my brainstorming.

Daria was there. Period. She made sure I had coffee, food, and she was insistent that irregular breaks were fine, but that I needed time away in order to mull over points and counterpoints. She became my sounding board. After all, she was a logical person, and the aforementioned plan would not be a document written in stone. It would be open for discussion, deletions, and improvements, depending on the insight of my people. In the end, I was quite sure we would have not only a fully operational plan, but an almost perfect plan. I use that word with apprehension. Perfect plan. Knowing that perfect does not exist in this world, or in this instance.

I attended one more of our formal dinners, and announced that until I could get this plan set up, I was retiring to the war room. I explained to them, "If you guys need anything, that's where I'll be, but talk to Daria. I almost tore her pretty little head off her body this morning when she had inadvertently disrupted my train of thought. If it's something that you need, talk to Daria. She is in charge of that too. I know you guys want something to do. Practice what you do. Practice on each other. Find the stairwell and quit riding the elevator. Work on moving silently within a closed environment, like the stairwells. Close the doors and listen to how you move. Stealth and silence is what we need. We have three floors to control full of bad guys. Braveheart, take Bronc and Sandman. Preacher, take Banger and Slick. Attack each other, but silence is the rule."

"Gotcha, boss!" was the chorus of voices.

Tonight Gregor was joining the clan for dinner. Daria explained my position quite succinctly, to the point Gregor queried me on the possibility that I had worked out a plan. I explained that the plan was within the throes of creation, and would be complete only when it was correct. He agreed that to be hasty would be inherently bad for all those persons who would inevitably be involved.

Dinner proceeded without further query or comment. Not to say it was not as normal. After dinner, Daria and I escaped the clan and Gregor. My first thought was, "Good. They can amuse Gregor and each other." I needed only one person in my life at this moment and time. My friend and keeper, Daria.

I sat down and went to light a smoke. I found I was out. Daria turned from the table. Not only did she have a drink for herself, but one for me also. It was Scotch, my favorite. She handed me a pack of cigarettes. My brand too. I withdrew one and she already had the lighter flaring. I lit the smoke and knew it would be alright. I didn't know how I knew, I just did. It was indeed a truly great way to feel.

Sitting in the war room after nine days of near twenty-four hour days, with a haggard and much frazzled, Daria by my side, I looked at the plan. Still a little rough, but there it was. An evolution. A way to recover what we wanted, our package. I gently touched Daria's shoulder and she awoke. She looked up at me, "Are you okay, Boots?"

I answered her, "Yeah babe, never better. Would you like to go for a walk with me or are you just too tired? You look like I feel, and I feel shot, but let's go for a walk to the roof."

"Yes," she said excitedly, "To the roof. We have been absent from everything and the places we are accustomed to being for days." She fairly bounced out and grabbed my arm.

"Geez," I exclaimed, "You're a game young lady Daria! I just put you through what most men can't complete. When I plan, I have a tendency to be a very ungentlemanly fellow, cussing, screaming, and in general being a very unfriendly person. Most people shy away from me, in fact most people won't come near me when I'm in this stage of planning. It will be hard enough during the basic run through of a training scenario. Most don't want the double whammy that I dish out. I demand maximum effort from everyone, and even more from myself. I live with a drive and a code that tells me failure is not an option. I learned this from childhood in Alaska. To fail is to cease to exist. If you fail in the north land, you most certainly will not survive. My father and grandfather taught me this lesson. One of the most valuable of my one-hundred codes that I live my life by."

It was time for the clan to sit, hear the plan and see the papers; it is, after all, their lives and their decisions.

Gazing over I said, "Daria, would you do me a favor, babe? It will be time for Preacher to leave in the near future, with an arrival time of early in the a.m. Check to make sure we can book him on the red-eye to London and then from London to Amsterdam." "Okay, babe," she answered.

Still looking at her intently, I continued, "And Daria, thanks. I mean, really, thanks for putting up with me."

She smiled at me saying, "It was my pleasure. It was an experience that as I understand it from Bronc, that no one has ever been able to deal with, and I was determined to experience something like this. Boots, when you plan something do you know what happens?"

I was very serious with her, "In a way I do."

Daria continued, "Whatever you go through, I do not believe anyone can express that much emotion or intense pressure for so very long as you have. I had to admit that I wanted to run, but I stuck it out. To realize you must die a hundred times, and the pain you must feel remains when you are fighting through everything to get your way. Thank you for allowing me to witness this thing you do. It was exhilarating and humbling."

I don't have any idea of what she's talking about, but my wife understands it well, where no one else does.

Speaking directly to Preacher I said, "Preacher, as you know, Daria has booked your flight for five nights from now. You will, of course, have the time to look over the plan, but we need the rest of the intelligence material in order to refine this evolution. First things first. Work your way in, and make them think of you as a harmless preacher. I know you have it under control Preacher. What I need is the stairwell information, then find Svetlana. After that, a full report on distribution of their bad boys and the locations of their layout. Where their top people are. Their communications and the hired guns and thugs. I know it can't be done overnight and I don't want you taking unnecessary chances, but ASAP on the stairwell and body locations, okay?" He answered, "You got it, boss!"

Locking eyes with him, I said, "Thanks, Preacher."

He laughed, "You would do the same thing for this job, That is, if they would let a heathen like you in!" We both had to laugh at that statement!

Preacher, Daria, and I walked down to the war room only to discover the clan in place, and in heated discussions and frantic pantomimes already heavily in progress. I spoke loudly, "What's up guys!" Of course, everyone spoke at once.

When I yelled, "Is this a town meeting, or do you guys have a spokesman!"

They all just stopped talking, everyone laughed, and then Braveheart began, "Boots, you are assuming (a word that intimates of making an ass of you and me!) that there will be two exits of choice, and Boots, after looking at picture three, I disagree. The vehicle lot in the rear would impede an impending disappearing act with Boots and company. If you look you will see that there are two vehicles and an innocent vehicle. This lot then becomes a trap. It is too far to run to a vehicle, especially if there are bad guys who are inviting us back for a rematch."

Eyebrow lifting, I said, "The idea, Braveheart, was to ensure that there would be no pursuit."

His eyes widened, "Am I to understand that we will be killing all of their combatants?"

"No, Braveheart," I answered, "the presumption would be to disable all of their combatants."

He answered quickly, "It can't be done, Boots. Not with the present amount of manpower that we are planning to use."

This was something that merited further discussion, I'm afraid. I looked around the table, "At this point, who else has an opinion?"

Banger raised a valid point. "This is still a subjective plan. On the outside, it is a good plan. However, with Preachers imminent departure it will be a more solid plan when we get the intel that we require. As far as egress is concerned, I think out the front door is a very sound plan. We can electronically stop most traffic from advancing on our buses by means of directional spike units. You know, just like the ones they use on the cop shows we see on the telly all day."

I answered, "You're right. But that means someone has to deploy them."

"Then let Czar do it!" Banger retorted, "He'll get a big kick out of it!"

That being said, I asked the question again. "Is there anything further on this point?" It was done, and it was written onto a final sheet.

Preacher looked over the plan and he had only one comment. "You guys are too critical and too bitchy, but since you are that way, I can look at this plan and know it is the basic plan and will, in all actuality, change very little. So, I can go to Amsterdam and begin my arduous task with a clear conscience, so I can feed you guys and Boots the information to finish the evolution. With that said, I will begin to prepare for my little trip coming up in a few days. I'll see you guys and Boot's assistant at dinner." Preacher left.

I turned to the rest of the clan, "Okay guys. Point one of one-hundred is solved. Let's get busy with this and knock out the rest, and then go get our girl." The job began in earnest.

CHAPTER ELEVEN

Our day began little different than what seemed usual, but this day would not be business as usual. Slick had worked his magic again and gotten Preacher a one-hundred-eighty day visa for which he received the gratitude of the clan. Something seemed different though. It was apparent that an air of excitement pervaded the very atmosphere around us. It was with a new dedication about what we did that was apparent. There was no feeling of business as usual.

There seemed to be something different in the house. It showed on Daria's face, but her actions were more point specific, as though she expected a bomb to go off. I glanced over at Gregor. His face also seemed to show the same intensity. As if they had a secret. I don't like secrets and surprises infuriate me. The whole feeling made me apprehensive and on edge. This is not conducive to a clear mind or clear thinking. The reason for this apparent change would become exceedingly clear after lunch. Up until that time I continued to feel a lot of mixed emotions.

Lunch was finished and I looked at Daria and asked if she would accompany me to the glass fortress. She agreed, but seemed preoccupied with some thoughts of her own. We walked along towards the elevator. She seemed to grow more apprehensive.

I stopped and looked into her eyes, "Daria, do you not want to go to the roof?" Thinking my breath was bad, I had placed a mint in my mouth and repeated the question. She answered, "Yes, I would be more than pleased to."

She was definitely nervous as we entered the elevator she turned and looked at me and grabbed both my arms. She pulled me down a little bit and kissed both of my cheeks. It seemed odd, but enjoyable.

We reached the glass fortress without further incident. Daria had brought both of us a cup of coffee. I went to light a smoke and found that I was out again. Daria brought out a pack of smokes. I did notice right away that they weren't quite crushed, but they had definitely been worried a little. I took one out and Daria lit it. After we finished the first cup of coffee, Daria immediately poured two more and I lit another smoke. After I had taken a second drag, Gregor entered the fortress, and not alone.

There was a woman accompanying him. She was approximately thirty-five to maybe thirty-nine, maybe even forty. However, this was an extremely beautiful woman! The first thought to enter my mind is that Gregor was concerned by the way Daria had attached herself to my being, and maybe he was trying to interest me in someone else! He couldn't have been more mistaken, and I was wrong about his motives, way wrong!

Standing before me, as I said before, was a startlingly beautiful woman. She had green eyes. Not ordinary green, rather they were iridescent green. She had sandy blond hair that would've drug the ground if it had not been styled the way it was. From the way she looked, and the figure she portrayed, by all rights she could have been a Playboy bunny in her youth. She would have needed a bodyguard, no pun intended. I must have been somewhat transfixed, because Daria had to try more than once to get my attention.

This woman didn't have to get me to stand, as I was already standing out of respect and shock. Gregor and this woman walked in and came closer to me. Then they were standing two feet in front of me. In reality, the woman and I had locked our eyes for last fifteen feet of her journey. Gregor started to speak which broke the spell.

He said, "This is my sister-in-law. This is Sasha, Boots. She is a new arrival to this country. A fledgling American. She arrived three days ago from the Ukraine, in Soviet Russia. She doesn't speak much English, but then, of course, you speak Russian. She had a great desire to meet you and thank you."

I had to wonder why she wanted to thank me. Was it because I was the first real American man that she had met? It just didn't make sense, yet.

"Boots, I want to introduce you to Svetlana's mother."

This was his declaration. I was stunned and shocked into shame at having thought anything else, but it brought it all home like a jet crashing in front of me. I stuttered for words as Sasha came over to me with tears in her eyes and on her cheeks. It came home with a vengeance like I hadn't felt for quite some time. I do not believe that there were any dry eyes on this rooftop, nor should there have been. This mother was counting on the clan and me to free her daughter from a horrible situation. To return her as intact as possible, back into her mother's arms and to the bosom of her family. It was a humbling experience. All of a sudden I felt inadequate for even standing here. Even worse, was the feeling of abstract helplessness that this mother felt. It was a message shot straight into my heart.

Suddenly, I wanted to run away like a nine-year-old who had been caught in some peccadillo, or the thirteen-year-old who still swore he hated girls, only to be caught holding hands and kissing one by his friends in school. From these feelings, slowly came a feeling of anger. It grew until I was disgusted and angry. Why would Gregor do this? Did he not know how much I cared? Did he have any idea at the responsibility I felt? That when I engaged the clan, they could lose their lives on my watch? Personal safety meant nothing to me, but there were huge responsibilities inherent in this endeavor and extreme danger to the clan.

I stopped, as furious as I was, I said nothing. The only one who had an inkling was Daria. She had begun to figure out how I would react, but would never make a public issue of it. Time passed with Sasha. She, of course, only wanted to thank the clan and me. It's the connotations that hurt beyond reason. I can't begin to explain the tremendously wide range of evocative emotions that I felt. The only one to notice these emotions was Daria. She instinctively knew because of the experiences she had with my nightmares. I had unwittingly prepared her to read this from me.

Gregor and Sasha then withdrew because they had business elsewhere. I heard the elevator start on its way down after they left. Then it began. Something that happens to me when I am under tremendous strain. After the situation has been taken care of. I'm told it happens to some people, especially those in a constant state of extreme tension.

The rage I felt rose like the high tide engulfing the shore. Daria sat, and patiently watched. She made little noises as I swore and spouted off at myself, at mankind, and half the world. As these things do, it ran its course, until in the end I realized what was happening and squelched it down.

I turned and there was Daria. The Daria that could only say, "Do you feel better now?"

As fast as this rage began, it stopped and the tension broke. I looked at Daria and I knew that this girl was good medicine, and a lucky charm.

She didn't even ask. She got up and put ice in two glasses. She added vodka to one and scotch to the other. These were no normal drinks. These were full glasses. Even though I had never seen Daria drink alcohol, I had suspected she might. She could drink. She drank hers down without turning around, and then poured herself another. She then returned to our chairs, handing one to me and sipping hers.

She sat down and said, "You are like Russian man. You have bad temper like one. I'm sorry if seeing my aunt was wrong."

I had to catch my breath and told Daria, "It was not wrong Daria. It just made me realize how important it is to make this thing in Holland happen, and the tremendous hope your aunt has for her daughter, and for us to be able to do this mission."

Daria leaned over and kissed me and said, "You're truly a kind and caring man, Boots. You surround yourself with men who are like you in so many ways, but no one can measure up to your standards. Not even yourself. But, I know you can do this. I believe in you, Boots. You don't know how to quit, and you don't know how to lose. You're not built to lose. Are you sure you're not Russian?"

I told her, "No, I'm Baroque. My people come from the eastern end of the Pyrenees Mountains, starting around Lourdes and going east. We are as stubborn and pigheaded as Russians."

She laughed and then finally so did I. For some reason, probably good sense, we decided to call it a night and start back to work in the morning. Besides, I decided Preacher would be beginning his journey soon, and there was much to do before he left.

The next morning the meeting started, but there were no comments. I told them, "Yesterday afternoon I had the good fortune to meet Svetlana's mother. The bad fortune was after she left I tripped and blew a gasket. That's why I didn't make dinner. I'm sorry to all of you for being angry." Out of nowhere there was a noise. It was the telephone. Daria answered it and began to speak Russian, which made me smile. Now she was getting phone calls in the war room.

"Boots, it's for you." she said.

I answered the phone and a familiar voice boomed in my ear, "Friend Boots, you have Russian girl secretary, not wife no more?"

I told Czar how this young lady was a voted member of the clan.

He started right in, "You need to know this before you plan. I wanted for to tell you. Look around I did."

I thought to myself, "Please settle down Czar."

He began again, "Your favorite package is on the third floor, the controls are on the fourth floor. But know this, the second floor is pure poison. On the left, facing the front above the first-floor. There is no door on the stairwell until you get to the third floor. The stairs going to the fourth floor has a door. Your package is on the third floor, through a door. Go to your right. The door to the left has more prostitutes, but they are not the high dollar soldiers on the second floor, but they will yell. If you go through the left door on the second floor, you're dead. All dead. Through the right door are supplies for the whole place. There is an elevator. There seems to be large crowds on most nights."

With this information we would have enough Intel to complete a working plan. "Hey, Czar," I said, "Preacher is leaving soon."

Czar said, "I know friend Boots. Little Russian girl call Czar.

Tell me same. Is she cute?"

I had to laugh, "Damn straight!" I said.

He laughed in return, "You lucky old son! Two Russian beauties you have!"

I replied, "Thanks, Czar." We needed what were the missing pieces to our puzzle.

"Good," he retorted, "Hurry up, friend Boots. Much want to sail North Sea. Fun we will have."

Smiling, I said, "It's been a long time since I've been sailing, you crazy Russian!"

Czar's voice boomed back, "Problem solved friend Boots. No worry, Czar have control."

I asked him, "Czar, call me when Preacher gets in and if you should hear anything else."

"Can do, friend Boots. Das ve danya."

"Das ve danya, Czar." and the line was dead.

The Czar, in his own way, was helping far beyond what we expected, although I don't know why. I would think that he would have a hard time finding what we needed. Leave it to the Czar to save my butt and cut our time down!

I went back to speaking to Preacher, "Preacher, the Czar has it figured damn good! With what he just gave me the plan as you saw it, albeit not completed, it will be eighty-five percent of the final plan. Just be careful, and get in that door, brother."

Looking straight at me he said, "I'll do it, Boots. You know I can."

I told him, "I know that. If anybody can get through that door, you will, you silver-tongued Baptist devil!" The room burst into laughter.

After twenty minutes the room was dead silent. Gregor had brought Sasha to the war room. I let Daria translate what Sasha said. "The men in this room are brave. They are courageous. They are generous and they are kind. They have earned much love from my heart, and from other peoples of Russia. I thank you."

I had to break in here. "Sasha, my lady, please save your thanks until Svetlana walks through Gregor's door and into your arms, and then we can think about licking our wounds and a big party."

Little did I know Daria had heard mention of a party and in her mind, she would make sure it was a blow out. By the time everything was said and done we could move on, it was time to get cleaned up for dinner.

Everyone filed into the dining room. There was a pervasive feeling of the need to get busy, but first things first. I had no idea what to expect at dinner. Would Gregor come? Would he indeed bring Sasha? I didn't know, but secretly I hoped not. It wasn't a matter of being uncomfortable around Sasha, but I had enough pressure to deal with. The clan felt it also. You could see the strain on all of us, including Daria.

It made a decision I was contemplating much easier. I announced that tomorrow would be a day of rest or whatever for the whole crew except me. I hoped they would all just go somewhere. Period. And, to leave me alone to do my work. To plan this mission. After all, Preacher was leaving the day after tomorrow. It would be a good day to go to the war room and work undisturbed. I wanted Preacher to have an evolution to look at before he left.

At breakfast, most of the clan said how they planned to go to Broadway, catch a couple of shows and dinner out. That suited me fine. It meant only I would be here the majority of the day. Preacher would be flying out at 21:00 hours the day after tomorrow. A good man going into a bad situation. Before he leaves we will have a long talk about his objectives. I decided right now, that I was going to grab Daria and head for the fortress within seconds after dinner was done.

It has been such a mixed day of emotions with all that has gone on. Someday I'll let Daria show me her part of New York City, but until that day there is too much to be done. After dinner Daria and I headed to the roof to smoke, and just talk and to try to shake off this day. As we sat, I felt compelled to hold her hand, just to hold a hand and nothing else, and that's how it was taken.

It was a horrible night of nightmares with Daria winding up back in my room at 02:15 hours. That would be it for sleep for both of us. Two hours and roughly twenty odd minutes. She just let me cry and no one else showed up, thank God. It was a crappy thing for a friend like Daria to watch me cry. Although, she was crying too as the pressure of yesterday wore her down at last.

CHAPTER TWELVE

Breakfast was quiet and uneventful. Everyone seemed to be ready to be gone for the day, including Preacher. What they had planned no one was discussing. I knew these guys needed a break and I needed a break, so I could get some much needed work done. There were a couple of lists to be made and a departure schedule, along with the beginning of the final plan which seemed extremely clear in my mind today. My guys began to filter out. They went in two groups. Preacher, Bronco, and Sandman laughed as they left, and around fifteen minutes later, Banger, Slick, and Braveheart went on their merry way. Daria was nowhere to be found. Well, off to work!

As I got to the elevator, I was alone and there was no noise. There wasn't anyone but me around. I could see Alexi coming down the hall and asked him where Miss Daria was.

He replied, "She left twenty minutes ago, sir, on her excursion." I queried, "Is there anyone else here?" He said only the help was still there.

"Alexi," I said, "Could you bring me a carafe of full strength, black coffee down to the war room? Better yet, if you will make it, I will come up and get it myself, so you don't have to come down."

He asked me, "Aren't you going out, sir, like everyone else?"

I answered, "No Alexi. I am not. I have far too much work to do. Could you do me a great service? If anyone asks about me, tell them I'm not here. You know it's not true, and I know it's not true, but this work has to be completed."

He just said, "Very good, sir."

I pushed the elevator button and proceeded down to the basement where the war room was located.

A baseline evolution is just that. A beginning, and as facts are added, along with applicable suggestions, changes are adopted or discarded. The mission plan would evolve, hence, the origin of the word evolution. I read reports and studied maps. I concentrated on the things we did know, were added to the list of materials that would be the information to build a plan. The fourth floor would have to be neutralized without wanton killing or destruction. The second floor was identified as an area that not only needed to be controlled, but the extreme threat the people on the second floor posed. I deemed it necessary to eliminate these threats from engaging in the scenario. Elimination was a possibility, but not a probability. To eliminate this threat would take the input of everyone involved. That is how I saw it at this point.

The next morning we all convened in the war room. When everyone was seated, I began. "The clan will proceed to the building. Some of us alone. One group of three, one group of two. We will proceed at five to fifteen minute intervals. Banger will be the first in, heading for the third floor where Preacher will already be in place. I will proceed later in the tail-end-charlie position. Bronco, you are to proceed to the base of the stairs on floor one and lean against the wall. Sandman, I want you to start up the stairs, stopping in the middle between the first floor and the midway landing. Slick, you are to move up and take station on the landing above Sandman. Braveheart and the Czar will ascend the stairs to the second floor to control the enforcers. Braveheart, you will be carrying a package designed to stun and immobilize the enforcers. Banger is planning the package. It will be constructed at the Czars. Czar will back Braveheart up."

I continued, "This is not only our way in, but our only way out. Control must be kept in this area. When you have all entered the building, I will proceed on my way towards the entrance. At a pre-selected spot I will deposit a communication interference transmitter, better known as a white noise machine. It will begin its job at 20:00 hours. I will already have gained the place where this promenade will begin. From 20:00 hours we will have a nine minute window to complete this evolution. From start until the buses arrive we will have ten minutes to complete the promenade. It can be stretched to twelve minutes, gentleman. That will include collecting our package and loading it into the delivery van. We will then proceed to the docks, dumping the buses, and moving to the escape vessel and be underway. We have a total of twenty-one minutes. At this time, it could change, depending on new information that the Preacher uncovers, and what the Czar says."

The day I spent in relative quiet writing this evolution, I had a deep satisfaction at knowing that the clan had been running training scenarios all day, every day starting in forty-eight hours after their arrivals. They had good-naturedly groused, but after they study the evolution, they will be pleased their leader had thought to make stairwells the import of their training. Now we had to practice the evolution, and do it on time, every time. Preacher will be able to see the evolution and know his job from that document. All of us will finish the evolution and be highly trained in its fine points.

After the clan had seen the plan, without comment to date, we were getting ready to deploy our first man. Preacher would be leaving us in thirty minutes, going once again into the breach. But, he was not to be without an ally. Czar was picking him up and taking care of him. He would also back Preacher up in every way possible.

The time flew by and Preacher's gear was loaded into the town car. Goodbyes were done and I stepped forward, "Preacher you take care, my brother. Do your job if you can, but don't get dead or your wife will kill us all. I wish I were going instead of you Preacher."

He laughed, "Ah Boss, you couldn't do my job!"

He was right on this one, I could not do his job. Preacher entered the car to a chorus of goodbyes and Godspeed. I leaned in and told him not to be a wayward child. Call home, even if he hadn't found anything out yet. Just call home.

"Preacher," I said lastly, "Go with God, my brother." With that, Preacher was taken from our midst.

Surrounding me was the clan, disturbed in some aspects, nervous in others. But then, there was a prevailing aura of excitement and danger. It had started. This operation was now not on paper, but ramping up to the finale. Only how would we get there, and in what shape would we come through it all.

Things had settled down from the preceding evening with Preacher shipping out. Now, it was time to begin training in earnest. We went over the scenario and watches were checked and made to conform. When we began the first time, I was the coach. I must say that Gregor's house was a very good training aide and with his permission it became the standard of training for the mission. It was ideally suitable. It had a stairwell system similar to the other building and with area marker ropes and signs, it became the building in question. We laid out this area as close to the real thing as possible.

When Bronco entered the area, I told him to go to the bar and get a drink. Alexi the butler, handed him a coffee. After he received his drink, he got into position.

I said, "Bronco, remember you are the gate guard. You're the first defense going in, and you're defending the stairwell so the clan can withdraw."

He answered, "You got it, boss."

I told him, "With that cowboy hat of yours you will start this evolution. When you tip your hat up, it's a done deal. Watch your tick-tock. Three minutes after you see me the game is on. Sandman, you would have already been inside. Proceed up the steps midway."

I reminded him to relax, saunter, and be alert as he gained his position. Banger radioed he was in the attic and had deployed his package, and retreated to defense with Preacher (who was played by a valet). Slick, without being told was on station, as was Braveheart. The only one late was me.

"Is everyone's shielded communications on?" Through the talkies, there was only one comment, "Damn, the boss is right. Yeah, he's always right!"

These men were wearing the latest in personal communication equipment. It was shielded against white noise. It was designed that way. Everyone was equipped with a micro-wireless earbud that could not be seen, and a wireless microphone that looked like a button for the collar of your shirt. There was one on each side of the shirt. The small but extremely powerful transmitter was designed to transmit one-thousand meters in all conditions and environments. To know what a team member was up to, or into, could spell the difference between success or failure, or even life and death. Not only for themselves, but for the entire clan. There were two missing, Preacher and the Czar. They would have to be brought up to speed after the evolution was refined to its final disposition.

"Okay, guys," I said, "Let's run this scenario slow, and by the numbers. There is no hurry. Get the placement correct, and we can work on speed as we go. Is everyone ready? Let's do this! On my mark! Go!"

Their professionalism kicked in, and the two weeks of practice that they had while the plan went from a thought to an evolution, was time well spent. Although, the first nondirected run was a time-consuming failure. It was the first step. Much like a child's first step. Progress is made by repetition. The more repetitions that were completed the better you can walk, or the better you can complete an evolution. These were baby steps. The road might be long, but it is not interminably so, and we had began to build.

It had taken the clan, at least by my stopwatch, twenty-seven minutes to attain their positions. We would need far more practice and a lot of refinements in the application phase. This is what would occupy the clan for the next six days. It was what the clan did. Having heard from preacher and the Czar of his safe arrival, and how he was now a tourist, of sorts. The Czar, of course was being the tour guide, along with his girlfriend, Heilgrid. It was to say the least, not a five star Condi Nast tour.

The Preacher however, commented on the country, its beauty, and, "if you've never been here it's something to behold. It's a beautiful country!"

I made no comment. It might be beautiful, but it allowed heinous crimes to occur.

Preacher's voice sounded serious, "The Czar's boat needs some work before we join the regatta."

"How much work will it take, Preacher?" I asked.

Preacher sighed, "It will probably take the clan a week to get her ready for the sea."

I, of course, would have to allot the time to prepare this vessel. Whatever it needed, it would get, from the bottom to the crow's nest. With this information, in some ways, I was relieved. But, I was still concerned about the extra public exposure of the guys. It could be done. It would have to be done.

We practiced the evolution for a total of five more days, and it was time to begin improvements. Sandman stood at our first meeting after the base plan had been in play for eleven days and outlined a slightly different deployment procedure. He thought it should go from the top to the bottom instead of the way it was planned. In other words, Bronco would still act first gaining his station, but as that was done, Banger should go thirty seconds after that heading for the third floor. Braveheart and Czar to proceed to the second floor forty-five seconds after Banger started. Then Slick ten seconds after that, and himself twenty-five seconds later. As it was written down, he knew that we would be trying his revised plan.

We broke for lunch and Daria expressed a thought. We did not have to break for a meal, as meals and anything we could possibly need should, and could be made available in the war room. Most nodded to me in agreement and I turned to Daria and thanked her. I asked her to make it so. After lunch break, and for some of us, there was a chance to escape and have a smoke or two, and clear our heads. Daria would escort all of us to the glass fortress, making sure that coffee or anything else we would require was readily available. In many ways this was a preferential way to do things, however we would still have formal dinners in the dining room under the watchful eye of Gregor and Daria.

We began the new deployment plan and it worked in a much broader sense than anyone in the clan could have guessed. After running this scenario six times in a row, it was apparent that this deployment plan was far superior than in the original plan. After six runs we had reduced the time without going to full combat mode, down to sixteen minutes. It was a welcome suggestion that we reworked into the master plan. Training would continue until the time we needed to use it was attained. There were many other items to be worked out, but that part of the plan would have to be discussed in the a.m. Dinner was approaching and there was no further time left in this day for training.

The morning started as usual. The time had come for everyone to meet in the war room. As everyone found their places, the discussion turned from the plan to an operational name. It seems all of our missions received a name, and from an odd person, out it came. From Alexi, the butler. When he said the word he grew very self-conscious, because he was only a butler. Of course, my opinion is different. This man, at least to me, is the salt of the earth. One of us. The man who makes it all possible with his contribution to life. It was simple, not unique, but apropos. He had only said "angel," and it was unanimously adopted. "Operation Angel" had begun.

The drift of the clan was more on what we would need as far as equipment and supplies. I listened and simply spoke to Slick, "This is your department, partner. It's your specialty."

With that said, Slick arose and went to the blackboard. He took over from there. He stood and said, "Gentlemen, shall we begin? I had planned for, and inspected a quantity of firearms before I disembarked from my home. I perceived we would only be as good as our weapons. I came to the conclusion that we would need a quantity of pistols. I discovered that I would be able to procure a quantity of composite pistols in caliber forty, so I purchased these, along with ten, twenty round magazines for each. As I said, I looked at many weapons. I then procured five mack ten submachine guns, and then purchased fifteen fifty round magazines for each. These weapons are not unfamiliar to us and will be a serious threat to whomever we face. I tried to standardize ammunition, however, composite pistols come in nine millimeter and forty calibers and mack ten's come in nine millimeter, but I found them chambered in forty-five caliber, so I procured them, of course."

Slick continued, "Heavy weapons are plentiful in many models, but wanting certain capabilities, I chose to purchase eight Heckler and Koch model ninety-one battle rifles in seven-point-six-two by fifty-one millimeter. Each of these are accompanied by a drum magazine holding one-hundred rounds of ammunition, along with five magazines extra for each battle rifle. The ammunition will consist of armor piercing rounds and Hydro shock hollow points and some explosive tip. I've ordered enough for a small war. Since it was decided we would be leaving Holland by boat, I called my business associate and explained that I would need a defense weapon for a small craft. It will be shipped when I call. It is a long barrel fifty caliber anti-aircraft weapon. The ammunition is armor piercing and consists of belted boxes of five-hundred rounds. They will ship ten boxes."

Slick paced as he spoke, "I considered the need for demolition and acquired forty pounds of C-four. I ordered twenty contact fuses, twenty burn fuses, but I located thirty-eight light beam detonators along with three-hundred-fifty feet of armored twenty-six gauge wire. With the thought of having to disable personnel, I acquired twenty-five concussion grenades and five fragmentation grenades. As would be required in any operation, there are always things you want to leave no real discernible trace of, so I acquired three pounds of magnesium powder, mixed with white phosphorus, along with six timers for those nasty surprises. A white noise transmitter was located and acquired. A friend of mine made a copy for further need some day. Fighting knives are Gerber. I acquired one dozen. If we don't want them for us, I can give them as gifts. If you require something other than I have explained, tell me what we need, and it will come."

No one had anything to say, or their questions had been answered already. I patiently waited for the others to speak, but they did not. So I did. "Slick, what's the state of our paperwork? As I see it, this is what we're going to need. We can use our passports for official travel upon leaving, and then switch to false ones to check into Holland. We will need real exit visas and stamps on our real passports. We will also need exit visas for our package, but I would like to plan on more than one package, just in case. We will need no hassle entry and exit stamps for the country we decide to transit through."

"Let me interrupt, sir," said Slick. "If we go to France I have many friends who can help."

Looking around the room, I spoke, "So, is there any doubt about where we should sail?" No one disagreed, so we were going to France. "Okay Slick, let's go to France!"

"Very good, Boots. When we leave Holland, we will be fine.

I guarantee it!"

And Slicks guarantees never failed.

It was agreed it would be a long trip, but what the hell. I've always wanted to go back to France. I asked the room, "Is there any more business in this area? Does anyone have any questions, or needs?"

Bronc spoke up and asked about the kind of holsters that Slick had purchased. Slick stated how he had purchased ambidextrous combat shoulder holsters with magazine pouches concealed for the correct amount of magazines. Those who carried the mac-tens would be wearing the same type holster with vertical magazine pouches.

"Some of you," I said, "will be wearing both. It won't be comfortable, but it will give you tremendous firepower capabilities. Okay, is there anything else? Are these weapons and arrangements satisfactory?"

Everyone in unison said, "Okay."

"Next," I said, "Braveheart, since you're taking care of ground transport, what have you been able to arrange?"

Braveheart stood to speak to the guys when the phone rang. When Daria picked up the phone, she glanced at me. I told her to put it through on speaker and vox voice activated, so I could speak to whomever without having to hold the receiver. It was Preacher.

"Boots here, Preacher. You're on vox brother, talk to me."

"Well Boots, here's an up to date. I've been inside. They're still jumpy, but it's going to be fine. I haven't got up the stairs as of yet, but they are leaning towards me being able to. There will be an exception for a while. I won't be going into the side with the package just yet, but it is moving along very well."

Preacher continued, "Well, I've been to the boat. It won't take that much to get it ready. The sails are good. The Czar and his two friends are cleaning the inside and decks in preparation of you guys getting here. Czar thinks at least some of us should stay on the boat. He's got some blank lease papers, so he's going to lease the boat to one of us, which is done quite often. At least

to tourists, and let's face it we're tourists."

With that, he laughed along with all of us.

"But really, Boots, when you get here, we could get done what needs doing and supplies in about a week. It's a real heavily built boat. It's wide. Lots of room down below, at least enough for maybe twenty or twenty-five people, so there's room. You should see the engine room! This is not an average sailboat. It's not even an average sport fisher! I think it's faster then she should be, but very lacking in electronics."

"So," I said, "Are they available?"

Preacher replied, "Everything you might want for a boat is right here and available for the right price."

I asked him if he could tell us anything new about the building.

He said, "No, the Czar was pretty right on, but I will have to see when I get to go to the floors above, but I think the Czar was right on with his description. I will tell you this guys, the people who run the building have tentacles everywhere here from the government to taxi drivers. So, remember this when you come to visit."

"Okay, Preacher, thank you for calling."

"See you on the flip side, Boots."

I answered, "On the other side, my brother," and the line went dead.

"Well guys," I said, "he's in and if he thinks it looks good, I've got to believe he's right. As you know, Preacher won't give false information or hope. It is now 17:00 hours and I for one want a cigarette, but then I plan on returning to the war room. I think rather than dinner I'm going to beg off and asked Alexi if he would mind bringing me a couple of sandwiches and a salad, along with a drink. I want to continue working. You guys can do as you please but some of us should appear for dinner."

Most of them decided to go to dinner and resume in the morning, however, Sandman and Daria decided to come back to work. There were things to do and I couldn't leave one stone or question unturned, or not answered.

We headed to the glass fortress. Daria, myself, and Sandman.

Daria asked Sandman why he did these things.

He asked her, "What things?"

To which she answered, "Rescue people and children without pay. You could be so rich."

Sandman smiled and said, "Is it not written in your Bible, we are our brother's keepers? It is written so in the Koran. Mohammed preached mercy, to take care of our brothers was demanded. Is it not so?"

Daria answered, "Yes, it is like that in our Bible."

Sandman continued, "Then, where is the problem?"

"Well," Daria said, "You don't earn any money doing your job."

"I earn other things Daria," he stated, "as Boots does. It is a richness of the soul, not of the pocket."

She looked quizzically at him, "But you could be rich, and have all of the finest things, cars, and houses, or anything you want, as Boots would say, and he's wiser than most."

Sandman answered, "What could pay more than a smile, or to know what you do is dedicated to a principle of his God, as is mine. That God raises up the man of war to a level where his war skill is useful for other things than to take life. In doing these things we bring glory to Allah or God, whichever you call him. Boots also taught me that God is God, no matter what his name is."

I never spoke or glanced at these two who were discussing the why of it all, but I felt a deep appreciation for what had been said. It was the way I believe God has made us all, and gave us skills. I chose to do this, and it chose me.

In the war room, I asked Sandman what he thought of everything up to this moment. His only comment was he found it to be more than satisfactory. In a small way I was pleased. I was working on timing schedules and in order to be on time things would have to be planned plus or minus thirty seconds, which on the outside, and to a layman might seem impossible, but it's not.

I spoke to Sandman saying, "Sandman, this is how I got it figured. If we were to start the infiltration at 19:10 hours with me bringing up the rear tail-end-Charlie style, I will drop the com box and 19:51 hours. It will begin its job of communications disruption at 19:57 hours. The Czar has a friend who can take care of disconnecting ground lines at 19:58 hours, and I'm in the door. Bronco would already be in position, along with everyone else, or within ten seconds of my entry of our target building, and eight minutes later we are out the door and getting on the buses, and skating on out."

"That's a tight schedule."

For the first time in all the planning and training Daria had spoken. I was stunned and Sandman was shocked. I asked her what she knew that we didn't.

She answered, "I don't know anything else, but there's no safety margin. What if the buses are held up in traffic? If the stairwell is more busy than planned and other things. I don't do what you do, but I go shopping and find this, that when I'm on a tight schedule there is always a holdup. Something that takes more time."

Sandman had to admit that it was true, and so did I. There were too many variables and there was no slack time. The place didn't close. This would require more thinking and planning, however, we would stick to the original timeline.

Sandman looked somewhat concerned as I told him, "It's no big deal Sandman. Nothing goes off perfect, unless it is meant to."

It was time to relax a little. It was 22:00 hours. At the least it had been a long day with much accomplished, but as I've said so many times in my life, 04:00 hours comes early! I just wanted some time to just be me. I headed for the fortress with Daria walking quite silently. She was not her usual talkative self. We sat down and Daria apologized for butting in.

"It's all right," I told her, "You said the right things, kid, and you're correct in your observations. Nothing is quite what it appears and things have a tendency to work against a timeline. I should've taken a traffic problem into consideration before I was bold enough to write down a timeline. It's not like me to assume the best, only the very worst.

So don't fret yourself, ma'am! The rustlers won't get the cattle!" and I laughed out loud, thinking to myself, "I almost made a serious error in judgment."

I awoke in the morning and showered and shaved. I walked over and shut off the alarm before it could bother, or wake another soul. I was ready for the day. Was it ready for me? Shoes in hand, I opened my door and quietly proceeded down the stairs, careful to avoid the squeaky steps, and headed into the kitchen to rustle up some coffee. I found Alexi there.

"Don't you ever sleep?" I asked.

Alexi answered, "Yes sir, but not much."

I asked him why, and he said, "Well, it's a long story that I'm not comfortable talking about. I see you don't sleep much either, sir."

I told him, "No, I don't. It's a long story that I'm not comfortable talking about either. I don't talk about wars."

Alexi nodded, and with a knowing look said, "Neither do I, sir."

Changing the subject, I asked, "You got any coffee there, Alexi?"

Alexi answered, "Yes sir!"

"And Alexi," I said, "don't call me sir, I'm not the boss. I'm Boots, man, and I prefer being called Boots."

Alexi looked slightly uncomfortable, "We went through this before Mr. Boots. If I get used to calling you by your name, I might slip in front of the master, and that would not be very good for me, sir."

I gave him a knowing nod, "I got you Alexi, but know this, and I will consider "sir" as Boots, because you're as good as me, if not better."

With that, I received a pleasant smile with coffee. He was a good and kind gentleman, and I liked him very much.

I reached the war room and began with the plan, adding the timeline, plus or minus two minutes. There was a solution here, and I was determined to find it. As I thought, it dawned on me, if the buses were disguised as delivery vans, they could be parked there before the operation began. I was sure delivery trucks would be dropping off supplies to some of the places all of the time, but at different times. I've got to run this by the guys. I needed to know what Braveheart has in mind, because he was in charge of transportation. Anyway, it would be very important to know more than one route to the Czar's boat. I do not think we should leave our buses next to the finger pier that his vessel was moored at.

When we got there I would have him lay course to Cherbourg, France, just in case. It's a long ways down the coast. It could seem that we would be lost to the world for quite some time escaping by sea. That means, we will drop off their radar screens, and hopefully be far safer when we got there. Since I skipped breakfast in order to write a new list "of have to be completed", Daria and the clan came into the war room. Daria was beside herself that I would once again not come to the morning meal, but I had things that had to be completed.

Time was slipping by. In reality, Preacher had been gone for thirteen days, and twenty-five days had come and gone, since the day I arrived. It would probably be another eighteen days before Preacher had enough information and ease of movement to help the clan to help Svetlana.

The clan filed by the coffee and began to sit. I got up and said, "You guys talk among yourselves and discuss everything. Right now, it's my break time and I want to smoke and clear my head."

I left the war room and Daria decided I had been punished enough after her sharp rebuke about being a no-show at the morning meal. As usual, she was talking to me and I was on auto answer. Not that she bored me, but like all commanders time was my enemy, and was just passing quicker than I had hoped. I wanted to just have silence. Then she caught me. I said, "Uh-huh" when I should not have agreed. She started on me about how unappreciative I was, and I agreed with her. At that moment I didn't care, and told her so. She was shocked. "Good," I thought, "maybe she'll listen now!" I asked her what the hell the color of my curtains had to do with much of anything. She began to cry as she explained she didn't want me to be bored, and she was only trying to help.

I told her, "Daria, you do help. The changes in my room help, but it just doesn't matter to me right now. It is a nerve-racking time for me. What I'm doing is very time consuming, and with that responsibility comes stress. A lot of stress! I'm not trying to ignore you, or be mean.

Just bear with me and my moodiness. I'm sorry, babe. Please forgive me."

It was like I hadn't explained anything after the apology. It was just the same. She never missed a beat. I guess my apology was accepted after three cups of coffee, along with two cokes, and I would hazard to say seven cigarettes.

We returned to the war room where an argument was going on about something totally unrelated to our present mission. I blew my top, and proceeded to scream at the guys to shut up!

Sandman stood up, looked at me and said, "Fellas, we got big headman with stress, just like he always gets. Let's give him a break."

They all looked at me and Banger had to say, "Geez, Boots! Take a chill pill or something!"

That broke it and everyone in the room laughed out loud, long, and hard. Daria looked totally bewildered, which made every man-jack of us laugh all over again. It was good to be with my guys and the people who know me!

A little more relaxed, I said, "Guys, it's a pleasure to know ya. But, if you will look at the mission status board, here is a timeline.

We know the plan now, we have to make it work, right?"

I heard, "Okay, Boots. Let's get to it."

I looked around, "Thanks, Slick. Everyone set your watches." Everyone set their watches and I held the stopwatch. "Here's how it's going to work," I said. "This time guys, from the side door. It is clearly within the area we have designated the training area. We will start from the door, work through till we have reached the other doorway. Let's do it slow and by the numbers. The only thing that will not be included yet is the gradual infiltration inside the building, which will be added later. But first, we have to get the promenade down, and I mean we need to be able to do it in no longer than ten minutes. After that time, I'm afraid we will start being targets and not rescuers. Once we get it down to fourteen minutes, I will ask Gregor if we can use some of the staff as patrons."

Daria popped up with, "I'll be Svetlana!"

I laughed and replied, "I was just going to suggest that, dear." I must admit, this seemed to please her very much. I interjected, "I do not expect this to happen the first time, but I believe the more we run this scenario, the faster it will become."

The first time from the door had taken sixteen minutes, and that's half way. I looked for ways to make it faster, and slowly, it did become faster. This was not only from my suggestions, but each member of this team had a suggestion, and some worked, and of course, some didn't.

Bronc thought Banger and Slick should go up together. It worked, and shaved fifty-five seconds off our time. Why? I still haven't completely figured that out. Since I had the longest run from zero, and was last to move, I had to learn to move faster without drawing undue, or adding unwanted attention to myself. It wasn't easy. In the end I visualized my wife on the third floor, and it worked. It had taken eleven days to reach fourteen minutes. Too long of a time to be successful. It was time to get some bodies in the way!

The staff not only helped to set everything up, but willingly played the people. People we would have to go around or rescue. We could draw no undue attention from them. The attention part wouldn't work with these people. They were far too fascinated by what was going on around them, to not watch absolutely every move we made. What I had expected would be longer elapsed times, however, proved to be quite false. We went from fourteen minutes to eleven minutes in five days. The reason was under my nose. The times before, people were involved were longer. The difference was now everyone was trying to go unnoticed, instead of just going. It was gratifying, to say the least.

There wasn't much to critique. It was just a matter of making the operation automatic. The less we thought about what we were doing, the more deliberate every move became. The human mind and body economized everything. This process proceeded. The times grew shorter from eleven to nine minutes, which in a matter of time I believe could be reduced by those two minutes. If it was important, then I knew without a doubt, this group of men could accomplish it. We had now been training in earnest for approximately twenty-five days, with more of these days to come. Part of this time, by the nature of the mission, was spent in redesigning the plan. The base plan still stood, albeit much improved from the constant input of professionals and their experiences.

Dinner was dinner. It had become a routine, and one I seldom attended. Not from lack of interest, rather from an overwhelming feeling of expedience. I much preferred a light meal in the war room, much to the disappointment of Gregor during the times he attended, and Daria, who wanted to be near me at all times. I found that thinking was much easier when I was alone, and it seemed answers to problems came easier also, because it was. However, things and people who can distract you when doing something important can inadvertently get you killed. In this case, more than me could and would get killed, or worse, become enslaved. I felt the need to work alone while problem-solving.

CHAPTER THIRTEEN

For me sleep is short and days are long. It's been that way from the time I was a child in Alaska. Morning had started for me an hour ago at 03:30 hours. Old habits die hard. I did my morning calisthenics and had already shaved, showered and got dressed. I wondered if I would find Alexi in the kitchen, and like most mornings I would go in search of coffee. If there was no fresh coffee, I did have instant. After finding coffee, or not, I would head to the war room, where I felt a driven need to be. To make sure again, that nothing, no stone had been left unturned. While I was sipping my coffee, the phone rang. I answered and it was Preacher.

He started right in, "Hey, Boots. Sorry I haven't called, but I've been busy doing ministering to the souls of lost ladies, ladies of the night."

"You made it Preacher?" I feigned surprise.

"Sho' nuff, honey child!" he said.

I laughed, "Damn! You're good preacher!"

He laughed back, "Don't flatter me! Shower me with money, jewels, what have you."

I replied, "What I have is deep thanks and appreciation, along with a healthy dose of gratitude."

He just said, "That'll do son, that'll do."

I asked, "So, what's up Preacher? Talk to me brother."

He began slowly, "Where to begin? I guess at the beginning. I met with the headman. I told him what I was about, my mission, and preached to him. He not only likes me, he likes the idea of me ministering to the ladies. He gave his permission, but I wasn't let into the right side where our package was wrapped up." He took a long breath.

Exhaling, Preacher continued, "Three or four days passed and I went back to the head man and asked why. He didn't know, but he would fix it. Even whores need to believe in God! He was sure that they needed the word of God." "Amen brother," I answered.

He began again, "The next day I was allowed access to these kids, but the personnel have this need for ministering too, at least the boss, Illyavich, thought so. For the last nine days, it's grown progressively looser for me. I can almost come and go when I'm needed, or if I need to help one of these wayward girls. For some reason they see me as a friend. There are a total of seven girls on the right side. All of them are young. I think our package wouldn't knuckle under to them, Boots. She would do as she was told, but just barely. She still doesn't trust me, but it's better every time. She's the oldest. They get younger, until we have a little French girl who is twelve years old. I'm taking the little one. Period!"

What could I say to this? "Okay preacher."

Preacher was very serious, "Boots, there may be more volunteers than I thought."

I asked, "How many?"

"I'm not sure," he said, "but the two for sure, maybe three or four. I don't know. Here's the scoop. On the fourth floor, that's where the bosses are, it's for sure you have to have a key to make the elevator go past the third floor. There is a stairwell door, but it has a sign that says "broom closet." It is hidden in plain sight. The catch to the third floor is you have to buy your ticket to get there. It's two-hundred U.S. dollars for the left side, and five-hundred dollars for the right. You get a temp key only. The deposit is two-thousand U.S. dollars. You get your money back from the client desk when you come down. You do the math, Boots."

I asked him, "Preacher, what can you tell me about the second floor?"

He said, "It's pure poison, Boots. If you turn right, you won't get in. It's a supply room. You know clothes, linens, food, and booze. They've even got a drug vault in there! If you turn left and open the door, there's twenty-five, armed killers in there. From what I've heard Interpol's crack unit won't tangle with these guys."

The Russian mafia has a long reach and plenty of horsepower.

Preacher told me, "Boots, I could find nothing on communications so far."

I replied, "So Preacher, what you're telling me is that there aren't any surprises for us. It's pretty much what you and I doped out from the intel Czar sent to us. Do you know where the passports are kept?"

He answered, "On the fourth floor, Boots, but I don't think it's worth it. Tell Slick."

I had to agree with him, "Is there anything else Preacher?" "No," he said.

I asked him, "When are you going to be ready for us, Preacher?"

"Anytime, after one more week, and when will you be ready, Boots?"

"You and the Czar should be receiving care packages within a week, and with luck, we'll be ready to start the dance in fourteen days, Preacher, with a promenade date in twenty-one days, if there are no hitches. It will be stretched over four time periods. Itineraries will be shipped with flight plans and airport info when we are ready. It will come DHL. Is that satisfactory?"

"Fine," said Preacher, "It's a pleasure doing business with you, sir."

I replied, "Be safe, Preacher."

"Back at you," he stated, "See you on the flipside, Boots."

I answered, "On the other side, brother."

The line grew silent. A serious bead of sweat ran into my eye. Damn! This crew just ain't gonna catch a break. Although, it could be worse. It can always be worse.

I had no plans to let anyone but the clan and Daria know, and if anyone finds out Daria will be blamed, and the mission will be scrubbed, for a while, which meant most certainly costing a few lives, and I don't mean ours. I contemplated what I had written down from Preacher. I was itching to go now, but if nothing else I have learned to be patient waiting for the odds to favor victory, rather than defeat.

After the morning meal, which I did not attend once again (I had already had breakfast with Alexi), the clan filed in. I sat staring at them. I didn't utter one word. I just had to look as Daria began to speak. She said little after she got a look that would freeze water. I just sat there and wouldn't talk. Bronco suspected, but no one else did. They got coffee and milled around. I stared. They were still talking to each other, and not too seriously. I watched Bronco. He was unmoving. All of a sudden, I think Sandman sensed something. He looked at Bronco and then me, and grew still and quiet, as the others with no proclivity to get it together, in a sharp as a razor knife, barely audible voice, I told them I would no longer deal with undisciplined and rude personnel! Slowly, with many valuable minutes lost, I waited for the problem to rectify itself. In the end, it didn't. I lashed out like a grizzly bear, throwing a bolt of lightning.

I got their attention. "Gentlemen, what are we doing here?"

They answered, "We are here to set up a rescue scenario."

"Correct," I said. "Is this evolution done?"

I heard, "Well, good enough."

I felt my anger rising, "Wrong answer, boys! We will be perfect or we will be dead! Does anyone have any additional comments? None? Well, then that's settled. Gentleman, Shall we begin?" It had to be right.

This day turned out to be ten full evolutions. It was enough, so that in the morning they were ready for work. I will not tolerate lackadaisical attitudes. I will not suffer fools.

I told them, "We are here for a specific purpose, and by God, you'll live up to those expectations or I'll know the reason why!"

There was not a word. I stated, "Gentleman, this meeting will reconvene at 06:30 hours in the morning. Put your game faces on and bring your best game. Moving day has changed and we will be ready."

With that, I walked out knowing these people who knew me, and knew my reputation, would not come for a coffee klatch, but ready for business. I walked out taking my notes and the messages, heading for the fortress. No one followed for quite some time. First were Bronco, Sandman, and then Daria, very quietly and timidly. I had made my point. For what it was worth, some had understood. The others would, or leave. It was worth the risk. Putting innocent people at risk was unacceptable to me.

Bronco broke the ice. "Boots, I'm sorry. I don't know what it is to be in command. I know you commanded Alpha for three years in Vietnam. I know you graduated top of every class, including boot camp. It's not easy to be top of your class in Force Recon. Rumor had you in another outfit at the top of your unit. It's amazing that you're alive at all after the Tet Offensive of '68. You and your team, along with Preachers and Schwartz's teams, spearheaded taking Hue City. The three-man teams were the best of the best. If the rumors are true, your team was way beyond the Recon units. It is common knowledge about Kai-San, Hill 881, Alice in Wonderland, and you were in Connecticut and Louisiana. Up and down the trail, and you played in North Vietnam. I do know you transferred up to more important duties after the Marines, and made a reputation for yourself. There. I'm sorry if I seem less than focused."

I glanced at Sandman. I could see he was stunned, and Daria, had no idea. "Bronc," I said, "It doesn't matter. We now have between seven and fourteen days to get this thing right. I talked to Preacher this morning. It's not much less than we thought. There's very bad medicine there, and there can't be any mistakes in performances, or attitude. What I saw this morning was no attitude, like it was a cakewalk. They're living the high life, and playing at their jobs. I try to make allowances for youth, for horseplay and for not knowing, that to act like it's just another gay party, it twists me out and burns my ass! What the plan stands for is unconditional love of children and our fellow humans. We stand for the rights of people who have no rights, or are enslaved with no one to free them. But we will. Many people think I must be rich because I work for the government, and rescue people and children. Bronc, you know something? When I joined the Marines I made twenty-four dollars and fifty cents every two weeks, and it's not much better now. As far as charging to rescue humans? We don't charge for our services. We've taken cases that we paid for! The clan gets it done without receiving a damn red cent! I don't want to go into this with guys who aren't serious, because this is serious business. I expect a certain amount of respect."

I continued, "You've both worked with me before. Sandman, for you this is your third time, and I hope not the last."

Sandman answered, "It won't be the last evolution, Boots."

I looked over at Bronco and said, "But you, Bronc, you've worked with me six times. You know what I'm all about. When it's time to work, that's what I do. When it's time to play, I play hard. It's a simple thing, and it's impossible for me to accept less than the best."

I turned to Daria, "Daria, you are my joy and my friend, but sometimes I need quiet. If it seems like I'm picking on you, I probably am. But, in your own way you make it worthwhile and I appreciate the attention you give me. It makes an old war dog like me feel pretty special, but the stress of the mission burns me up and it twists my guts into a million knots."

With all that said, I asked Daria to join me, and she said, "Yes." Then I said, "Guys, I'm going to sit here and talk and smoke for an hour with this beautiful friend of mine. If you care

to, there's plenty of room for all of us."

They declined my invitation and left.

Daria asked, "Did you mean what you said, Boots?"

I answered her, "Daria, I don't lie and I don't use people to get what I want. Not booze, not dope, not anything. Personally, I think you are quite beautiful, and without a doubt you make me feel good. You are a breath of fresh air in a world of pollution. Okay?"

"Thank you, Boots," she replied. "I am so very glad. I enjoy being with you. You are not like anyone else I know".

I laughed, and so did she.

When I returned to the war room things were, to say the least, quite different. Not one of them was anything less than attentive. They were all business. Evidently, Bronco and Sandman had plenty to say when they had returned to the war room. It was a day of attitude changes. At last, they were more of a team, after I blew up without an apology, but they hadn't earned one. As the day came to an end, with hopes for a brighter tomorrow, I tried to relax. I needed sleep, but sleep was elusive. I managed to get a couple of catnaps, but not enough.

I got up dragging myself, and only when it was time, once again, to begin the training exercises did I find myself ramping up. I was determined to succeed in obtaining our goal of seven minutes. We were going to work six a day exercises. I was responsible for these men and the success of this mission, but I needed intel from my own men.

I had just told Banger to keep working on refinements to this evolution, and asked him if I could have some of his time.

Banger said, "Sure, boss. What do you need?"

I said to him, "Banger, here's our problem. We have a stairwell that needs to be blocked off, but we can't just blow it. We can't hope to hold it by force. We don't have enough men. It would be inadvisable to kill all of them, because the Dutch authorities would be less than pleased. Remember, they held the trials after World War II, not only in Germany, but at The Hague. This building houses courts and an international court. They also have a rather nasty prison there. So what can we do?"

Banger replied, "Here's what I can do as far as the stairwell, Boots. I can set up laser light beam detonators in a myriad of configurations. They will all be wired, but only two will cause detonation. When someone is faced with a maze, it's not easy to figure, and you don't just charge ahead and find out which one detonates when you break the light beams."

I asked, "How long would it take to deploy it, Banger?" He answered, "I don't know."

I asked him if he could figure it out.

He retorted, "Yeah, but I need to go to one of your electronic stores here just to get laser eyes with return receivers. Boots, over here you use them for intruder alerts, or security, like in museums."

I said, "Well, hell! Let's go get what you need!"

Banger explained, "I will have to create a pattern where it will interlock, and is tall enough it can't be jumped over and low enough as to prevent going under it. Placement is not that hard, Boots. I should be able to install one every two seconds. You stick the light and line up the receiver on the other side, but you can see the light on the wall and slip in and place the receiver. If it's all pre-wired and the wire is loomed into the C-4 explosive, it takes no time at all."

I just looked at him and said, "How the hell are we going to control twenty-five odd soldiers in that room, Banger?"

He laughed, "Just like the fourth floor. If they get out, we're in deep shit! I know that, Boots, and I have a solution, but you might not like it."

"Okay," I said, "Well, try me."

Banger continued, "I could string together a sequence of concussion grenades, and at a predetermined time one wire would be pulled and then tossed through the door. They would detonate, shutting down their response time for ten to fifteen minutes."

I asked him, "What kind of damage are we talking, Banger?"

He said with a laugh, "Not too much, but it will need paint! It would depend on cubic feet within the room. If there are walls, the effectiveness is reduced by a large percentage. Almost forty percent. Only having two different charges would do the job then. Worst case scenario on damage assessment would be any structural damage and missing parts of wall, etcetera."

This made me smile, "So, you think it can be done without knocking the building down?"

"No problem," he said, "I just need to know the interior dimensions, boss and I can fix you up!"

I had to ask, "What do you think, Banger?"

He replied, "I would rather have to throw grenades, boss. I don't think we could do the job and handle twenty-five bad-asses who'll come boiling out of that door with us standing there, being right behind us."

It sounded good.

I knew he was right. "Okay, Banger. Set it up. Do your best, but don't take any chances."

Banger asked, "Is there anything else, boss?"

I answered, "Yes, there is. You're good with timers and gears. Well, I need a machine to come on automatically after it's placed in position."

Banger said, "That's not a problem. We'll use a jiggler, which starts a timer and turns on the machine."

I continued, "I also need this machine to self-destruct twenty minutes after its job is done, but it can't go boom. It has to melt down and become unrecognizable and untraceable."

Banger nodded and said, "I think it can be done, I know it can. Just let me work on this stuff, boss. I won't let you down."

I looked him straight in the eye, "It could mean our lives, Banger, let alone our package."

Banger replied, "Okay, Boots. I'll figure it out, and be able to build it before we rotate."

"Thanks, Banger."

"My pleasure, Boots."

I wondered about Bangers solutions. It was important to remember what we were after. Not the destruction of Amsterdam, but the building. If it wouldn't be full of people I'd shoot a charge that would lift the whole damn building off the ground and stack it on the ground in piles!

I said, "Thanks Banger. I know you will do the right thing."

He just said, "Thanks, Boots."

I thought of what we had gotten done, and yet we had so much to do. It was somewhat overwhelming trying to keep it all straight, but I would, with help from my friends, I could.

Tonight dinner was exceedingly formal. Gregor had invited several of his friends and colleagues. It was formal, but uncomfortable for the clan. It even appeared to be uncomfortable for Daria. It was time for Gregor to introduce his security force. I took umbrage at the very thought, but I reasoned that he had to explain our presence in some way, although I was not comfortable with being thought of as a soldier for hire, and I believe that was what he wanted to portray. But again, I had to wonder as Gregor said the words private security force, Daria caught my eye. There was some kind of warning in them, and I would never find out the reason for this look. She would not talk about it. Yet, dinner went well, and none of the clan, including myself, had made a major faux pas at the meal. It was after dinner that things began to get strange. Almost like something untoward was about to happen. It grew until I asked permission to post guards, and the rest would retire. It was a game, but I felt Gregor wanted it that way. It would be the last time we fed his delusion.

CHAPTER FOURTEEN

The clan gathered early. We would once again practice by doing dry runs. The clan had made up its mind to gain those minutes that we would need just before the start of the second round. I decided to advise these men once again.

"Guys," I said, "trust yourselves as I trust you. Without reservation. Believe that you can do anything, and you will accomplish what you desire. Let your mind move you, not your will. It will work. Believe me, somehow it works. Are we ready on my mark, gentleman?"

Mark. And a flurry of activity began. The stop watch showed they were doing this evolution in record time. I gained the stairs and moved up the staircase, heading for my objective. I looked at men who weren't going to quit until it was right. A new picture of these men began to grow, along with deep respect. I glanced at the stop watch. My mind would not comprehend what my eyes had revealed. I had to check the watch face twice, and still it was unbelievable, but there it was. Seven minutes, ten seconds! It had been accomplished for the first time! The target time had been reached. We were on the right track, but that was only once. It's just a start. It would have to be done, again, and over again. Until the watch face would be a common sight. The elapsed time varied no more than thirty seconds. This was one of the main goals of all of our training. It was what would help keep us alive, and our package alive, and allow us to transport and escort her home to her mother's arms.

We had just completed our fourth repetition, when I called a halt for taking breaks.

"Braveheart," I called.

He replied, "Yes sir, Boots."

I asked him, "What are you planning for buses, buddy?"

He answered, "I've been thinking, but tell me what you think."

I told him, "My thoughts are to either build or appropriate company delivery trucks, the kind you see in small towns and large towns. If you have a business, you have to be able to procure and resupply. If you have nothing to sell, you're out of business. So, we get two large delivery vans and park them close to the front door."

Braveheart smiled, "On the whole, it's a good idea. What about drawing attention by having these vans out in the open?"

"Well," I answered, "according to the Czar it is commonplace for delivery vans to be there twice a day, at 05:00 hours in the morning and at 17:00 hours, with a quiet but steady intrusion of these vans twenty-four hours a day."

He replied, "What could you expect in a town like this that operates twenty-four-seven, Boots?"

I said, "I don't think it would be abnormal for these vans to be seen or in that area, parked with flashers on, however, I plan to thoroughly investigate this upon insertion."

"It's a superlative answer, Boots. If it can be done without too much attention, it would be infinitely better than having two vehicles charge up, or be late charging up to our extraction point. This would be a showstopper, with possible policia ramifications."

"That would be inherently dangerous. On the other hand if our vehicles should get stopped or held up in traffic, we could find ourselves at the extraction point with no evac vehicles.

Just standing there with our package, and an alternative evolution to activate and perform under escape and evade, with bad guys up and alert to what has happened. It could turn into an urban war zone. If it's possible Braveheart, make it so."

He exclaimed, "You got it, boss!"

I told him, "Good job, my friend. Let's go for it!"

Braveheart replied, "No problem, Boots."

After talking to Braveheart on transportation issues, I decided to run another evolution in fact, and sat the guys down to tell them we were close to being on the mark.

I asked, "What do you guys think? Do you want to go with this, or work on the evolution longer?" There was an uncomfortable silence. "What's the matter guys? Swallow superglue?"

I heard, "No Boots, were not the ones to decide. If you think it's good, okay. If not, Boots, let's get to work."

I took a deep breath and continued, "The best chance of success is the ability to perform in a superior position to your adversaries. I'm of the opinion that we should practice until our times are consistent to the plan. Seven minutes and twenty seconds is a good number, there's no doubt. But, the shorter our time can be made, the faster we can do our job. If there's a hitch in the recovery, if it takes longer to get the package, for some unseen reason, we will still have time in our bank to use. If we go over ten minutes, our chance of success approaches zero due to the Mafia's perceived ability to react by then, or due to official intervention. So, I would surmise that we should continue training for no set time. I know training can be tiring and boring, but necessary for our survival."

We continued to perform dry runs at the consistency that was required. Between training and updating the plan, time became less than important. Everything on this side of the world was progressing at a pace that put us on target for the date I had chosen. I had originally proposed a date in March. However, with the complexity of the mission, that date had been altered. The operation was set for the last Sunday in April, and we were on track for that date. We knew that we would have two weeks work in Holland. One week on the boat, minimum. I had already discounted and planned on twice that much time, because I am a person that checks things multiple times, so as not to overlook the smallest detail.

The training continued, sometimes with Gregor's staff, sometimes with just the clan. Our actions became automatic, almost fluid.

Everything was done without thinking. It leaves a huge amount of time and energy to perceive problems, and to perceive threats. The practice evolution had now begun to net us six minute and fifty second turnarounds. These evolutions would start from outside the side door. From there to the fourth floor of the house we occupied. Of course, we only trained in the stairwell, as that's where our ingress and egress would take place. I was convinced we were ready. Patience is a virtue, but mine was getting pretty damn thin. I was ready, along with the clan, to move to our new base of operations in Holland.

While I was thinking of what was left to do, the ringer on the phone brought me immediately back to my present time and place. I picked up the phone about to speak when Preacher's voice came over loud and clear.

"Boots, Preacher here."

I said, "Duh, Preacher. You're one of two people who have this number."

He retorted, "Okay, no lessons on phone etiquette, boss. I'm in, and in pretty damn solid. I have pretty much the run on this sleazy operation. There have been one or two surprises, but nothing to do with the mission."

I told him, "That's good news, Preacher."

He continued, "Boots, when are you guys traveling?"

I just said, "We've been waiting for the invite, Preacher. I figured that you and the Czar would know the proper time, and make the call. You're there, Preacher, and know the situation, the problems, and the general outlook. So, it's your call."

"Okay, Boots," replied Preacher, "Let's do this thing. The Czar is ready. He's got quite a crew, wait until you meet them!"

Little did I know that the Czar's crew would be two beautiful and buxom young ladies, who not only knew their way around weapons, but indeed knew their way around a sailboat, along with other attributes that I would hear about, but never know for sure.

"Do they know what they're about, Preacher?"

Preacher answered seriously, "You can take that to the bank and draw interest on it, Boots. They're that good."

"Okay," I said, "I will set up travel. Are you guys ready to pick up the clan?"

Preacher replied, "No doubt, Boots. We have three drivers, and they will get the tourist treatment. The Czar let it out we're having a reunion of sorts. Don't worry, Boots. It's some club he's a member in. I think it's some kind of world traveler by sailboat thing."

"Okay," I answered.

And Preacher replied, "So the word is go, Boots."

I told him, "You got it, Preacher. You tell that bear that we will settle up when I get there."

"Okay, man," replied Preacher, "See you on the flipside, Boots."

"On the other side, my brother," I responded. The call had finally come and things begin to ramp up from here.

Emotionally, the fuse was lit, and would rocket up. Things became pumped up. Abilities would become more efficient. It's just hard to explain how a person feels when you're as ready as you can be, and the situation you've been waiting for is finally at hand. Since it was late, and most if not all of the clan was either asleep or close to it, I would make the announcement in the early a.m. I was extremely pumped up and not tired, to say the least, so I decided to head for the fortress to have a cigarette, and a drink. I had to relax and do some thinking. It, for once was a self satisfying walk.

Rather than alerting the house to the fact that someone was using the elevator, I decided to walk up to the roof. I gained the roof, and before retreating inside the fortress, I decided to go and look out from the eastern side of the roof. I just wanted to see the area for what it was, rather than just a place. I gazed out and around, then I realized life was going on out there and families were being tucked into bed and some were being created. It was a very satisfying thought, and yet somewhat amusing.

I turned to proceed into the fortress, and there was Daria.

She spoke quite softly, "It's a beautiful world, Boots."

I had to agree, it truly was. I told her, "It's unfortunate that evil has to be here, but it's a reality. It was truly a paradise that was lost. I wonder if Adam and Eve ever thought of what they took away from us, Daria."

"I don't know," she said, "but I wish they hadn't done it."

"Me too, babe," I said, "me too."

We turned to walk into the fortress and she was once again holding my arm. In some ways it was reassuring, that there was a goodness here and it was worth fighting for. We sat down and I reached for a cigarette only to find once again, an empty pack. Daria took it, and handed me a new pack. I had to laugh, and so did she. We sat and had a couple of drinks and talked about a few things. Mostly, I listened and had a most relaxing time. The scotch felt good. The burn in my throat, in some ways, was very refreshing and stimulating. As we talked, Daria yawned and I glanced at my watch. It was 01:20 hours. 04:00 hours would not be long in coming nor would it wait for me to get extra sleep. What the hell.

"Daria," I said, "It's time for this guy to bed down for a couple hours, okay?"

She answered, "Fine, Boots. I'm really tired."

I told her, "You sleep in little girl. You look like you could use it." No argument. She was tired. I said to her, "Let's go, babe."

She was almost asleep on her feet, so I showed her to her door. She kissed my cheek and walked through her own door, and I through mine. I was beat.

CHAPTER FIFTEEN

There was this insistent and obnoxious noise in my ear, and then I heard a crash, and knew I needed a new alarm clock. Crawling out of bed and into the shower was a chore, but when I turned on the cold water, it woke me up completely. I had to laugh to myself. I thought, "Boots my boy, you single-handedly support thirty families in the alarm clock business!" That thought made me laugh. After my morning duties I decided to round up some coffee and went down to the kitchen.

I talked to Alexi and I asked him if he liked America.

Alexi looked at me and said, "I like it very much, but not like home, Mr. Boots. Home we farm and have animals, and much family. Here, I have Daria to look after. My wife, she gone now. Children everywhere on Earth. Some write, but not very much, and soon Alexi gone too."

I told him, "I'll bet you even money you outlive me!"

He laughed, and I laughed, and Daria laughed. Alexi looked embarrassed, but Daria went to him, "I love you, my good Alexi. Is good to see you smile and laugh, but be careful. Please."

Well, that seemed somewhat out of character for Daria, but she had a human side too, as we all did.

I looked over at Daria. I said, "Daria, what are you doing up?"

She glanced back at me and said, "Checking on why you threw your clock. It hit the 'tween door."

I replied, "Well, go back to bed."

She smiled, "No, I don't think so. Is there more coffee, Alexi?"

He answered, "Yes ma'am."

Evidently, something in what he said, or how he said "ma'am" seemed to hurt Daria. At least it appeared so. I never found out. We headed for the war room, coffee in hand with the promise from Alexi that he would bring more.

We sat drinking coffee and talking while I was looking at a street map of Amsterdam. I was trying to decide on travel arrangements when Daria just got up and left. I didn't know why, but I was busy and didn't have time to find out how I had once again offended her. Clan business precludes everything, even my own beloved wife. I had decided some of us would appear as businessman and we were! However, I felt no need to tell them, or anyone the true nature of our business with this country. Some of us would be, of course, tourists.

When the clan wandered in, and got their coffee, they then sat down. As I gazed at them it was with a certain amount of pride that I announced moving day. There were smiles, and suddenly, the very air was almost electric with anticipation and excitement. It was a pivotal moment for all of us to go from training to operational status. It is a feeling like no other for men like us. What seemed like endless and pointless days of training and planning will finally end by getting started doing what we had been asked to do. Although, this had taken more time than some of the missions. Some take a matter of days, or a long slow burn till it's done.

I began to explain my feelings on how we should appear, and duration in time. Along with routes it came out like this. I told them, "This is the way I've got it planned guys, and it has already been decided. Sandman, you will be flying from New York via red-eye, so you will arrive in London before business hours. You will be leaving London that night by red-eye to Stockholm, and leaving at night for Amsterdam. Via red-eye you will arrive in Amsterdam early in the morning, where you will be picked up by Czar or Preacher, or a combination of both. Of course, go with them."

I looked over at Bronco and said, "Bronc, you will get the same treatment, only you will leave New York red-eye to Los Angeles, from Los Angeles to Rome, and from Rome to Amsterdam. This will be one day after Sandman."

Turning to Slick I said, "Slick. New York red-eye to Paris, then red-eye to Barcelona, and red-eye from Barcelona to Amsterdam one day after Bronco. Braveheart and Banger, you two will fly from New York to Edinburgh, and from Edinburgh to Rotterdam. The Czar has your transport arranged. You will be picked up there. They will have a card with the Czar's first name and my name. It will also have one thing on it, and we all carry one. If you don't see it, you'll know it's a trap. You will be leaving one day after Bronc or four days into the promenade."

I heard, "Okay, boss, from all around."

I continued, "I will leave from New York going to Atlanta and then to Rome, Rome to London, then to Amsterdam, arriving two days after everybody else. Discreetly look around, but look at the boat. When I get there, we will be busy as hell, not only adjusting, but we all have jobs. Especially Banger, Braveheart, and Slick. So the promenade begins tomorrow. Gentlemen, let's do this right and party afterward, right here since all expenses are being paid. We will have the party here. Gentlemen, the gauntlet was thrown. Let's pick it up and slap the hell out of them!"

Today is Monday. Sandman leaves today. It was not all that easy to get flight arrangements and times as I wanted them. But, the travel agent that Gregor uses, and said for us to use, succeeded in getting it accomplished. Each layover was overnight. Enough to decompress some, but not much. These are the days we live for.

On the whole, I have little problem justifying what we do. I don't believe that causing problems for criminals is altogether not necessary. If a person has cancer and in order to live must have a life-saving surgery where he might possibly lose his sight, what would he choose? How many people faced with that decision, or something similar, would choose life and not death. Watching with his own eyes. As far as the right to act goes, if we do not act, is it not as barbaric as the act itself? As my comrades began to leave, my world grew smaller, and I was gently reminded that one would be left behind. She would, in some ways, be lonely and afraid, but she would be happier when we returned. And, with God's good grace, we all would, or be waiting on the flip side.

Today Sandman left, as all of us will. Without much fanfare or family, but we leave with a job to do and we do it with all of our might. There was not an awful lot to do now, except wait my turn to be on my way. Daria and I found each other's company to be very enjoyable. We didn't talk a great deal, but nonetheless it was comforting. In time, my turn came for me to be on my way to bring Daria's cousin out of slavery and humiliation.

Six days out, and it's my turn to begin the journey. Daria, of course, accompanied me. Gregor, on the other hand, was nowhere to be seen. This was with good reason. Gregor said this was Daria's job, and indeed it had been. When we left the car I noticed that Daria had a death grip on my arm. I picked up my boarding pass. We had time to stop and have some lunch. It was, of course, too early for a drink. We had coffee at the end of the meal instead. While we were sitting there, I found her to be starkly quiet. It made me curious. This is not a usual occurrence. People are usually happy that I'm leaving, because they know that if it is humanly possible I will return with their loved one, or loved ones, as the case may be. I paid the bill and we walked closer and closer to the boarding area. We stopped and I asked her what the matter was, and noticed she was crying.

I said, "What's wrong little one?"

She whimpered, "I'm afraid I got you and your guys into something that might get you killed."

I said, "Honey, you have, but it's okay."

She cried, "No, it's not."

I told her, "Darlin', let me tell you if it costs me my life, or Bronco's or anyone else's, as long as Svetlana comes home, it is the price we are all willing to pay."

I looked down at her and she kissed me, and turned and ran. Unable to look at me she just yelled, "I love you!" and she hurried away.

I was stunned. As I said, nothing could have prepared me for how Daria felt. There was no reason for her to feel responsible. It's our job. I turned to hand my papers to the flight personnel and a picture appeared in my mind of Daria's tear streaked face, and penetrating eyes staring at me. It was a picture I would remember, not only on this case, but others. My papers taken care of, I turned and began to board the plane.

CHAPTER SIXTEEN

"Good evening, sir," greeted the flight attendant. I answered back that it was indeed. I passed down the interior of the plane to the rearmost seats, because I do not like people behind me. A stewardess or steward does not seem to bother me; after all, I know why they are there. My seats were the last two on the right-hand side of the plane, facing the tail. They were both mine. I had purchased both of them because I had work to do, and had no desire for anyone to glance at what I was working on. I like to be comfortable, and had no need for an in flight companion.

The plane began to slowly back out of the jet way and the engines began to wind up. They reminded me that at home in my shop was a turbine motor ready to be installed in my son's car. We were now taxiing out and were in line for the take off. It never changed, and I hoped it wouldn't. As the plane began to pick up speed, I quietly said, "Rotate" and we lifted off. I was now in the air and truly on my way. All of this would be repeated in Atlanta, Rome, then London, and finally arriving in Amsterdam. My destination.

As I worked, and I wrote, "Need to get boat ready, update the electronics, provisions, supplies, clothes, robes, pajamas, slippers." The last four were in particular for Svetlana. I had received her old sizes from Daria. About the only difference was the bust. Svetlana's bust was larger. I would have to go shopping for her. I didn't think they would let her go shopping for the clothes that she would be needing to escape, and ply the waters of the North Sea with a band of armed brigands!

The flights were uneventful and I managed to get some sleep. It must be stated, if I was going to sleep, I locked my briefcase, then put my handcuffs into the handcuff attachment plate, with the other end snapped onto my left wrist. The stewardess knew what was up, somewhat. She had obviously seen other couriers on her flights, and paid no heed to it. On all of the airlines it seems to be somewhat normal. I must admit all the way to Amsterdam, the stewardesses were very nice.

I was presently on my fourth and final flight, inbound to Holland. I was actually very tired. Happy, but tired. We began the long slow descent into Amsterdam. The engines grew quieter, meaning the pilots were spooling down the power. It's at that time you feel almost weightless, and then the gravity seems to return. The plane had started its controlled crash towards Amsterdam's airport. The plane descended lower and lower. You could look out of your window and see the ocean, and then the land. I could feel the plane shudder a little as the flaps descended into their landing position. You could see people, like ants, and then another shudder, as the landing gear descends and locks into position. Then you're on the ground at full reverse thrust.

Others want off now, but can't. Most people can't wait to stand up and bounce off each other trying to scramble through the hatch in order to be the first person off the plane. I finished filling out my customs and immigration papers, so they would be ready when they were asked for. The plane began to empty out, and everybody was twenty-five rows ahead of me still bouncing off each other.

I finally stood up, stretched, and grabbed my coat. My briefcase was now unattached, lest it raise eyebrows. I got out my new passport, and had my papers and immigration records.

I approached customs and immigration, and handed my paperwork to the officer.

He began asking me some questions. "Is this your first visit to Holland?"

"Yes, sir," I answered, "and from what I saw from the airplane I should have come many times before."

"Yes," he replied, "it's a very nice country. Reason for visit?"

I spoke clearly, but lightheartedly, "I'm here on business. I have seven towns to visit, plus I'm going to spend as much time as I can just looking around. There is so much to see!"

He smiled at me, "The windmills, and you must see the dykes and gates."

I responded, "Ah, there is so much to see! I only hope I have enough time on my visa left after business."

With that, he leaned in towards me, "How long do you think you might need?"

I looked back at him, "I don't know. Do you think sixty days would be enough to take care of business and see very much of the country?"

He smiled broadly, "Well, for a small handling fee, I can assure you that you will have enough time."

Here it was, the spring for a payoff. "How much would it cost?" I asked.

His eyebrows raised and he smirked, "Oh, not a lot, for a business man like you. I see you do business in many countries. The charge would be two-hundred-fifty American dollars for ninety days."

"Well, yes," I said "I do travel a lot and that's not so much, but I hope ninety days gives me enough time."

He nodded back and said, "Well sir, if it's not, you can come to the airport and I would be glad to help you out!"

I thought, "Right buddy. How much does it cost?"

I smiled at him, "If I need more time, I would only deal with you, if I could. It's not usual to find someone so understanding in a foreign land."

"Well," he said "you're quite welcome."

As I handed him three-hundred dollars, I wondered which pocket it would go into, and thought, "I'm sure I can screw up this town in ninety days, old chap!"

He waved as I walked away, "Have a nice day sir, and a wonderful visit in our country."

"Well," I said, "you have a wonderful day and I hope to see you soon. As far as your country goes, I am quite sure I will get a real bang out of it" (if only you knew the truth you crook). I said, "Ciao, man," and I was away from the cause of one of the problems in a country that tends to look the other way concerning white slavery. It's for the buck.

I walked away before I said something to draw attention to myself. My thoughts turned to the mission at hand, and I wondered who would be picking me up. I went to claim my baggage and there was a bear standing there, with a most beautiful young woman. As I approached, a huge smile erupted from this large and handsome man whom I call friend. It was a warm and genuine reunion between two friends.

One of my bags reached the position where we were standing, and wanted to be recovered. One of the bags that had accompanied me all these long miles. I reached down and grabbed this one, but there was no sign of the whereabouts of the others, as of yet. As I sat the bag down, a huge paw reached out to grasp my hand and as we greeted each other, my hand disappeared from view in this man's grip. We shook hands and he pulled me towards him, and of course I received one of the bear hugs this man was known for. It was a warm and brief reminder we were friends.

As we talked awaiting the arrival of number two of three bags, a quite beautiful woman with blonde hair and blue eyes, who had a nice figure and a warm smile asked the Czar if this was indeed the infamous man she had heard so much about.

"Da, Heilgrid," said Czar, "is friend Boots from many wars, and many missions. We friends now many years."

Her smile broadened even more. She introduced herself, "I am Heilgrid. It is honor to meet you friend Boots."

I smiled back at her. "It is my extreme honor and a pleasure, Lady Heilgrid."

This made her blush and caused her to continue to smile. I spied my third errant bag and had a good laugh as I saw Heilgrid punch this very large man and tell him, "You did not say he gentleman and royal talker." The royal talker part would not be explained in detail until I saw the Preacher.

I snagged my third and final bag and the Czar grabbed both bags I had already retrieved, and we headed for the door. We approached a very nice BMW vehicle and I saw another woman get out and open the trunk lid. I was taken aback and I must say I was stunned, for there stood Heilgrid. But no, it wasn't possible. It then became apparent as Heilgrid introduced me to her identical twin sister, Heilvia. Heilvia introduced herself, as Heilgrid introduced me. This young woman pulled me toward her with amazing strength and hugged me. Then, she kissed both of my cheeks. There's that cheek thing again! A man could grow accustomed to this practice very easily.

She greeted me with a, "Hello friend Boots! I think we will become very good friends and we must talk soon. We must leave this place. There are many eyes and ears here."

So, it was true. There isn't an influence vacuum here. The Mafia had most transport under control, or at least had influence and the watchers were in place. This is something to be considered, but would not concern me.

We gained the semi safety of the car and I told Heilvia we would talk soon, but Czar was going to go off like a cherry bomb if he didn't get to talk.

"Boots," said Czar "we've been waiting for you and I'm so glad you are here. We all are. I had planned to take you to my home, but first we will go by the boat, and then you will be seeing your building. I do not believe is easy thing we do, but can be done with help from Heilgrid and Heilvia."

I must say as far as the beauty of this country, it was enchanting and stunning. If it wasn't for its transparent involvement in white slavery by ignoring it for financial gain, it would be a country that everyone should see and experience.

We proceeded down the highway, and while talking it came to light that one of the twin's best friends had fallen victim to this group of thugs. This meant they didn't have any compunction about helping. I asked the Czar if the twins could handle weapons. I was answered by Heilvia drawing her pistol. It was a nine millimeter, Smith & Wesson combat pistol. Likewise, Heilgrid had more than breasts under her sweater. She had a Desert Eagle forty-one caliber super mag pistol.

I asked, "Can they use them?" and the Czar explained that from the boat at approximately seventy-five yards, each could empty a full clip of ammunition into the target from the deck of a bobbing vessel. This was a singularly impressive statement. "How much do they know?" I queried.

"Everything, Boots," said Czar, "I did not keep any information from them."

I sighed, "In other words, they know the entire plan?"

Czar looked at me, "In a single word, yes."

I asked, "How do you girls feel about what we're planning on doing?"

They replied, almost in unison, "We think it's the first positive step against this group of thugs! Boots?" "Yes, ladies," I answered.

Heilvia said, "We want in all the way."

I was hesitant until they said please, and explained their girlfriend had been recovered from the Zieder Zee, beaten to death. She had been missing for over a year. In my opinion, bodies in the sea don't last long, being aware of the predators and creatures. So, their friend must have been murdered for not cooperating with them. This girl was twenty-one years old when they found her body.

"So," I said talking to the girls, "what you're telling me is you are both crack shots with pistols and you're experienced sailors. You have an ax to grind with these people."

Heilvia spoke first, "No. We want them hunted down and shot."

"Yes, that's what we want," replied Heilgrid.

"Well, ladies," I said, "you're going to be disappointed. If some of them are killed inadvertently it would make me happy, but we're not setting out to do anything but rescue prisoners." The girls were pretty quiet after that.

The town itself was not what I expected. It didn't appear to be unkempt, however you could tell it was not that well-maintained. We did not go past the building, on purpose. When we got to the docks and we were able to get out, it was nice to stretch my legs and smell the air. Heilgrid came around the car and whispered in my ear for appearances sake, and to draw little or no attention to us, I should drape my arm over her sister's shoulders, because there were several Mafia boats in this part of the marina.

"I hope that this does not compromise your moral values, but remember I'm the, as you call him, the Czar's girlfriend." She giggled, and so did Heilgrid.

He was living with both of them! This would indeed present an unusual wedding photo with two brides! At that moment all I could think was, "I gotta be there!"

We proceeded down the dock to a finger pier about halfway down on the left side, and there was the Czar's boat. It was indeed a beautiful vessel that I noticed immediately, although it had enough antennae for a radio-telephone, shortwave, VHF, and several others, he had no radar. I made a mental note to have this remedied by having an extreme short range and medium-range radar installed immediately. When we boarded her I noticed that she was very stable.

I asked, "Czar, does she have stabilizers?"

He answered, "No, Boots, but you will be surprised at how stable she is."

I asked him, "How long is she?"

With a wide smile on his face Czar said, "From stem works at waterline to stern, she's forty-eight feet, eight inches and she's eighteen feet wide amidships."

He had claimed he could get thirty-five people on board. We will see. We stepped into the wheelhouse and I saw all of the bright work was brass. Everything that was woodwork was African mahogany or elm. When we went down the stairs into the main part of the boat, it was immediately noticeable that this was an awfully big boat below the main deck, reaching far below the water line.

I turned around and the Czar was opening the hatch that led into the engine room. Here were no surprises. I found a very powerful high-speed diesel that was connected to a cruising diesel. The high-speed had four-hundred horsepower and it was connected to a dual drive gearbox. Also, hooked to the gear interchange was a four cylinder seventy-five horsepower cruising engine. However, it was a sailboat. Heilgrid said it was fast under sail. In the engine room was a desalination unit and a very small generator for power requirements when she wasn't under mechanical power. There was a small wind generator that would at least keep the batteries charged.

When we went into the salon the first thing I saw on the left was a pretty nice galley. Here was everything a person would need, including a small microwave. To the right was seating for eight. At a dining settee forward was seating for more with a stereo, a TV and movies. There were four small staterooms with double bunks and two heads in the bow. There were six V berths.

The Czar said, "In a pinch we can bunk down twenty people."

I asked him, "How long can you provision for?"

He answered, "It depends on how many people."

"Well," I said, "say you had twenty people and it was an emergency and you all had to sail. How long could you sail for without resupplies, keeping in mind you want to eat very well."

Czar replied, "If we take on maximum supplies we could stay at sea for thirty days, Boots. So, let me ask you. Why thirty, and why extended sea time?"

"Czar," I began, "I plan for the worst and if it's better than that, it's a good day. Didn't you ever carry extra ammo after someone told you that you'll only need this much because it was only a two day mission?"

He nodded, "Da, friend Boots. I trusted my estimations better than high command."

"Well brother," I said, "this is my thinking. If we can get more than one girl to come with us, it could take Slick extra time on the radiotelephone to make all of the arrangements."

The Czar agreed "Is good thinking Boots, very good thinking."

I asked him, "Czar, would it be a weight or space problem?"

He answered, "Not to be weight. You right Boots. Storage space, maybe."

"Well," I said thoughtfully, "if we have to, we'll stack stuff on the engine room deck. Does it matter?" He smiled, "No Boots. It does not."

I told him, "There will be more later, but at the moment it escapes me. I'm a little tired and I will have to think about it."

When we left the boat for the car, there were several gentlemen watching what was going on. For some reason my combat radar went up and I was in full combat mode. Before I could take another breath, Heilvia sensed it around her, but mostly from me.

She pulled my head closer to her so she could whisper in my ear, "Mafia enforcers, be careful, Boots. My pistol is under my left breast, just in case."

However, fortune was looking down on us when one asked Heilvia, "what was up," and she blithely replied that we were going sailing on our honeymoon and there was a small sailboat for rent down there. There was, but at that time I had no idea if it was true, we evidently did not raise an alarm or their suspicions. I turned to Heilvia to comment, but she just looked at me. It evidently was not an appropriate place or time to say anything. As we got into the car I could see the strain was apparent, especially from Heilvia's hands. When she put her hand upon the steering wheel there was a definite tremor there.

While we were driving out Czar said, "Boots, those guys are only here if their bosses are down six piers from my boat. The

big boss has a mega yacht at the end of the pier."

This gave me something more to worry about.

When we got back on the road the Czar said, "Heilvia, please go by the building in question. We will go past it both ways." "Okay, Czar," she answered.

We turned onto what appeared to be a main road through town, but Helvi (what I had started to call her) said, "No. The main drag, as you say in the states, is over there three blocks.

This is a road that is termed to be 'pleasure alley'."

Then the Czar cut in, "On your right, at the second building from the end, is our target."

As we approached this building, I could see Preacher getting his back slapped. He was smiling and waving like these people and he were the best of friends.

"Well Preacher, it's your job, although it's very distasteful, it was a critical part of the plan and we are glad you could get it done, my friend." I would tell him later.

There was plenty to see, however. There were women. Young women and teenagers, along with young girls in various windows dressed seductively, or nude. It infuriated me to see a girl who wasn't even old enough to have breasts, sitting spraddle-legged. I would hazard a guess at the girls' age to be between ten and twelve years of age. But, it was not just little girls. There were also young boys. By the time we had passed this building twice I was enraged at the way humans had just become pieces of meat to be had for a price.

As we proceeded to the Czar's house I was visibly sickened, and madder than hell. We pulled the car into the driveway and unloaded my gear. I walked into the Czar's house and was confronted with the eyes of the clan.

I walked in and said, "Hey guys. How's tricks?"

Bronco was the first to speak. "Well, Boots. I see you got the million-dollar tour. How did you like the show?"

I glared at him, "Don't go there tonight."

He persisted, "We would like to know."

I shook my head, "Don't get me started, don't even get me started. What I need is some coffee, a carton of cigarettes, and a case of scotch. When is Preacher due back?" "In thirty minutes," said Bronco.

I answered, "When he gets here, there are a number of items we need to discuss and there are things we need to be doing. Has anyone besides Preacher been in the building?" "He's the only one, boss," was the reply.

"Okay. It's okay, guys. I'm going to get me a cup of coffee, and then we'll sit and wait for Preacher."

While the coffee pot did its job making the required beverage, Heilvia came up to me and asked, "Boots when you get your

coffee, would you go outside and walk with me?"

I told her, "I would love to, Helvi."

As the last throes of percolation slowed to a stop, Helvi brought me a cup and then poured it for me. It was cooling as we walked out of the large door into the garden, which I had admired as we drove into the Czars place. I was so upset I hadn't really looked at my friend's house. I saw that it was most certainly not a dump. It was a beautiful Dutch country home. A two-story house that was a somewhat distant relative of what we in the states call a Dutch colonial home. From the front it was a tall beautiful home, painted white. The shutters and trim were an almost Kelly, or Irish Green. It really rather stood out.

There were four large multipane windows on either side of what could be considered the center line of this magnificent home. The windows on the bottom floor seemed to be identical. At the center line of this house stood a four foot wide door, with a porch styled roof. I found it to be quite an effect, with what looked like a red tile roof and all copper flashing that had aged to perfection. As you looked out from the porch, you could see down a short path that reached out through a sea of flowers. All of this was contained within a white picket style fence, approximately three feet high. In the backyard, there was a very large covered patio that had also been screened in. Outside of this was a brick work patio, along with the patio there was a six by fourteen foot fishpond, with fish in it. The flowers were incredibly brilliant.

Helvi and I walked along in the garden and she said she was interested in America, and of course I was more than willing to tell her to please go and visit. Although, the walk through the garden was like pulling a cork from a seltzer bottle. I found myself decompressing from the whirlwind of jet travel, emotions, and just being dog tired. I turned to Helvi, and had to ask how this business could thrive in a civilized country.

She looked me dead in the eyes and said, "Is it not the same in your country in places like this?"

She was right. I said, "It is prevalent in the states. In fact, it thrives in twenty major cities in our country. I'm sorry Helvi. I should have thought more about the crime and less about where it was."

"It's okay," she answered, "it bewilders me also, Boots. Why would anyone need to rape or molest little children?"

I shook my head. "I don't know. I just don't know."

We continued to stroll along and began to discuss different subjects, including art and great works of art. She asked if I had ever been in the Sistine Chapel.

I told her, "No Helvi, sadly I've not taken the time."

I heard a familiar voice. "Well, it's about time you made the show, Boots."

I didn't even have to turn around to know that it was Preacher. "How's it going, brother?"

He said, "Okay, man. I hate it and it's disgusting, but I guess you could say, okay."

He came abreast of Helvi and me. I turned and hands shot out to grasp each other, not unlike the two men who were attached to those hands.

"My brother," I told him, "I'm sorry you drew this job, but I couldn't trust this to another soul on earth."

"I know, Boots. Please believe me when I say this is one job I would gladly give up."

I looked at him knowingly, "I can only guess, Preacher, I can only guess."

"Boots," said Helvi, "I have to thank you both for what you do, along with how you say, the clan."

"It's what this man does." Preacher was speaking of me.

I looked at him, "I'm not here alone. Well, shall we get back to the house and the guys. We have to talk before I get much more tired. I could actually use something to eat and a shower, and it probably would not hurt to try to get some sleep." But, I doubted that sleep would be easy to come by.

Helvi began to apologize for not thinking that after my travels I might be hungry.

I told her, "Don't worry about it. I'm not in danger of dying from starvation."

She answered, "Well, what do you like to eat?"

Preacher laughed, "He will eat anything that doesn't eat him first!"

That made me smile to think he was correct in his assessment of my nutritional requirements. "I'll tell you what I could use Helvi, is another cup of your fine coffee, and to talk to all of you. Helvi, do you know where I could find someplace to boil my body, and get a real massage. I'm not talking about some abbreviated attempt to find sex, not that it's bad, but I need a real massage!"

Helvi smiled a big smile and said, "We have a sauna and a cold wash and I'm licensed to do this work. I work in sports facility!"

Somehow, it seemed like I should feel just a little uncomfortable, but we would see. We entered the kitchen and Helvi grabbed up the coffee pot and filled my cup. I proceeded to round everyone up and get them to the great room.

As they arrived, I began to speak. "We won't talk in detail about very much guys and girls (an afterthought with the girls, but these two young women deserved my attention and recognition no less than the clan). I saw the boat. Czar in the morning I would like to return to the boat, and with you and the girls, I would like to take full stock of what we will need. I would like to get radar units and a weather fax machine installed on your vessel. That's with your permission, of course."

Czar answered, "You have that Boots. My boat is your boat."

"Well," I replied, "you will have to decide where you would like them, and the most advantageous spot to have the radar screens installed, and where you could put a weather fax machine on the boat. Heilgrid and Helvi will help me, at least I hope they will, decide on supplies that would be needed on an extended voyage."

Slick popped up with, "That won't take that long, Boots."

I told him, "Well then, the Czar and his ladies don't have to stop and shop for a while." We all laughed.

The room became somber again when the Czar spoke up. Boots, do you remember who was on that dock today?"

I replied, "Yes."

"Well, they could be there for a while. Heilvia will be your guide and companion. Not only here, but especially in public. Always remember, friend Boots, they have many eyes and ears on the docks and roadways. Even as you found out at the airport. They are around every form of transportation. I think for you is dangerous. Do what Heilvia says and don't argue."

I saluted him and barked, "Yes Sir!"

Everyone in the room laughed, but it was more serious of a problem than they knew.

I spoke directly to the girls. "Heilgrid, Helvi. I want to have every consumable we will need for a max voyage. I'm talking good food and plenty of it. However, there will have to be special considerations for Sandman. He is a Muslim and he's one of us."

Turning to Sandman I said, "Sandman, would you give Heilgrid a list of foods and how your food needs to be prepared? I will cook it for you if you would prefer."

He answered, "I don't think Allah made any fast and set rules on Muslims that live like I do, running around the world saving the little ones, Boots. We will take it as it comes, but I cannot compromise on the foods."

Respectfully, I nodded, "I would not ask you to Sandman." Looking back towards the girls, I continued, "Ladies, we will need fish, beef and pork for non-Muslims. Also on the list should be pots, pans and utensils for Sandman. If unclean food touches his, or is cooked in the same pot, he cannot eat it. So, we will be very observant about the needs of our Muslim brother. We will talk about it." With that, a huge wave of exhaustion hit me. "Hey, guys. I got to get some rest and stuff."

They all understood. As the meeting was breaking up, the Czar came over to me and said, "Boots, you need workout and rest. Heilvia talk to me. Is okay, my friend. She work at the sports institute. You go now. Get boiled and fixed. We start more in morning. All will get done, Boots. I swear it."

I knew he meant what he said. With that said, Helvi reached out and grabbed my hand and guided me outside. I lit a cigarette for myself, and I saw she needed her cigarette lit also. We stood there smoking and laughing for no particular reason. It just seemed the reasonable thing to do.

It was a strange thing to be doing. Here I was, seven thousand miles from home, in a one-hundred-fifteen degree room in shorts, baking with a girl, not my wife, alongside of me and talking about the benefits of sweating until you're parched, and then stepping out and getting into a cold water shower. It was pleasant, but certainly not an experience that I would be willing to incorporate into my daily routine. Like I said, it was pleasant, but strange. After the cold water shower, it was off to a room where Helvi had a massage table. She showed me into the room and had me lay down on this table. Then she turned on Mozart, and excused herself.

She returned after approximately ten minutes. She'd gone to shower and dress. It was around one-hundred degrees in this room as she started. There is one thing worth mentioning about this massage. If it had a joint, it was Helvi's opinion, in fact, that it must be popped into place. I do not believe I had ever been beaten up quite this badly in hand-to-hand combat, nor had it hurt this bad! Even when I had to cut free of a parachute and plunged forty-five feet to the jungle floor in full gear! Anyway, it felt pretty bad at the time it was happening. I, of course, thanked Helvi and she kind of giggled. She knew that I was hurting pretty badly.

I crawled into a shower and turned up the heat. It felt exceedingly beneficial, and I was able to stumble to the bed and fall into its embrace. I barely had enough strength and dexterity to pull the blankets over me and I fell asleep immediately. It was 20:00 hours.

CHAPTER SEVENTEEN

I slept until 05:30 hours, the longest stretch of time I'd slept in eighteen years. I prepared to turn slowly. I knew there could be no possible way I would be able to move after the pummeling I had received last night. Slowly, as I sat up, I found that movement was not to be difficult or too painful. Well, I decided to rotate out of bed and try to stand up. Actually, I moved quite well and had not experienced any pain, as of yet. As I stood, I realized whatever this worker of miracles had done, she had done it properly. I moved with ease and with no pain. That was something which was unusual anyways. It was an exquisite feeling and I fairly jumped up and down.

I felt great! While I dressed I knew I wanted to hug this lady who took my body and turned back time. When I saw Helvi, I went straight to her and did what I had planned to do. I hugged her and thanked her. She looked somewhat bewildered, and then we both realized what had happened and laughed together. I had just hugged Heilgrid. Damn, near identical twins! I located the one and only Helvi, I had hugged the other one and I repeated my thanks to Helvi. I told her what had happened and she gave me hell! After all, didn't I know Helvi was quite a bit taller than Heilgrid! All of one half inch, and then we both laughed.

It was coffee time for me. I seldom eat breakfast and at the most a handful of grain and a piece of fruit. Not so with the clan. They could have wolfed down a cow, at least that's in my opinion. As we started the day, I had planned on the clan getting to know the area around our building. But, after listening to the Czar's warnings and admonishments, those plans were canceled until Czar had time to escort each of them through the area. He, of course knew what to watch for, and who to shy away from. No police. No unwanted attention was my motto and my standing rule, with no exception. Not even for me.

Preacher left for his rounds. The last place he was stopping at would be our target. He spent approximately four and one-half hours there, not only with the ladies, as they were referred to, but with some of the staff. It was a mystery to me how he did this. Czar, Heilgrid, Helvi, and I prepared to leave for the boat with the guys hanging out at the house. They would not have an inactive day as they would constantly go over the plan, talk to each other, and of course they were now beginning to assemble the gear we would need.

Banger and Braveheart were parked at a table working on the plans. They were responsible for the suppression of the Russian enforcers, and stopping the egress from the fourth floor. It would be easier when they had a full set of structural plans and adits of the building, but then they had the timer system for melting a certain transmitter, and a shock switch that would turn on the one and the same machine, via a timer. When it was dropped it would all trigger.

All Banger said was, "It's a piece of cake, Boots. We can do it. We're just waiting on some parts from France."

I told him, "Okay Slick, handle it." Right now it was off to the boat.

We got into the car and Helvi drove. I sat shotgun, right side and Heilgrid and the Czar bringing up the rear. I had my briefcase in hand. We would be working on the boat today and every day until she was fully equipped and provisioned. I planned to put enough supplies for a maximum trip. It was a very noticeable fact that our "friends" were around. We not only saw their footprints, there was a pair of them down on the docks about ten finger piers down from our boat. It seemed they paid little, or no notice of us, as we were all laughing, and Helvi and I were playing. It was not the most comfortable thing I had faced in a while, but it was not the worst, or the most difficult.

I asked the Czar, "Where can we get the equipment that we will need?"

He answered, "Well, there's a used electronics place close."

I told him, "Czar, we are not using anything that isn't new on board this vessel of yours, so where do we get them?" He spoke right up. "Hartvrieg Marine," he replied.

"You know this place, Helvi?" I asked.

She answered, "Yes, I do. It is where my father purchased equipment for his boat before the accident. His boat and all

hands were lost out in the North Sea."

I looked at her solemnly and said, "I'm sorry."

She continued, "Thank you, but he died doing what he loved. Not to say that he didn't love his family, but it was his way of feeding his loved ones."

I asked her, "Where's your mom?"

Looking unbelievably sad,

Helvi said, "She passed on two years ago, and now they are together, and very happily sailing the universal ocean."

I thought this to be an extraordinarily philosophical statement.

I asked Helvi, "Will you be able to negotiate the purchase and installation of the equipment we will need?"

She answered, "That's not a problem."

I looked at her very seriously, "You do know we needed these things yesterday and that stocking supplies will have to wait until we are assured no one will be coming aboard the boat."

There was no smile in her voice, "I know, Boots."

I told her, "I need to talk to you and your sister."

We went aboard the boat and after Czar unlocked the cabin, we went below. Heilgrid and Helvi sat in front of me. I had to find a way to explain my predicament.

"Ladies," I said, "here is my problem, and I think it is best suited to you girls and not a man. We are going to need clothes to dress our target, but here's the problem. She will need everything from shoes to a coat. I have her measurements from approximately sixteen months ago, but I'm not positive that they're right. I would feel just a little self-conscious buying bras and panties and the like."

They both said in unison, "We can take care of that, Boots."

"Well," I said, "I thought I better ask you two first, and then later I will ask Preacher before we buy anything. This is because I want to bring out more than one young woman. If I had my way I'd kill the whole damn bunch in that building, get all of the young ladies and gentlemen out of there, and blow the damn place into puzzle pieces! But, there's too much chance of killing an innocent person. In reality, if I can, I want to rescue as many as will come. When I talk to Preacher this evening, I would like you both to be there and help figure out all of the possibilities. So, what do you think? Will you be able to shop for these girls, and one in particular?"

They both said, "Well, sure we can, Boots."

I said, "Okay. We will take this subject up with the Preacher then."

Getting back to the other subjects, I said, "Supplies, babes, supplies. What are the most popular meats here?"

Heilgrid said, "Well, fish, chicken, some pork and little beef."

I told them, "Americans eat all of these, but steak and chicken are our favorites."

Helvi replied, "So, it is mine also, but it is very expensive."

I told her, "We're not going to worry about prices."

Heilgrid asked, "How long will we be out?"

I looked back and forth between the two of them. "We're not supposed to be out more than nine days, but I worry a lot. If we stock for thirty days, theoretically we should have a surplus. How big is the freezer unit?"

Helvi said excitedly, "It is really large. You could probably get three quarters of a large cow in it."

I smiled, "Good. Do you think you can figure out what would be needed for thirty days? That's breakfast, lunches and dinners and also mid rats. Mid rats are those ration meals that you can get to at night if you work odd hours. Pop and snacks. Also, I would think these girls would like some real food for a change, and plenty of it." They told me they thought they could figure it out.

So, it was back to the supply lists. "Okay, girls," I said, "we also need plates and everything for twenty people."

Helvi's eyes were wide as she said, "So many, Boots."

I nodded, "We hope so. If I can get them to come with us."

She answered, "I hope you can."

At this I replied, "Me too, babe, me too. I would like the list before you go shopping, and along with all that, did I mention ice-cream? If I didn't, now you know. It's a girl's comfort food, and speaking of comfort, it's been my experience that a female needs to bathe after an experience of being violated."

Heilgrid replied immediately, "There are two heads on this boat. Both of them have showers."

"Well, for you girls that's no problem. You can go in and go even if there is a shower going, but please keep in mind some of us cannot."

"There are four staterooms."

I turned to her, "I hope they are full of girls that we plan to take with us. I have a feeling that they might want to talk some.

Are you up to it?"

Helvi spoke, "We had already considered this to be a possibility, and both Heilgrid and myself have talked to someone we trust and have learned some ways to help these young ladies."

All in all, talking to these young women seemed to go the way I had envisioned, although you always picture the ideal scenario. It seldom turns out that way, but there is always hope. Without hope there can be no conceivable future.

As the Czar came in on our confab, he asked if there was anything he could do. I told him, "Not really, Czar. Have you figured out the proper placement of your new equipment?"

He said, "Yes, I did. Come and look to see, Boots."

I smiled at him, "If it feels right to you Czar, it's fine with me. You have to live around it."

He asked me, "Do you know how much this equipment will cost, my friend?"

I replied to him, "As a matter of fact, it's not important to me. This equipment could be vital on the sea, watching for trouble and staying out of the way of larger ships that could just ruin the whole damn trip, my friend."

We spent time going over the controls and handling characteristics of the tub. The Czar and I seemed to have never had a time lapse of when we were apart. We worked checking and rechecking fluids and wiring. It really was like we had never been apart at all. Everything we did checked out as we finished up in the engine room and storage bunkers. The ladies needed to talk, so they left the cabin.

The Czar said, "Boots, if the girls are going to take over the staterooms, Heilgrid, Heilvia, you, and me, along with the clan get the foreword area and everywhere else."

I had talked to Czar about this question earlier. It was the way he had decided it should be. It was his boat and I would never challenge him on this point. I might be the boss, but he was the captain of his ship. Period. It had been a great day with fine friends, but it had been a long day.

We left our escape vehicle and the Czar brought up a good point. "Boots, with the radar and weather fax, along with all of the supplies, the boat could become a handsome target for

thieves, and they might just take her."

"Okay," I answered, "what do you suggest?"

He told me, "Someone will have to stay on the boat."

"Well Czar, I guess it's the least I can do."

I like the quiet anyway and there was radio and television along with a plethora of films from all over the world. I certainly would not be bored, and if I needed something, Helvi or Heilgrid could bring it to me. If I was needed, Helvi could come and get me, but that would not happen until after the radar went on the masthead.

We decided we could do no further damage to the vessel, which brought a barrage of laughter, however, we decided to go to the marine electronics shop before we went back to the house. When we went in the shop, there were eyes watching, but this did not concern us much, as we planned to give too much information as to why we would need radar. We approached the counter and I realized I was out of my league here because I did not speak the language.

Heilgrid began talking, and Helvi translated what was being said. Heilgrid asked the man behind the counter about what radar would cost. I believe he sensed an extra buck here, because I could have bought the same radar units for much less. However, we weren't in the States right now. I must admit the radar units were top of the line. The discussion continued, and the price for each unit came down a little when he realized that Heilgrid intended to buy both and have them installed by his people.

The clerk asked Heilgrid why she would need these units and she neatly explained that she, her sister, and her sister's boyfriend, and her husband were presently preparing for a one-year extended cruise exploring the coast from roughly here, down the coast of France, through the English Channel, Portugal, to Spain and going into the Mediterranean Sea. We would go to Majorca, then onto the Riviera, and down to Tuscany, Italy and down the coast.

He approved and said he would like to do the same thing someday. "It must be nice to be rich," he stated.

Heilgrid smiled and pointed at me, "He's American."

The clerk smiled back and said, "Well, that explains it. Is your sister going to marry him?"

She laughed, "As a matter of fact, they are to be married in Naples, Italy."

He was impressed, and Helvi was somewhat surprised by this startling revelation. I was mildly amused. It gave us what we needed. There would be fewer eyes because of this story.

Heilgrid asked when he thought he could do the job. He thought for a moment, and then said because this was Monday the third, he could begin work on Wednesday, and could have it done by Saturday the eighth.

He said, "As you probably know, we will have to install a new antenna mount and two forward plate mounts for the radar rotators."

Heilgrid answered, "That will be fine, but this won't compromise the mast in any way or get in the way of the sails?"

The clerk retorted, "Absolutely not! I have done over five-hundred installations and haven't lost a ship yet." His levity was definitely inane at best.

Heilgrid decided it was time to talk of prices. She asked, "How much will it cost?"

His lips formed a tight smile as he continued, "Well, I don't know exactly, it depends. It should run somewhere between twelve-thousand and fifteen-thousand United States dollars."

Heilgrid feigned apprehension, but I told her it would be fine. She told him, "I will bring you the money in the morning after the bank opens."

He looked somewhat shocked, but he was satisfied with the deal. He told Heilgrid that the work order and the purchase order, along with the contract for installation, would be ready in the morning. He stuck his hand out for a key, but Heilvia was not about to give him a key.

She said, "We will be working on the boat all this week, and of course stocking it, so you will not need a key. We will be there."

After shaking hands and bidding our farewells, we were off like dirty shirts.

As we drove out Helvi playfully said, "You better do right by me!"

I promised her that as soon as we got to Naples in this boat, I would marry her. It made everyone laugh. My wife would never understand sharing me with anyone else, nor would I understand sharing her either, but it did make for a good cover story, and a great joke that we did not share with anyone.

It seemed like the next five days were a whirlwind of activity. I had no idea of what it would take in supplies to load this boat, but all contingencies had to be covered. Just as I had planned, the radars and weather fax were finished being installed on Saturday afternoon. After checking them thoroughly for any random signals or parts that were not in the original schematics, we felt justified in trusting these units. The loading and packing was completed on Sunday the ninth of April.

We would spend the next week studying. As was promised, the rotation began into town. The Czar wanted to guide all of us, however this would not be advisable. Because of the Czar being the only guide, our faces would be associated with his face, and that would appear to be unusual. In no way did we want to be associated with each other on the streets!

Preacher was a gift to us. He was not only an operational member of the clan, he was a wealth of intel and was good at discovering what we would need. When we met at the house, the Preacher was talking. "So far guys, I don't seem to be able to find a pattern to the shift changes."

Bronco stood and said, "Preacher, there's got to be some sort of a pattern. They just can't all stay on the job working."

"Well, Bronc," Preacher answered, "if there is a pattern I haven't been able to discover it as of yet."

I told him, "Just keep trying, Preacher. Remember who these people are. Look where you wouldn't normally. Take the time to look, and you will find what you were looking for all along. Also, pick three employees that you can easily recognize and watch them. Maybe they have a floating schedule run by the month."

Preacher smiled, "Good idea, boss."

I continued, "And Preacher. We have time, so don't rush and don't try too hard, or you won't find it ever."

He looked slightly relieved, "Thanks, Boots. I need to calm down and not worry so much."

I slapped him on the back. "Just relax. It's just the way things are, and the way they work sometimes. Go bless the chillins', man, and you'll get the information sooner than you think. Just don't be nervous."

CHAPTER EIGHTEEN

Today we received a care package from our friends in France. The box was clearly marked "machine tools." As we opened the crate, no one could avoid the mark on the other end that read "French Diplomatic Corps—no inspection—Expedite." Upon looking inside, we saw there were the tools we had ordered. We pulled back the heavy brown oil paper. What we beheld was sixteen brand new Smith and Wesson forty caliber gas operated semi-automatic pistols, fully made of composite materials. Also included, were one-hundred-sixty, twenty round magazines. On the other end were five mac-ten submachine guns, with a pared down number of fifty, fifty round magazines.

This was the first of our care packages from well-meaning friends. There would be more. Many more such boxes every day or so, all addressed to a Baroque diplomat. It never ceased to amaze me, and Slick always impressed everyone. They would all come by diplomatic courier, supposedly.

While everyone admired their tools, the Czar warned them to put them in his safe place. None of us knew where that was, but such was the inherent trust in a clan member. It was moments before everything was gone, and the rest was burned at the onset of this mission. We came to terms with the idea that the law would be fractured, but we never try to shatter them. However, it was always a distinct possibility. I think the twins were shocked with what just happened, but I'm afraid they had signed on with pirates and brigands. I hope they do not think badly of me.

Banger came to me to inform me he had finished the design for starting and stopping the transmitter. It was not particularly complex, but was technical and would work with the parts he had ordered. After studying the schematics and tech language, Banger had created a master plan from technical skill and know-how. Humans, given time and material and a basic knowledge can, I believe, accomplish the impossible, and if not, at least the improbable.

Helvi decided that my exile was more than one person should have to bear. When she drove me to the boat, she decided she was staying, so I would have someone to talk to. I told her I was fine, but this young woman was having none of that. She had made up her mind. Although it was pleasant to have company, it certainly was not needed. She turned out to be extraordinarily intelligent. She was a graduate of a University in France and she had a Bachelor of Science degree. She was quite interesting and it wasn't like there was a shortage of space aboard. She stayed for two days and then had to leave, because she was going to Rotterdam for three days. She departed and it felt like a boon for me. In many ways it would feel private again.

Transportation was a problem because I did not have a Dutch permit to drive. Due to security concerns, taxis were ruled out almost immediately. Due to these problems, I relied on Heilgrid, Helvi, and the Czar. Since Helvi was in Rotterdam attending a sports medicine symposium, the transportation duties would fall to Heilgrid and Czar. They came to the boat on Monday morning, the sixteenth of April. It was 07:30 hours. As they approached the boat, I popped out of the cabin hatchway and said, "Good morning, guys."

"Good morning to you, Boots," returned Heilgrid. "Were you lonely here by yourself?"

I smiled, "No, not really. I always have something to do."

"Are you ready to go, Boots?" yelled Czar.

"Give me a minute, or come aboard. After all, it's your boat anyways," I said with a laugh.

"No," he said, "we'll just wait here. Grab what you need and let's get going."

"You bet," I said.

I went below and grabbed my briefcase and put on my jacket. I came on deck, turned and double locked the hatchway, and proceeded to jump off the boat.

"Come on guys!" I said with a smile, "It's a brand-new day!"

It was not a reach to be a little upbeat. We were one day closer than yesterday to a solution as to the patterns of how the shift changes were organized. There had to be a pattern. No matter how smart they were, it was there.

When we entered the car, the Czar was talking about time. I asked him, "Are we too much trouble, my friend? I'm sure it's

very awkward to have so many people in your home."

"No, Boots," he replied, "I'm just getting antsy."

I looked at Czar understandably, "I am too, my brother. There is no doubt of that, as patience is a virtue only for those who have already been rescued. Those persons who have not been rescued, they have the time that they live on, also the hope and faith that they have not been forgotten, and pray for rescue. So, we're free and we have to find the tenacity to rescue them. We need to be upbeat about what we do, and whom we rescue, knowing full well that every one we save is one less prisoner in captivity."

"Since you put it that way Boots, there is a reason to be upbeat."

I sighed a long sigh, "Don't get me wrong, Czar. I'm not that happy about many things, but if we allow hope to fade, we would find ourselves feeling hopeless, and that is unacceptable. The people who find us have faith that we can return their loved ones to them. At least we know where this one is. It's unfortunate for her, given her present circumstances, but I have faith that somehow the clan will succeed in freeing this young lady. It's not going to be easy and it may not go clean, but I believe we will succeed."

Heilgrid turned and looked at me, "You think more than one would ever imagine, Boots."

I laughed when she said that. "I'll take that as a compliment coming from you Heilgrid. Thank you." The conversation seemed to quiet down until we reached the Czar's house.

I had made it a habit to enter this house through the back door, because the coffee is in the room that the back door opens into. I like kitchens. I have always liked kitchens. It's homey, the smells, the spices and childhood memories come back to me. Some of the very best memories of mine are locked firmly in kitchens. As I poured myself a cup of coffee, Preacher joined me.

"Boots, I've got to tell you that I believe Svetlana somehow knows I'm not just there for preaching. Yesterday she said something that caught me off guard. When I was talking to some of the other girls that were there, she came over to me, leaned down and spoke into my ear. 'When you go, take me with you.' I didn't know what to say other than 'good things come to those who wait.' I was just a little flustered when I left, but no one knew it but me."

I looked him in the eye, "Are you going to be okay going back into the building, Preacher?" I asked.

He replied, "I'll be fine, Boots. I just have to be. She's got a terribly haunted look. As I was talking to them, I just noticed this other girl, Boots. God, she can't be over twelve years old! I hadn't seen her before, and asked her where she had been. 'They had me in the window. They called me eye candy,' she said to me."

I heard Preacher's voice start to crack, and I told him, "When this rescue goes down, make sure you know where she is." "Okay, Boots," he said, "I think she's French. That's what she speaks and she's fluent in it."

I told him, "Don't tell Slick yet, Preacher. We can tell him the evening of the raid. Okay?"

Preacher smiled at me almost thankfully, "Okay, brother. I'm keeping it to myself and I'm going back just like normal."

"Preacher," I asked, "have you found any kind of pattern yet?"

He answered, "I'm not sure, but maybe."

I stared at him, "If you're up to it just keep watching them, but try to find out how it's done. If not, we're going in ice cold, and trust me, it won't be pretty."

Evidently, my whole demeanor had changed, as everyone moved away from me except for Preacher who just continued to talk softly until I asked what was the matter. I looked around the kitchen and saw that it was empty.

I said, "Where did everybody go preacher?"

He smiled crookedly and said, "You scared the hell out of them."

I asked, "What do you mean I scared them?"

"I saw this before," he continued, "it was just like in Vietnam. Boots, it's when you're on the precipice of going berserk. Like with the chopper. Like at the Citadel. Like so many other places. You just step out for awhile and a new guy takes your place." And then I knew.

"It's okay, Boots," he said softly.

"I know, Preacher. It's okay." As I turned to Preacher, I had tears in my eyes. "I'm sorry, Preacher."

He put his hand on my shoulder. "It's okay, brother. It is just fine. I'm glad you didn't go there. When I saw this before, you won medals. Lots of medal's, but they came with a price." He knew me well.

I yelled into the other room, "Come on back guys, I'm sorry.

Sometimes I get carried away."

Surprisingly enough, Heilgrid came in and kissed me on the cheek, and it was better. I turned and asked, "Preacher, can you handle this for a while? I need some air."

With a big smile, he answered, "Sure, boss. I got your back."

I grabbed some coffee and started out the door. That is where I ran straight into Helvi.

"What's the matter, Boots?" she asked.

"Nothing, babe. I just needed some air."

"Well," she said, "I'll keep you company."

I smiled at her, "I thought you were in Rotterdam."

She laughed a little and said, "They postponed the symposium. I'm going to get some coffee too, okay?"

I looked at her and told her, "I'm glad you are here. I just need some air and to walk, so I'll be waiting on the patio. Okay?" "Okay," she said, and went to get her coffee.

As I stood there thinking, many thoughts went through my mind. Thoughts of war and many friends who were gone. I even remembered the Citadel. I will never be able to figure out why I just charged the enemy, or how I didn't feel the bullet that tore through my arm. But, those were the days when the need was great for men, not just me, but many men to go above and beyond the normal boundaries of their abilities. I was a fortunate human. I survived. Not all of us did, and I mourn my friends that died to this day.

As Helvi walked through the door and came closer, she looked at me with a much more critical eye, I'm afraid.

"Well, Helvi," I began, "I'm sure you heard what happened, and I'm sorry. It just happens sometimes. I can't explain it and I don't try to."

"It's fine, Boots," she said. "Don't think about it. They will get over it."

"I know," I said, "but I never do."

With that said, I went out the door into the fresh air with Helvi. She talked about many things of which I remember very little, but it made me feel better to hear her chatter. It reminded me that the world is real and goes on. After my lapse into combat rage had receded, Helvi and I continued to talk about nothing really important. Something she said sounded weird, and I had to laugh. I wish I could remember what she had said. I'm sure it was funny, it had to be. Not much in my life is funny.

We walked back to the house and saw a very large courier truck in the drive. "Well, Helvi," I said, "It looks like the clan got mail, doesn't it?"

She laughed, "I think so, Boots."

When we walked into the house, we saw there were four crates. Three very large and one medium-size crate. These were the things that the clan had been waiting for. The first crate that was opened contained eight Heckler and Koch seven-point-six-two by fifty-one millimeter battle rifles with one one-hundred round drum magazine. Along with this were five extra one-hundred round magazines per rifle and our twenty-five concussion grenades and ten fragmentation grenades. There were forty laser eye detonators. There were also two reels of wire, along with connectors and timers. When we opened the next crate, it was full of ammunition for our forty caliber pistols. The count was five-thousand and five-hundred rounds. It also contained seven-thousand and five-hundred rounds of forty-five caliber ammunition.

I said, "These things must weigh a ton!"

I turned to the Czar and he said, "They do, brother, they do."

The next crate contained the needed C-four explosives and one white noise transmitter, along with our communications gear. It was quite a load of assault gear! We all hoped that in the long run, it would just be dumped in the ocean without being used, but you just could never tell. It's better to have a weapon if someone's using one against you, than to need a weapon and not have one within your grasp. It's better not to have to need one at all, but this is not an ideal world.

The last crate we opened, and then we closed it immediately. We would have to get this to the boat. It was the ships defense weapon that Slick ordered without asking. He had been correct in ordering it. I probably would have been hesitant to order one, but, after all, he is just a little brash and flamboyant.

We had been trained. We had all proven our metal in combat. We now had the plan, along with the tools. Now, everything hinged on what Preacher could discern from his visits to the building, a lot of luck, and the mercy of God. Preacher continued his surveillance of the building and his discussions with not only the women, but some of the employees. Slowly the hypothesis that these people used a floating shift change began to prove up to the maybe stage. As always, time either comes at you like a freight train at top speed, or it flowed like a lazy southern river. At this juncture, it was from the Deep South and time went on endlessly slow.

We had dismantled Slick's ship defense weapon and taken it in many pieces to the boat, where at night before I went to sleep, Helvi and myself reassembled it. It was a beautiful weapon! It would be a sad moment when this went over the side, but it had to go eventually, along with everything we had that was weapon related except for the forty caliber pistols. They were legal and above board and all we needed was the proper paperwork. We all had that set of papers years ago.

As another week crept by we found we were all getting antsy to get this done, and go on to the next mission, in God only knows where. The clan has collectively touched every country on this planet.

To date, I had avoided seeing the interior of this building on the advice of the Czar and Preacher. But, that advice and those conclusions had now changed since preacher was already there, and to come into this world could prove to be disastrous for him and those young lives. These were the lives we planned to change back to a better life. It could possibly cost us all our lives, but I didn't think so.

The Czar had decided to take me to this place. We, of course, would only have a drink, but it would give us an in depth look at the tactical situation, and what could happen from which directions. I found it to be pretty much the way that preacher had described it. From his diagrams he was pretty close, but there were some subtleties that had been missed.

Where Bronco should and would be standing, there would be to his immediate left, an elevator that said private. This was not by any means an original item in this building. It was new and fairly modern. This building would not have had an elevator when it was built. In my opinion, and later in the Czars, this elevator was for the enforcers, and mostly for the key men on the fourth floor. I would have to ask Preacher if there were landings on the third floor, and indeed on the second where the enforcers were stationed.

This in itself changed little. Bronc could handle the elevator along with line of site threats. Still the most dangerous places were the second and fourth floor. I needed to talk to Banger and Braveheart. Having a mental picture of this pit, I felt it was time to go as I didn't want to be in sight too long. I didn't want to be recognized when hell came to dinner, or for them to think anything about any of us.

It was an utterly silent trip back to the boat. I had much to think about. When I exited the car, I thanked Czar, and told him to have a good evening. I turned and headed toward the boat deep in thoughts of my own. I stepped onto the deck and knew the locks would be off. I had a boat mate. Helvi would be there. As I stepped on down the stair well, a wonderful smell permeated the air. I reached the cabin level and there was Helvi cooking and humming. I glanced at the table and it had a full complement of knives, forks, spoons, plates, bowls, and cups. To the side were two glasses. One was for wine and one for either water or milk.

As I walked into the cabin, she turned with a big smile, "I found a recipe and thought you might like to be my guinea pig."

I suddenly realized a kind of magic had happened that can only occur between two people, brought together by unusual circumstances and who must be virtually inseparable. It is not love. That magic has a name. It's called true friendship and devotion. A type of kinship. We were together a lot, as much as I had been with Daria, but I never felt this kind of kinship with Daria. I believed that somewhere in my mind I thought Daria had wanted more than a friendship, however it could have been just an insecurity problem.

We sat down to eat and I of course, helped seat Helvi. By the look on her face I could see this seemed to please her a great deal. Being the good guinea pig that I was, I ate the experiment. I discovered it was indeed very good, but had a strange flavor (some kind of fish dish!). It was most certainly not unpleasant.

Dinner came to a close and I got up, and poured each of us a glass of wine. We proceeded on deck so I could continue my bad habit of smoking. We walked around the boat and I began to talk to her about my thoughts and worries.

"It bothers me, Helvi, that some people think of these rescue missions as wrong, and that it would be better to let the police handle these problems. They don't realize that the police are so tied up with rules and regulations they don't have the authority to act without a huge amount of evidence and permission. In the meantime, the damage is done."

Helvi looked quite solemn as she said, "That is a philosophical question, Boots. Does it bother you how people view what you do?"

I had to answer honestly, "Not really. In the long run I don't give a damn."

"So," she said, "in truth what you're asking then, is why things aren't clearer for everyone else as it is clear for you."

I nodded, "I guess that's it."

Her face softened, "Not many people, in my opinion, care like you or the guys do. They do not care about children and people, they just talk a good story. They would just as soon not hear about it, and certainly not see it. They won't talk about it. If they maintain this facade, they don't have to make the tough decisions. I must admit Boots, when I first found out about you I had huge reservations about you. But, today I trust you with my most prized possession. Me. I know you wouldn't hurt me. I know you wouldn't rape me. You believe all humans should act humanely, and not like sheep. You believe humans have a fundamental right to be treated as humans, not as property. Does that about size up your question?"

"Yes," I answered, "thanks sweetheart."

Helvi smiled. "Boots, you will always be welcome. Do you want to know what I think?"

"Absolutely!" I said, "I'd love to hear it."

"Well," she replied, "You and the guys you are like knights living in a realm that needs them, but refuses to believe in them. People believe there's no room on this earth for you, Boots. It seems to me that the things we need the most, we are trying to get rid of, and your breed is one of those things they want gone."

I knew she was right and what she had said was correct. "Helvi," I said, "You're a peach in a lemon world."

She laughed at that. "That's funny, Boots. That was what I was thinking about you."

I smiled back and said, "Let's go below, babe. To hell with everything tonight."

We descended into our private world. When I shut the door, what was outside did not exist. At least not tonight.

CHAPTER NINETEEN

In the morning I was no longer in the black funk I had been in. The night had been kind to me. Helvi and I had sat and talked, laughed, and listened to the opera Carmen on the entertainment system on the boat. I was actually in the rack before 24:00 hours and had gotten four and one half hours of semi sleep, that was as good as the company I had kept the night before.

After I cooked breakfast for Helvi and myself, I cleaned up the joint. Not only from breakfast, but the night before. She just laughed and it amused me. She would be going to work after dropping me off at the Czar's. She seemed happier than normal. She was getting ready to take a six-month sabbatical from work. In Holland, they can take one every four years, and she was taking it now. "Well," I thought, "very cool indeed."

I hoped that today would be the day that everything would break for us. I had now been engaged in this for well over two months. Not long, but long enough to want to achieve the goals that were set down some time ago. I am an optimist. It is a conundrum to what I do, but it was a much needed specialty. As Helvi pulled into the Czar's driveway, I felt a bounce in my step and I went around to open her door.

She had rolled down her window and said, "Boots, I have got to go."

"Okay," I replied, "that's fine Helvi."

I leaned down and kissed her cheek. There's that cheek thing and now I'm doing it too! Very strange indeed! While heading to the backyard, I turned and waved to Helvi and she was gone. I came in my usual way and grabbed some coffee. Everybody was at the table. They looked at me expectantly.

"What?" I said and looked down. No, my zipper was up and my shirt was clean. I repeated, "What?"

That's when I decided to go into the head and look in the mirror. There on my cheek was a perfect set of red lips. Heilvia's.

Well to Hell with them! I didn't wash it off.

I walked back in the kitchen and repeated, "What?"

I heard, "What on earth have you been doing Boots?"

I responded, "Why? Because of the lips on my check?"

The retort was, "Well, it does pop into one's mind."

I laughed, "If you knew how many times I had to wash my face so Helvi could try again and again until this set was on! She thought they would make you dirty old den mothers talk! It took over an hour to make it this perfect. Deal with it guys!"

Everyone began laughing. The terrible tension that had been building up over the weeks of constant training and studying to rescue Svetlana was broken. It was gone. Now the clarity of thought and purpose had taken over in all of us again. It needed to happen and Helvi had done it. I was relieved for the first time in eight weeks. I must remind myself to thank Helvi in a special way.

It was fairly early and Preacher's duty would not call for another two and one half hours. He was more positive of the shift sequence, but it would have to be observed for five more days in order to make the ultimate decision. Day after tomorrow, the Czar would be taking the boat to the fuel docks to top off his fuel tanks. This included the reserve tank along with the range tank and auxiliary generator tank. His vessel was equipped with a water desalination plant that had just been serviced, but there was also emergency water onboard. None the less, things were coming together.

It was with hope that it would only be as I surmised and that a target date could be set in five days. We would have to be careful about pushing this faster than it should go. Time was not the goal, success was. It seemed like a day would start out and in the blink of an eye it was gone. This one was gone already. Tomorrow morning after Helvi and I were gone is when Heilgrid and Czar would get the boat taken care of. I told him to go ahead and have all the fluids changed, so the boat would be busy for the day. I felt it would be better than later saying "Man, we need oil," or anything else after we had already embarked on our flight to avoid the Mafia!

Before the Czar took the boat I asked him if there was anything else that needed done or should be checked. He told me that the only thing left was of his twelve batteries, one was weak. I looked at him and told him that if they were available to put in all new ones, especially if they were over a year old and in the end I would be satisfied with everything.

Everything that we could do with the boat had been done. Even down to spare everything. Ropes, lanyards, blocks, filters, pulleys, rollers, and anything else that could be thought of. When he brought her back he was happy, and so was I. The light bulbs were even new! Czar had got her all the fuels, oils, and filters, plus their spares, and twelve brand-new batteries. He even replaced the old batteries with larger and more powerful ones. He did a good job!

Banger had the circuitry worked out for the stairwell bomb. Braveheart and Banger had somehow figured out the stairwell size from the first floor stairwell. They figured a pattern of detonators that would, as Banger said, 'Would bloody well confuse me!' They had used all forty detonators and had practiced deploying them in the Czar's stairwell. If Preacher could help him, the unit could be deployed in thirty seconds. It was hard to believe, but I watched and timed them. It was indeed thirty seconds! Then the wire was draped and loomed and the package was connected to the power pack. It all took fifty-one seconds. When it was deployed for real, I hoped that it would do its job in causing the leaders to fail in being able to descend into the lower floors. We did not want them to be able to figure out what had happened and rally some kind of troops.

Banger said to me, "Boots, I've got the stairwell covered and a rough plan for knocking out the enforcers, but I haven't had time to think about the transmitter yet. It will take time. I'm sorry, but these are not normal items that are being planned and constructed. We are in a basement two-thousand miles from the supply house and we don't have any catalogs! So, it just takes thought and a lot of time."

I told him, "It's okay, Banger. You're doing a hell of a great job, man! You come up with one new style doorstop and I know you'll come up with the rest as well. Time we got. I know you don't want to disappoint anyone, but my friend, I don't think anyone will be disappointed in your ingenuity or in your construction. Let alone the results you'll get when everything is deployed and in use. So, you just do what you do best, and we will wait. We would rather have stuff that works well and works right instead of crap you might as well leave at home. Okay, bud?"

He just said, "Okay, Boots. Thanks for having faith in me."

I looked at him, "Banger, do you think I'm one of the best?"

He laughed, "There's no bloody doubt!"

I stared at him with intent. "Do you know why I'm the best? It's because I only work with the best, and in your line of work, my friend, you're the very best. It is so far over the limit it's beyond the best. I only work with the best, Banger." With that, I bid him adieu and went to see the clan.

I walked in and said, "Hi, guys. What's new? Are you guys bored?"

They all looked laid back and lazy, "Well yes."

I felt a little peeved. "Has anyone thought to break out the weapons in order to do a weapons check?"

Their response was, "No we haven't."

Now, I was getting just a little upset. "What if you need to use those weapons?"

Bronco said matter of factly, "They are just guns, Boots."

I could feel my temper rising. "Has anyone ever handled a composite forty caliber?"

In lower tones they all said, "No."

I threw my hands up and told them, "Talk to the Czar. I'm going to want you in the shop downstairs, and not the one Bangers in. He's up to his neck in work! I want you to check out your personal weapons. Right down to the serial number! It's your's and I want you to tear it down, clean it, reassemble it, tear it down and put it back together. For a full day! I want you intimately acquainted with your weapon! Your life could depend on how clean it is and how it feels in your hand. They are one third of the weight and a more accurate than standard pistols."

Bronco laughed, "I suppose you'll be giving a test later?"

I felt myself getting really angry. "Piss me off and I will, smart-ass! Bronc, I'm serious. I've used one of these weapons.

They're incredible, but they feel different."

He looked down. "Okay, Boss."

I continued on, "When we get done, after a couple of days, we will start on the mac's and then the H and K's."

Bronco looked stunned. "You talk like we might be here another two, maybe three weeks."

I said, "It's a possibility, and if we're not ready, we won't go. So, get ready and stay frosty and on the bounce. Our client, Svetlana, expects a good show, and by God, she'll get one!" I half stomped out and almost ran right into Helvi.

"Hey babe," I said, "What's up?"

She answered, "Just coming home."

"Good," I said, "How about a cup of coffee?"

She replied, "God, that sounds great. What's with the guys?"

I shook my head, "They were on some kind of 'I know everything and I don't have to train no more' kind of thing."

She nodded like she knew, "I overheard what you said. Will they do what you say?"

I replied, "Of course. They're my friends and they are professionals at what they do."

Helvi sighed, "That's good."

I smiled and said, "You better hope so, sweetheart. You're putting your butt on the line."

She laughed, "Yes, but I've got the antidote to creeps." I had to smile back at her. "I forgot you carry a gun," I said.

"No," she stated "I've got you, and so do those girls."

I took a deep breath. "I hope it's not misplaced. Even I make mistakes, you know."

She nodded and quietly said, "I know, but I've heard and seen a glimmer of what you are capable of. I don't think I would want to be your enemy."

I did not want to think along those lines. "Let's change the subject. I told you I owed you anything you wanted. Have you thought much on it?"

She smiled, "A little. I'm not going to waste this. I am going to think hard before I ask. There is so much I want and you're not playing fair. Most people get three wishes or wants, and I only get one. So, let me think a while longer."

I just smiled, "You want to go for a walk? I need some air." "Okay," she said and off we went.

We strolled on out to talk and wait for Preacher. Helvi relayed to me, "The Czar said you and he met in Greece."

"Yes," I responded, "We most certainly did. We met once before that, but we were not formally introduced."

Helvi laughed, "He said something like that. How did you meet in Greece?"

I told her, "I had just finished up a rescue and was tired, so I stayed in Greece for three days. I ate in the same bar as he did, and one thing led to another. I introduced myself and he did likewise. I would say that we were friends from that day forward."

"How did you meet Preacher?"

I answered, "I met him in combat in Vietnam." I could see where this was going. "Helvi, I met most of the clan either in combat somewhere, or through someone whom I met in combat,

and I really don't like to talk about it."

She smiled slightly, "Okay. What if it was my wish?"

I was very serious with her. "Then I would give you a blow-by-blow description. Is that what you want?"

"No," she said, "I was just curious."

I told her, "Please don't be about that, okay?"

The conversation kind of dried up for a while, at least a little.

We continued walking and we talked about everything, but combat. She asked where I had grown up and I told her, "I grew up between heaven and hell in a place called Simpson Island,

Alaska."

She asked, "Is it a big island with lots of people?"

I replied, "No, it was my great grandfather's island. I was born on a fish float house anchored to the shore, along with thirty-two other families. All of different nationalities and religions. It was a great life. I went to school on water. We had a small schoolhouse built onto a float and it was anchored in the middle of the float houses."

She looked very interested. "Where was the closest town?"

I answered, "It was Wrangle, Alaska. At that time its population was one-hundred-forty-six. The big town was St. Petersburg. It had a doctor and it was only seventy-five miles by water. It was also across the passage and the Stikine Reef. We were what you might call a remote village. We had great Christmases because everyone had some special foods or traditions. We even had Sinterklaas come one year." "He's Dutch," said Helgi smiling.

"Yes," I said, "the Dutch family lived two floats down from us. They were a family from old Holland. We had families from Norway, Russia, France, Greece, and Portugal. Families from many countries. Although I loved them all, I loved the Dutch family very much. But, my grandmother got sick and my grandfather bought a ranch for her.

When they found out she was dying they sold everything and moved away. I was devastated when my grandmother died. My grandfather died six months later. He couldn't live without her. He died of a lonely and broken heart. Enough woman! I don't like talking about myself. It's like,

I don't know, I just don't like it!"

She said, "That's fine, Boots, just fine."

I have to admit if Preacher had brought bad news I could have taken it better then personal stuff, but the time was gone and Preacher was home. He came straight to me like a heat seeking missile.

"What's up, Preacher? Is something wrong?"

He said, "No, Boots. We're going to catch a break, I think, if we're up to speed."

I faced him, "Spill it, Preacher."

"Well," he began, "I overheard an enforcer and a bartender talking in confidence about the changes coming with time off."

I stopped. "What does that mean?"

He continued to tell me, "Three Saturdays from now vacations start and since there's not too much trouble to speak of, one

third of the enforcers are going to get a week off."

I was flabbergasted! "You're kidding me!"

He looked me in the eye very seriously, "Not even, boss. It spread quietly. Evidently, if the enforcers get time off, so do some of the bartenders, etc. This means we would only have to deal with about sixteen enforcers and inexperienced help in other areas. If we dress similar, no one will know who are the bad guys or the good guys."

This was a break! "Come on, Preacher. Helvi. We have got to talk to everyone else."

As we hurried towards the house my mind kicked in. "Preacher, you sure it's not some story from them to maybe get someone to do what we're planning? Maybe just to find out who's arrayed in opposition to their business."

He was completely serious. "I don't think so, Boots. If it was a ploy I would think that it would have had a somewhat louder declaration. I only heard because I was coming down the stairs and noticed the confab and stopped to tie my shoe."

"Hmm," I said, "This is something to think about, though other than that your job remains the same."

"Oh," replied Preacher, "I figured that, Boots. You are too thorough not to keep an asset in play."

We reached the house, but there was no one around. I noticed the door to the basement was ajar and hollered down, "Hey, you guys! We need to talk now, if not sooner." The edge in my voice evidently alerting them to come and the herd was on its way.

When everyone was either sitting, or at least in the kitchen, I told them, "Preacher has something he wants to say to you guys and gals."

Preacher looked around at everyone. "Here's the skinny." He then repeated what he had told me, to the clan plus two. One of which had also heard earlier. It was strongly suggested that it would depend on Banger's bag of tricks.

"What do you think Banger?"

He replied, "I'll have 'em ready in a week, Boss."

"Okay," I said, "that would be great but don't hustle too much."

He smiled, "Gotcha, Boots."

I looked around, "Well guys, talk to me."

The Czar spoke up, "Let's see what Preacher can find out. I love having you guys here and I don't care if it takes much longer."

That's the Czar for you. Anything for the clan and the ideal. I told him, "I hope it doesn't Czar. I've had another call and I'll tell you all about it later, if you're not busy I could use some help."

The only ones to say anything was the Czar, Heilgrid, and Helvi. "We want in!" was said in unison.

So, I had some people already and two raw recruits. That was okay. No one in the clan has to feel bad about a turn down. There were other clansmen and women, and others. A turndown did not have to be explained. With this group the reasons would be valid, but it did not matter. When they were available I would work with them, in another arena, in a new fight. Thanks guys, for being on this one. And that's what was said. So be it.

I sat down with Preacher. He wanted to explain why, but I already knew. His wife was pregnant and due in two months. Also, Preacher wasn't just a nickname, it was an important job he did, and I told him so. "Preacher, after this, go home and stay home until the baby is born. That is, until you feel the need to be on sabbatical again. Whether I got you or not, you're my best friend. Look at my phone bill and it will make you a believer."

"Boots," he said, "I know that's the truth. Look at my phone bill!"

We both looked at each other and the memories flooded in.

"Let's let it be, Boots."

"I'll second that Preacher. The new mission will be less without you, but it's cool, brother. I got the Czar and now I need to train two recruits!" We both laughed some and then got down to business.

I thought for a minute of the new mission, code-named Jamie. It had been in the news. A boy just vanished into thin air with his parents not far away. So much for being safe in Italy. I'm glad I have some friends in Palermo, but enough. This one isn't done, Boots. One at a time. Save them one at a time.

I put my hand on Preacher's shoulder, "All I can say is stay safe. Don't take any risks, but if you get the chance, then find out. If you can't, just listen to the talk around breaks or passing meetings. I'm tentatively setting the clock for the third Sunday in May. If I have to I'll change it, okay? If you see Svetlana, and you believe she knows, reinforce without a hope, if you get my drift."

Preacher nodded, "In other words, Boots, don't tell her what we're up to, but that miracles do happen."

I answered, "That's about right, Preacher."

He nodded, "Okay, boss. Back to work tomorrow, but I'm going to pull a late shift. I won't be back here until after 21:00 hours. I want to see what goes down at that time. In fact, I think I'll do that for a week, if that's okay with you."

I told him, "It's fine, Preacher. You're in it, man, and doing a great job. Don't change anything, but you run on your own schedule. We'll talk later, except, have you worked with the new forty?"

He said, "I own one in the states, Boots."

I smiled, "Well, never mind then. I'll talk at you later, brother." "Okay, my brother," he replied.

I stood and talked to the rest of the room. "Hey, guys. Before you wander off into something else, who hasn't worked with their fortys?" Out from under everyone's shirt jackets came brand-new Smith & Wesson forty cals, each pulled from brand-new holsters. I could tell they had worked on them thoroughly. New holsters are stiff. It can be difficult to get a pistol in and out of them unless you have oiled and stretched the holster.

"Start on the mac's, boys," I said, "I think you've got the hang of it. Are they loaded?"

"Damn right, Boots," shouted Bronco, "An unloaded gun is just an expensive club!"

"Okay," I laughed, "I'll talk to you later. And now to my main subject with the Czar and company. Helvi, are you out of your ever loving mind? And Heilgrid, what would your mama say if she knew you were out traipsing around with a pair of worn-out old war dogs, like the Czar and me?"

Heilgrid quickly looked at Helvi questioningly and then back at me. "Our mother is dead. I thought you knew."

I felt their sadness come over me and I took one of each of their hands in mine. "I remember, my girls, and I'm heartily sorry for you both, but if she were here what would she say to both of you young ladies? You can't make a living doing this."

"No," said Heilgrid, "but you can make a difference."

Helvi spoke up, "Boots, you said it. One life at a time."

God, I thought, "Did they listen to every word I said? How was I going to change their minds, or should I?" "Czar," I asked, "What do you think? They have no combat experience."

Czar smiled a crooked smile, and with one eyebrow raised said, "I think that they will get it just like you and me, Boots, and they will learn."

I slowly shook my head, "Czar, I don't even know the setup yet. We will talk about it at a later date. Let's get this one done first."

"Okay, Boots," he answered.

As things slowly returned to what one would deem a semblance of normalcy, the job at hand went back to where it belonged. At the top of the heap. That was where it should be, and it would stay there until this mission was successfully and satisfactorily brought to a swift conclusion. The swift part seemed to be a little lacking. The price tag was going up. I was glad we were not paying for this one, like we paid for Mission Manila or Mission Thailand. Those had been very expensive. But, not unlike this case, we don't spend money easy and we make it count, no matter who pays the freight.

As it was getting very late, and I needed to sleep, I went and got Helvi. "Come on, babe. Bed time."

She yawned, and we bid the clan good night and farewell. On the way out I yelled to the others, "Remember, tomorrow is another day in paradise."

Since we ate at the house, and I wasn't even sure what it was, as my dinner was as busy as the rest of my time, Helvi had to remind me to take a bite. Thank God for friends who care.

CHAPTER TWENTY

Morning began with the customary scream. Although, I had never screamed in any combat zone. That's just the way it is. As I came fully awake and alert, I realized where I was and began to relax. 03:40 hours is early. When I left my cabin I realized I had not disturbed Helvi's sleep and made a pot of coffee. I needed it.

While I sat waiting for it to be done, I looked at the papers that were sitting on the table. I began to read every entry. These were personal papers. It was my journal. I had kept a journal since I was nine years old. The reason escapes me now, but it became a habit to write everything in my journal. Who knows, my grandchildren, or great-grandchildren might get a kick reading them. I had learned to write in detail, exactly like the books I read, so they were pretty detailed and interesting. Just the facts, but they were certainly not a dry read. I had written about the good times and the war times, leaving out nothing. Hell, it was a habit. I finished my journal on yesterday's events and glanced at my watch. It was 05:20 hours.

Damn, I better get some more coffee made. Helvi should be awake in about ten minutes, and she was a bear without coffee in her cup. In that, she was just like me, and so I usually made the mud. As the coffee perked and was finishing dripping, Helvi exited her cabin. She walked into the galley. Her mug was steaming with the hot liquid. She sat down for a minute and grumbled a little, but after several sips she began to come around.

"Good morning, Boots," she finally said.

"Good morning, Helvi," I replied, "Did you sleep well?"

She smiled slightly, "Yes I did, Boots. How did you sleep?"

Although I was sure she knew, I said, "As always Helvi, it never changes."

She asked, "What's on the agenda."

I told her, "I'm not sure. We will see when we get to the house."

It was not exactly the truth. I only had some ideas, but they were only ideas.

After breakfast we left the boat. Helvi and I ended up taking a side trip. She wanted me to see where Heilgrid and she had been born. It was almost an hour away from Amsterdam. We pulled into a strange driveway and much to my surprise, I saw one of the windmills that this country was so famous for. She turned off the motor.

All she said was, "Come on."

We got out of the car and proceeded to the mill. We arrived at the door and found it was ajar. When we walked in to this magnificent piece of history, I saw several workmen. One man detached himself from the group. He walked over and addressed Helvi.

"Miss Heilvia, it's coming along very nicely. There was much to be done, but we are on target and under budget."

I had to reappraise Helvi. It seemed that she was trying to save this piece of valuable history. As we climbed the stairs, that were ornate as well as massive. She started to explain that her father was a miller as well as a fisherman, and his family had been millers for ten generations at least that she knew of. Her father's family had lived here, not only milling grains, but pumping the incessant North Sea back out where it belonged. I had seen no power lines, yet there was electricity. Helvi explained that the mill had a power plant hooked into the shreft.

I asked her, "What's that?"

She laughed, "Well, I can teach you! It is the gears at the point where the wind shaft transfers power to the grist mill below." We laughed together and she was quite pleased.

We walked around the third deck and she took me into an impeccably restored room. Helvi stood tall and with pride in her voice, she said, "This was my grandfather and grandmother's room. My grandfather had been part of the Dutch resistance in World War II. Boots, my father's oldest brother had been killed as a runner for the underground. It was a very terrible time."

I nodded and softly stated, "I agree, Helvi. It was a horrible war."

"Boots," she continued, "I wanted you to see that not all Dutch people like what's going on here. I wanted you to know my family was, and is, a good and God-fearing family. We have pride and honor, and do not like what is being done in this country."

I took Helvi's hand and looked into her eyes. "Helvi, I have never for one minute believed that all Dutch people were happy with what's happening here. It's like my countrie's politicians. It's about the power and the money, and to hell with the people! But, like Marie Antoinette, they could lose their heads over indifference and greed. It has happened before and it will happen again."

Helvi gave my hand a squeeze and said, "I have one more place to show you."

We walked up to the fifth deck. There were six decks, but the sixth was the power plant, gearbox, and other things that were dangerous. The fifth deck was much different. It was split into just two rooms. One was Heilgrid's and the other was Heilvia's. She opened the door and it was like a fairytale room. The bed, armoire, chairs, and dressers were all made of hand carved black walnut. You could see the delicate cuts made from a master wood smith's carving tools. The intricate design was more than just decoration, it was incorporated with the family crest on the headboard. The linens were lace and silver-blue brocade.

Helvi told me how her grandfathers back five generations had made all of the furniture. It was breathtaking and made me think of the love and work that went into this room. It was incredible and a monument to the ability of man to give. Helvi looked at her watch and then looked around her room. She told me that her daughter and son would be raised here in the old ways. I could find no words to speak. No words came to me at all. As we left this place, I had a new perspective on Heilvia and the Dutch people. Certainly not on the whole, but these people who cared about their past and their future. It was to look into the soul of not only my companion, Helvi, but a look into the soul of the real Dutch people. It was time to get over to the house.

We were just pulling into the Czar's drive and I asked, "Helvi, whose house is it that the clan is staying in?"

She smiled and replied, "Does it matter so much?"

I raised my eyebrows slightly and said, "Yes, Helvi, it does to me."

She answered, "It's mine and my sisters."

It was like opening up a box marked truth. It was Helvi and Heilgrid that were responsible for providing the clan with a base. I had to look at her and apologize for thinking they were only along for the ride.

"Instead," I said, "you were in the driver's seat and steering the whole damn bus. For that Helvi, I thank you and I will thank your sister. It changes my way of thinking about Holland. It's like in the States. There are people who want the right things to happen, but no one in power has the guts to change it, or they are growing too wealthy and fat to want to change things. You have given me faith in the good people of Holland."

With that, she leaned over and kissed my cheek and said, "Thank you, Boots. That means a lot."

When we walked into Helvi's house I told the clan that I wanted to talk to them behind the house, quietly without the Czar. It was there I informed them of who had actually made a safe house available for the clan to use. Not one word was said, but the actions of my guys showed that they understood the truth of it all. From that moment in time, the Czar lost nothing, but to my knowledge neither Helvi nor Heilgrid cleaned house, washed a dish, or cooked anything unless they chose to. The clan pays respect to those who deserve it, and disdain to those who warrant it.

Things settled down and it was time to check with the specialists of the clan. I proceeded to ask Slick, "Are we all set with the exit visa stamps and replacement passports from Russia? And what about our landing permits?"

"Yes, Boss," he said, "It has all been done and what's better than that is they are all legal. The only thing that has to be done when we get to France is submit to the inspection of the vessel. All gun permits have been obtained and are documented with the proper authorities. I have a friend in a ministry of great power. You know him, Boots. He has helped many, many times in these cases and is a highly thought of person. He has been authorized to help at every juncture and in all cases for the clan. We have a home, Boots, along with it, Sicily and Uruguay, so no matter where, the clan has friends. We are quite well thought of in many circles. I believe France has decided that you are, or should be a French operative."

I laughed, "That's impressive Slick, but then I expect the impossible from you and you're good at it."

I faced the clan, "Well guys, talk to me about the weapons. They are nasty looking. Are these new units?"

Slick interjected, "They are the new model made by Israel for their shock troops. If you will notice, on the right side of the weapon there is a new switch. On the left, you have a lever that goes from safe to semi-automatic and then on to full auto, but in the full auto position you can activate the right side lever in two different ways. To leave it where it is, gives you what is available with the left lever. If you're on full automatic and you push the lever forward on the right side you will get five round bursts. If you slide it back to its rearward position it will give you three round bursts, thus, getting the job done instead of wasting ammunition, it conserves ammunition. I thought it would be a much wiser use of firepower. So, it will just take dry run practice to get somewhat used to it, but I think it's better because the damn thing will fire at its maximum cyclic rate of twelve-hundred rounds a minute. With a rate like that, a fifty round clip will last only two point four seconds, and with the recoil it could be unmanageable." These were quite the mechanic's tools.

Bronco left the table and went to the vault. When he came back his only comment was, "I'll be damned."

"Well guys," I said, "what you thought you had under control, was not quite factual. I guess we all learn something new every day, so get used to the switches, levers, and feel of these bad dads." I looked back and asked Slick, "Are there any other revelations, Slick, or did you have anything else to add?"

He looked sort of sheepish, "No boss, I don't, except I tried one of the macs. It is an impressive weapon. It's at least a thousand times better than it was. When they added the switch they also lengthened the barrel by two point twenty-five inches and reworked the recoil compensators. It is a very effective weapon in a fight within forty meters or about one-hundred-sixty feet." We were all impressed.

The Israelis were tops in weapons technology. I looked around, "Has anyone got much else to add? Well, what do you

think guys? Should we train on Helvi's stairs or what?"

I heard, "Let's train, boss!"

I continued, "We can't count on any breaks and if we plan on them, we won't be ready for any surprises. Well, let's get to it guys. With any luck it won't be long now. If Preacher's right, two weeks. Preacher has two more days to nail down this rumor or information, and then we call the shots, with or without. We all have things to do after this mission. Most of you are going on several other operations with other clansmen, and some just need to be someplace else for a while. Me, if I can, I'm going home for a month before I go on my next job, but that's just me. Well fella's, get to it, but don't damage the nice lady's house."

I pulled Czar aside and told him, "Disengage from training with the rest and instead try throwing a whammy at them. See how they react. If they fail to react properly, smoke 'em man!

Pump them up, get them frosty and on the bounce for this."

Czar replied, "You got it, Boots!"

I turned back just before leaving, "Oh, Czar. Try not to hurt anybody, okay?"

He just laughed.

I headed down the stairs to the basement lair of the mad inventor. I could tell that things were progressing nicely because I heard Banger saying, "Damn right! It will work!" As I entered the laboratory, as we called it, there was Banger with a string of canisters.

He saw me and said excitedly, "Boots! I'm building two of these things. All you have to do is pull one cable and all of them come out. Not together, but one at a time. It will work like carpet bombs. I'm building two because of the size of the room and there are partitions from what I could see with binoculars. The first one the Czar will throw. The second will be thrown by Braveheart. The Czar's has to make it to the other end and Braveheart's will go in fifteen feet or so. The concussion will immobilize the enforcers for around ten to fifteen minutes, not just from the concussion, but from stuff flying through the air because of the detonation."

I said, "That's great Banger, but will it work?"

He smiled, "I hope so. Everything I've planned and know about this stuff tells me it will work."

I told him, "Well, were counting on it and we have faith in you and your abilities. It will work. How about the transmitter?"

"God," sighed Banger, "you're relentless! I give you two miracles and you want another."

"Yes," I retorted, "I depend on it." That is what I wanted, a stack of miracles from my Merlin of the twentieth century!

"Well," he said, "the destruct system is already in and the timer just needs to be set and armed. It's all in the shock switch to start the whole sequence working." I stopped him, "Can I butt in?" "Sure boss," Banger said.

I continued, "How about a triggered mercury switch locked into place by a bar. The switch should be spring-loaded, so when the bar releases, the spring forces it to invert, completing the circuit and starting a sequence. If it turns on the power to the timer and then it is taken out of the circuit, it wouldn't matter. The timer is started on its way and that turns on the transmitter."

Banger laughed, "Are you kidding me? Where did you get that from? If you got it from your brain, it's either luck or the work of a genius."

I smiled, "I'm no genius Banger. Just a guy who's desperate for an answer to a question that needed to be solved. Well, will it work?"

He nodded his head, "It should, Boots. Man, wait until I tell the clan."

I chuckled and told him, "You're not going to lay this on my doorstep partner. You're the man with the big bag of tricks. I'm the guy who puts them where they need to go. Other than that, Banger, drop it. Okay? Forget it."

"If you say so, boss, but I can't take the credit."

"Then give it to Braveheart! I don't care, just not me, brother. Keep working on that idea Banger, and when you get it together we're going to practice a full deployment. Albeit, a somewhat different environment than the building, or Gregor's house, we should get a reasonable facsimile. We'll be able to judge its application when the unit is deployed. Our other item we will be able to judge in its application when the spider is deployed."

With its laser eye detonators, along with its wires and central body, which is the explosive body, it was nicknamed the spider by the Sandman. It reminded him of the spiders in the sand of his homeland. I've seen them! He is not too far off. They're huge! Around two feet long, or across as the eye might behold them.

I told Banger, "When you practice deploying the spider, I want Preacher and myself involved, since we will be on the third floor with you, we will also be trained in its deployment as well as you just in case of an unforeseeable problem."

No one had to ask, but if he was shot, either Preacher or myself would deploy the spider, with the other using cover fire to assist whomever was deploying the unit. All of us had been trained for that particular situation. How to lay down cover fire, so it will do the most good.

"I would also like for the Czar and Braveheart to practice with something of the same weight, tossing their respective packages through the door. You will have to mark the spot where you want them thrown, Banger. If nothing else, there's a horseshoe pit out back. You might have to tape horseshoes together to get the weight right. Mark the spot, and when they can hit that mark every time, then it's good."

Banger seemed pleased, "Okay, you have a plan, Boots, and a good one."

At that moment the Czar pulled something, and I heard the yelling.

"That's my cue Banger!" I said rushing out the door, "I'll catch you later."

I raced up the stairway to find a huge argument going on. As I walked up I yelled once, "That's enough! Stand the hell down!"

That was all it took. Professional soldiers who are well trained, trained to have manners, and to obey the man in charge, stood down as ordered. "Now," I said, "what's going on and what's the problem."

Braveheart's face was red and he was huffing and puffing, "The Czar jumped out and attacked me! We were practicing and he jumped out and grabbed me!"

I asked, "What did you do?" It was easy to see Braveheart was still mad.

"I started yelling at him!"

I turned to the Czar. "Talk to me, Czar."

Czar spoke, "As I jumped out and upon him, he was confused."

Braveheart yelled, "Damn right I was! What the hell!"

I raised my voice to him, "Enough, damn it! Please continue, Czar."

Czar began again, "As I was saying, I think he was totally unprepared. In my opinion, he was killed on the spot."

I turned back to Braveheart, "Is this true?"

He was still a bit angry, but under control. "Czar just jumped me. We were doing what you told us to do. He had no right."

Now, I began to feel my temper rise. "You're telling me about rights. What rights do you have inside that building? I'll tell you. Nada, none, zip is your rights. The Czar was doing what I told him to do, and you were unprepared. You are dead. Your team is now in jeopardy and you shall be judged that way. You failed to adapt and overcome. How do you plead?" He had no chance to open his mouth. "The findings are, I guess you are either not as good as they say, or you've been duping everybody for too long. Never mind you are dead along with half of the team. The mission is a failure! You, mister, you caused the death of your team and the victims we were rescuing! I'd put you on trial, except you are dead and that means we are all dead. Now, what have you got to say?"

"I'm sorry."

"Sorry ain't gonna cut it! What the hell are you going to do if someone jumps you? Are you going to yell for your mama, or are you going to fight? Answer me god damn it, or I swear I'll beat the hell out of you!"

At that moment Czar touched my shoulder. I almost swung, but didn't. "Slack up a little, Boots. Go on down and get some coffee. Talk to Heilvia and leave this to me, Brother."

I was hesitant, but I also saw the sense of it. Czar knew I was angry. He also knew a long time ago, a man, he had choked like this and I lost him and three of my best friends, I was also wounded seriously enough to be in a hospital for an extended stay. It was a fight to live, let alone function again.

As I gained the area of the kitchen Helvi only said, "Here's some coffee. You look like you could use some air, babe."

It broke the brooding. I only brood or become like this in training. In the field I am relaxed in a way that can't be explained by me. While we walked and I continued to cool down, I started laughing about it all, but it would be a while before Braveheart laughed. He realized what had happened and vowed it would never happen again.

I came back into the kitchen with Helvi behind me. Braveheart stood and apologized. I told him no harm, no foul, but I owed him an apology also for overreacting. Not for being wrong, or for being too tough, I just couldn't allow stupidity. It could be the end of at least nine lives, and it wasn't going to happen on my watch, if I could help it.

I was speaking to everyone in the room when I said, "Gentleman, you were all there. You know what I expect and if the shoe were on the other foot, it's what you would expect. If I was out of line, now is your chance to tell me." There was a long silence. "If that's the way you feel, fine. Let's have some lunch and try it again. Shall we?"

Things went back to zero, like nothing had happened. That is what it takes. Trust in your commander that he knows the best way to get things done and tolerates no slack. Period. After lunch I talked to Braveheart. He promised me it wouldn't happen again.

"Braveheart," I said, "don't make me promises. Actions speak louder than words. Show me. Show the clan. We've got faith in you. I've got faith that you're going to be fine and do your job to the best of your ability, and there will never be any question." It was time to get back to business.

CHAPTER TWENTY-ONE

After one week of training, there were only two incidents noteworthy enough to be written down. The two extra days were up when Preacher approached the house. He had a bounce in his step. The Preacher was happy about something, however we wouldn't know why until he was here. Helvi and I entered the kitchen and saw the Czar was there.

I said to him, "Czar, I think you need to get the clan rounded up."

He answered, "Okay, Boots. Can do."

Just at that moment, we heard the front door open and then close hard. When Preacher entered the kitchen he was bubbling over, "Boots, it's true! Helvi, it's true!" He almost ran right into me.

I said, "Slow down, Preacher. Wait until the clan gets here and tell us all at once."

As the clan filed in, I was once again taken back by these caring men who put up with me, and the world. "Okay, Preacher. Let's have it."

Everyone was listening attentively when Preacher said, "Guys, as of Sunday after this one, vacations start. I was talking to one of the bartenders and he asked me why I was there. I told him I swore an oath to take my vacation and minister to those women who made their living in the world's oldest profession and this year, I drew Amsterdam. He confided that he was coming due for a vacation. It was without pay, but it was a vacation. So, I asked him what he was going to do on this vacation that was as of yet to be named. He told me he already had a specific date, so he knew he was going to get to go. He said Sunday after next would be his first day. He would be getting a vacation along with others. I asked him how many others were going to get one of these richly deserved vacations. He told me that almost a full third of the people who work there were going. I nonchalantly asked him where he was going. He got really excited and told me he was going to France. I told him that was great and asked him if everyone was going to France. He said, 'No, many are staying home or are going all over.' So, I asked if he at least would get a full seven days. I looked a little forlorn at him. He spoke right up and said, 'Don't worry, Preacher. I will introduce you to whoever replaces me. That way you can at least get free food and anything you want to drink.' I thanked him and he said, 'it's the least I can do after all that you are doing here. Even the bosses like you. They think you improve the ladies moods.' I told him that was what I was here for. I couldn't change their choice in life, but I could make them feel better about themselves. He answered back with, 'That's what's good about you, Preacher. You don't judge. You help. Don't be surprised if in a couple of weeks, when everything is back to normal, you might get to visit the fourth floor. Maybe they will give you a job.' I said that was something to be considered and I would, of course, consider it."

This was a perfect turn of events. It ran through my mind that I didn't think they would want him to work for them if they found out what was coming their way. "So, what do you think Preacher?"

Preacher's face tightened and he said, "Boots, I think it's got to be in eight days, when there is confusion from everything that's going on, and the change in personnel."

I looked at him seriously. "What makes us believe they won't bring in extra enforcers?"

Preacher replied, "There's been no major trouble at the place for the last seven months."

I asked him, "Do we know what that was about?"

Preacher kind of laughed and said, "Harassment, as they call it. From the constabulary and Interpol."

Interpol. An international law enforcement agency better known for not getting the job done, and the locals probably went because they were forced to go.

I looked around at the expectant faces, and then turned and looked at Helvi, Czar, and Heilgrid. I took a deep breath and announced the following, "Ladies and gentlemen. As of this moment, set your watches. The clock is ticking. On Sunday after next, the clan, in conjunction with patriots of the Dutch people's freedom forces, will engage the Russian mafia at the Pleasure Palace in a bid to take back certain human beings that are being held against their will for the purpose of a sexual nature." With those words, the clan grew calm and dedicated to pulling this operation off without a hitch.

There was an excitement in their voices. It was 22:00 hours and they wanted to train. I told them to rest. That training in earnest would began at 09:30 hours the following morning, but right now it was time for rest and reflection on what our job was, and how best to bring about the results we all wanted and knew were possible.

With that, I bid them all good night and grabbed Helvi, "Let's go home, babe."

Without so much as a word, she retrieved her things and kissed her sister. She looked at me and said, "Come on, hon. Let's go."

The drive to the boat was animated with questions and excitement. Helvi asked, "Aren't you excited?"

I smiled at her, "Oh yes, I am."

If she knew the truth she wouldn't have thought I should be. Eight days and I felt like a ton of bricks were on my shoulders.

Eight days and I would know if we were up to the job. Eight days and I wondered if one, or all of my friends would be dead. Or, if I would be dead. There was a nagging in the back of my neck. It had a tingle in it, along with what felt like shards of glass. An incredible pain, and my head full of doubts. What if the information was passed to Preacher? Had they found out? Had I been right? Was I right? Would Braveheart fold on this one? There was too much stress and strain. It was nothing new. It happened just like this on every mission. It was a living hell at times. I needed a neck rub and wondered if Helvi would oblige.

Helvi was eyeing me quizzically when she said, "Boots. Where are you? You seemed a little lost."

"I was just thinking some," I answered.

She looked a little worried, "Are you hungry, Boots?" I told her I was, a little.

She smiled sweetly and said, "We've got some Dutch sweetbreads. Would you like me to heat it up and put butter and cinnamon on it? We could eat that and have coffee."

It sounded very good. "That would be perfect Helvi. I was wondering if you could take the kinks out of my neck."

Her faced relaxed and she smiled again, "I would be pleased to do that for you. Although, Boots, you need to let me work on your feet and also your upper back. Then your neck."

I began to relax and smiled back, "Whatever you say, Helvi. You're the doctor, and Helvi, I thank you from the bottom of my heart, my dear." After what seemed like a long time, we arrived at the boat.

After we were inside, I decided to help with what we were going to eat. I made the coffee and helped to butter the sweetbreads. Then I set the table, but after looking at it, it seemed to be in the wrong spot. I moved the settings to the table in front of the settee. It gave me a feeling that it was so much more appropriate, and I got a vote of confidence from Helvi.

When the coffee was done I went to the refrigerator freezer and got ice cubes for the coffee. It cools down quickly and doesn't ruin the flavor of the coffee. I remembered the cream and sugar. Helvi took both. I just wanted a little sugar with my coffee. An odd habit, but I had it from when I was a child. We sat down to our snack and ate without talking. I have to be honest, it hit the spot! The part that I particularly liked was the honey that Helvi had brought for the sweetbreads.

After we ate, I took the dishes and washed up our utensils. I wiped down the table and as I came back to sit on the settee, Helvi looked at me and just said, "Waist up. Strip. Shoes and socks off."

"Helvi," I said, "at least let me take a shower, so my feet are clean."

She smiled and insisted, "Don't worry about it. Most people, it seems, don't even bathe before they come in for me to work on them. I think I can stand yours one time."

By the time I could say, "Thanks, babe," I was on the deck of the boat and Helvi was popping my toes.

She was interested in my scars, "How on Earth did you get almost identical scars on the top of your feet?"

I grimaced while she stretched and massaged my ankles. "They were run over by an M-sixty tank in the battle for Hue City."

She clicked her tongue and said, "That must have really hurt. You must have been laid up for months."

I told her, "No, what I did was have my teammates help me. There were no replacements, so I sat down and loosened the laces and then retightened them enough to hold everything in place. I continued in battle for twenty-three days. By the time we could get medical treatment, there wasn't much they could do."

Helvi's brow was furrowed as she asked, "What about the scars on the ankles?"

All I said was, "Bullets. They are part fake, now."

She shook her head slightly, "And the scar on the back of your neck?"

I took a deep breath in, "Two chopper crashes, a plane crash, and two car crashes when I got back to the world. Don't let

anyone ever tell you a broken neck doesn't hurt!"

She worked on my body for ninety odd minutes.

I felt somewhat better. Helvi told me, "A lot of your pain is coming from stress."

I smiled at her, "Well, babe, I'm stressed because of this mission. I worry about everything."

She laughed softly, "And you roar like a bull too, but it does you no good. Boots, it's time I shared my philosophy with you. If you have done everything humanly possible, there is naught for you to worry about. You have trained your men. The plan is good. You waited until they would be at their weakest and most vulnerable. There's nothing more a human can do. No matter how hard you try and no matter how much you want to make it perfect with a guaranteed outcome. No matter what you try, there is nothing you can change. Trust in your men, and most of all trust in yourself and it will come out the way it's supposed to."

She was right of course, but I have a hard time letting go of the feeling of responsibility, and of feeling I've left something undone. Sometime later while I was thinking, I fell asleep right there on the deck. Helvi must have covered me up, because I awoke with blankets over me. I looked to my right through the hatch, and there was Helvi asleep on the settee. I got up and checked to make sure she was covered. She was sound asleep, so I tiptoed into my cabin. I needed clean clothes and my kit, so I could shower and shave.

When I came out of the shower I could smell the aroma of fresh coffee, and yes, the other shower was being used. I sat sipping coffee and it all rushed back into my mind. It was not the things I had no power to change, it was the things that needed to be done.

Helvi came out bouncing and in a good mood, "Boots, you look much better. Did I help your back?"

I smiled broadly at her, "You bet your bippy, girl! I realized exactly what I needed to do. Not try to make the things I've already done to the best of my ability, better."

Her smile was bright and exuberantly she exclaimed, "That's the spirit! And Boots, thank you. You helped me to realize I can make changes in people."

We had breakfast and I remarked that it was a great day and she nodded in agreement.

"Helvi," I asked, "Do you know where the Czar keeps the charts?"

She asked, "Do you mean where I keep the charts?"

Another revelation. "Yes dear, where are your charts?"

She had a number of charts, but not in the direction we would need to go.

I said, "Okay, skipper. Where do we find charts? Lots of charts. I need them for this mission, along with my personal collection."

"No problem," she replied, "Tell me the areas and when we get there, I'll help you find what you need."

I told her, "The Mediterranean."

Helvi giggled a little, "Which part?"

To which I retorted, "All of it."

She stopped in mid step and said, "You're serious. Okay. What else?"

I told her, "Charts from Amsterdam out the southern North Sea, the English Channel, and the coasts of Portugal and Spain until we would get to the Mediterranean."

She looked at me kind of funny, "Is there something I should know?"

I shook my head. "I don't think so, but I'm playing a feeling. A long shot feeling, but a feeling none the less. Okay, babe?" "Okay," she said.

When we left the boat we saw there was a watcher. Not in particular looking in our direction, but to play it safe Helvi and I became entangled. We wondered what this fool was up to. No good, I'm sure, but then I'm the curious type. In any case, as we reached the car and jumped in and started it, we both smiled. The only ones with a clue were us. We drove to the other end of the harbor and found the right shop.

We pulled in and got out of the car. Immediately, we were entangled again. We went into the shop, and as Helvi began talking to the counter person, the other store owner who sold us the radar gear and then installed it was standing there. We began to look at the master chart catalog and started requesting numbers correlating to charts.

The counter person was apprehensive until the other store owner said, "Hild, they are serious. They are going on a sailing adventure all the way to Italy to be married in Naples, and then they are going on their honeymoon all around the

Mediterranean."

Hild hastily began pulling charts. In all there were seventyone plus harbor charts. It came to a grand total of one-hundredseventy-four charts. Since we were buying so many, it would only cost us four-thousand-seven-hundred dollars U.S. A bargain, as he said. Only because of our impending wedding. Right!

The man seemed a little self-absorbed, like we could not afford this amount.

Helvi looked at me. "Do you want to pay him, honey, or would you like me to pay for it?"

I smiled tenderly at her, "I'll pay for it, babe." Turning back to the counterman I said, "You do take credit cards, don't you?"

He replied, "Of course we do, sir."

I handed him the card and he ran it through the card reader. He looked shocked. I knew what was making him jumpy. This card was guaranteed for one-million dollars per transaction.

Gregor told me so, and I believed him.

He handed me a pen for my signature and returned the card to me. I thought it was odd, but did not question that he had not asked for any ID.

Hesitation ceased and he asked if he could help find something else, anything.

"No, that will do for today," is what Helvi said.

All I did was smile. I didn't speak much Dutch, that's for sure. As we left with our booty laughing at the stupidity of this man and at ourselves for having so much fun doing it.

As we got in the car still laughing, I asked Helvi who was going to lay out the courses.

She looked at me and said, "Why you, me, and the Czar." That pleased me some, but it was Helvi's boat.

She stated, "If all three of us plan the course, then we would all know it and could follow it. Along with that, nobody feels inferior."

I said, "Well, Helvi, I wouldn't, but the Czar would."

Very seriously she answered, "He's not as self-confident as you might think."

I don't think I ever thought about the Czar's ego before, but I'd be willing to bet she was right and what she said made sense. No one person could sail this vessel twenty-four hours straight without some sort of break. This way it was three who would know.

I smiled at her, "That's a very good idea Helvi. Damn smart of you."

When we reached the house we brought in the charts and the chart key, so we could see which chart would fit in which section.

When the Czar saw the charts he said, "Ah, my charts."

I said nothing and neither did Helvi. I said to him, "Czar, I thought since all three of us are experienced sailors and skippers, it might be best to have all of us plan the course and see, so we could all take a turn at the wheel, and no one will have to stay on the wheel with nothing to eat but coffee and cold sandwiches and little sleep. Czar, you must see the truth of it."

He nodded at me, "You are right, Boots. Absolutely correct. I would not to be at the helm of a ship for more than eight hours, let alone twenty-four hours."

I smiled at him, "Right you are, Czar, so let's do some planning. We know where we are and we will have to sail to the dyke and catch the shipping channel out through the flood tide dyke gates. Its one-hundred miles and two dykes and flood gates to the ocean. In speed alone, we make what Czar?"

He answered, "With the chugger we can make seven knots. If we put up sails we can make fourteen knots, and with the runner we can make almost nineteen and one half knots. So, which should we use to get out of the harbor? We will have to use the chugger under sail. It's night. We have to be careful."

I asked him, "Why, Czar?"

Seriously he said, "It is hard to see other boats."

I laughed, "That's why I had the radar put on. What do you think, Helvi?"

Czar made some noise, but I ignored it.

Helvi said, "I think we can get the boat out of its slip with the chugger and then when we get to the channel we could put up some sail, if we have a good wind. If not, maybe the sails will bring us to maybe eleven knots."

Czar spoke up, "No, we use runner. Get out quick, Boots."

I said, "Helvi, what is your opinion?"

She shook her head. "If we use the runner, as Czar suggests, we will draw a lot of attention to us. Not a good idea."

The Czar was trying to be stubborn. When I asked him if he wanted to be caught, he hung his head slightly, "Well, no."

"Okay," I said, "if you had a chance to sneak out without anyone suspecting us, why would you want to draw attention to us? I think we will stick with Helvi's plan. We can't sail out if we have no good wind and we won't be able to tack properly, given the traffic and depths of the water, as this chart indicates. We draw fifteen feet of water without bounce factor or swells."

Czar said, "We draw fourteen feet six inches."

"Czar," I retorted, "I'm not going to quibble with you over six damn inches. As far as I'm concerned, we draw seventeen feet and there won't be any mistakes. What do you say Helvi?"

She smiled, "I think you're right so far."

Czar looked angry when he said, "I am captain of vessel. I say what is best."

I never even missed a beat, "Czar, you're fired."

Czar's voice rose, "You can't!"

Helvi said, "He just did, Czar! Work with us. Work for all of our sakes and the good of all. If you can do that, be captain, if not, I am captain."

The Czar thought for a moment. "We do this. We get vessel from dock to cut on chugger then into channel. If wind good we sail. If wind fair, we help with little motor to push big boat. What you think?"

I told him, "It sounds fine to me. Helvi? It's a perfect plan, Skipper."

The Czar got his pride back and we got the safe way Helvi and I wanted.

After Czar had left I said, "That was a skillful thing you did, Helvi."

She laughed, "No better than you. Halfway firing him."

I told her, "You played his ego Helvi."

She shook her head. "No, he played his own, into the right plan."

I smiled, "You are a good girl."

She answered, "Thank you, Boots."

I returned with, "My pleasure, my lady."

I bowed and she curtsied, and we both laughed. And the planning went on. It took two days to plan and get a proper course and method for getting there. We all agreed that the runner could make the difference if the clan was in trouble, and it might well be, if everything doesn't go as planned with the course laid to french waters.

I asked Slick if he was going to let us know what port we would be heading for. Cherbourg. With that said, we had our destination, however the rest of the information would remain undisclosed.

I asked him, "Slick, why won't you give me the rest of the information?"

Slick answered, "Boots, it is my friend. A network. It has taken me years to build these contacts. If you know who it is, and you are captured and made to talk, not that you would, but if you were to talk, the whole network would be in jeopardy."

I admitted he was correct in his reasoning. "But, what if something happens to you, Slick? You are going to participate in the raid. What if you get hurt or you're killed?"

He smiled slyly and said, "Then my friend, you only have to remember your favorite book of Shakespeare, and when you read it, the answer will be within."

I nodded and replied, "Well, Slick, if it's that important, we have no choice, but to agree."

Slick was to help in the raid, and then fade into the night. He would then fly to France, and handle the other end of the mission from there, just in case it would, or could need some fine touches.

"Okay, Slick. We play it your way. When we set sail, it will be to Cherbourg, France." Damn. I wish I had it all, but I don't.

It would be a balancing act for Slick, but then I thought of him like a cat. He always lands on his feet, and most times on the run. Nothing ever seemed to perturb this man, unless it was a woman. I know this, if he didn't have to be in France, he would gladly have been on the boat, just in case he had to defend it. He did arrange for the defense weapon, and I'm sure it wasn't purchased with someone else in mind. I had an inkling of where the information was to be found. When I had time, I would find it.

As I had mentioned previously, with the course laid in, it would now be our job to figure the transit times. At eleven knots, we would be in transit in Dutch international waters for one-hundred-three miles before we could turn roughly ninety degrees in order to go between the mainland at Den Helder and Texel Island. We would transit the Maasdiep Cut. It is a small channel, but it gets us to the North Sea faster.

The transit time was the stressful part. At eleven knots it would take approximately seven hours to reach the Maasdiep Cut. The tide tables said it would be outgoing. From the cut to the border with England, it was an additional seventy-five miles. It would take an additional five and a half hours to this point, under full sail. From the Maasdiep cut, we would steer a heading like we planned to visit Great Yarmouth, England. Then at borderline, turn ninety degrees and resume our course. We planned on staying within two miles of the international border, just in case we had to avoid unpleasant entanglements. If the Mafia deduced we had left via vessel other than commercial, they would be like bloodhounds on the trail very quickly, and they had boats also.

It would be impossible to fly out with our package. Likewise, any form of commercial transportation would prove to be problematic, and it would be dangerous to use the roads. Not knowing the Mafia's reach into their departments, it would be foolhardy to say the least. The boat, even though a slow form of transportation, and the façade of a wedding and honeymoon trip, was the groundwork that was laid for the use of this form of escape. It was the best plan at the time and place, but an unnerving and bold plan, if indeed it was successful.

CHAPTER TWENTY-TWO

We were four days out from the mission, and Preacher had been brought up to speed on the spider. He could deploy it in fifty-three seconds. Almost as fast as Banger. Training went on, but was becoming a moot point. We had been at this for two and one half months. I believe you cannot be over trained, but men get bored doing the same thing day in and day out without culmination for their trouble. Life was much the same throughout, but for a few moments of arguments and overreactions, by me definitely included.

It was time to send a telegram to the war room. It would be carefully worded, of course, but Daria would know what it would mean. It read, "Daria sweetheart. Sorry I am not home. Stop. I will be having dinner with friends on Sunday. Stop. Hope to meet some new friends. Stop. Hope they appreciate my work. Stop. Will be home as soon as possible. Stop. Keep the home fires burning and a candle in a window for me. Stop. With love, your loving other. End." It is not so cryptic if the person who receives this message knows the score, but I wouldn't think anyone else would have a real clue as to its meaning.

Friday, Helvi and I left the boat to find a bon voyage message on the bow. It was from the working people in the harbor who knew of our plans to leave on Sunday night for our adventure. This message reinforced our resolve we had done a good job, and that no one, not even the watchers had been able to find a chink in the story. We were seldom apart at the harbor and always seemed to be entangled in one way or another. We would be whispering secrets around people, or showing affection in public. We both had a genuine affection for each other, however it wasn't the kind of affection one feels when they're in love, rather one of friendship, trust, and conspiracy. But, the others watching us did not realize that. In the end it would be a great triumph, or a friggin' Greek tragedy. I believed it would be a triumph, and Helvi did also.

When we went to the car we found there was another note. It read, "We will miss you. See you when you get back!"

As we got into the car Helvi's only comment was, "We've done it Boots."

I had to agree. It looked good, but was it good enough?

Helvi and I drove out and the subject of vehicles came up, and when she said it, it made sense. Czar, Braveheart, and Heilgrid had made arrangements with some friends of Heilgrid's for what we would need. When we got to the house we found a beehive of activity going on with men sneaking out to attack each other from odd angles and from the rear. It was truly amazing to see how much the guys had taken to heart the dressing down of Braveheart. He had single-handedly decided to take over practice and was throwing every dirty trick in the book at them. They were overcoming every scenario that Braveheart threw at them on a continual schedule.

We fully entered the kitchen, and Braveheart came over to us, "What do you think, Boots? Miss Helvi?"

Helvi said, "I think you're doing a fine job."

I smiled and slapped him on the back, "A great job. I couldn't have done better myself. Braveheart, where is the Czar and Heilgrid?"

He told me, "They should be coming down and in a few minutes, Boots. If you will excuse me."

Braveheart went back to his crusade of jumping the men. I think they all were just having fun, but then who am I to say?

Heilgrid and the Czar came in and immediately the subject of vehicles was brought up. Heilgrid and Czar sat down and Czar said, "Boots, after studying the situation, and after your conclusions about the vans, Heilgrid has some friends who are what you would call anti-Mafia, along with being in Slick's line of work, only not in as sophisticated a way. Heilgrid and I went to see them, and without saying what we were doing, we asked for their help in obtaining vans, but that they needed to look like delivery vans. They have two. One has been finished, and one will be done today. Boots, they look exactly like the vans that park up and down that street. The people that I talked to were more than willing to do the acquisition and work to change them into what we needed. It took major work in converting these vans. They had to weld on replacement panels over where the windows were, and then installed some armor three quarters of the way up the inside of the vans. With the added weight, the

suspension would have to be changed."

I asked him, "What do they get out of it?"

The Czar just smiled and said, "They get the vans." He continued, "The vans will disappear after we are done with them. The logo stickers peel off, so when we're done they will pick them up and strip off the logos. Then they can use them in their own operations. As I said, these are one ton vans. The motors are bigger. Almost twice the horsepower. They have twin battery systems and gun racks. The seats were put against the vans exterior walls. There is full communications. Also, you can get to the driver's compartment by sliding a panel. These guys do good work and the vans will be kept in their shop until we need them. We paid for all modifications, from top to bottom. Even the tires are high performance and get great traction. If you want we can go see them."

I shook my head, "I don't need to Czar, but it might be a good idea for Heilgrid and you to go make sure that they are up to all the standards we require. Something to consider is that the girls will be driving these vans." "Da," replied Czar.

"Well," I continued, "they can't possibly carry the battle rifles, magazines, and ammunition into these vans alone. Do you trust those guys enough that the tools and equipment could be

installed earlier and would still be safe?"

Czar nodded, "I believe so Boots."

Heilgrid spoke out, "You can trust them. I know these people."

That's what I needed to know. If these people were trustworthy, they very well could lead to being allies, and in a sense they already were, among the clan. We would look upon this fact with much appreciation, and I was sure that in the future these gentlemen would be remembered with affection on my part.

There were fifty-two hours until it became a reality. The moment I had sweated bullets over and the clan had ran themselves ragged for, trained and practiced, and invented equipment for. That reminded me to see Banger, and Slick pulling his magic act getting things here and working within a system to obtain the proper, or improper papers to allow us to complete this mission. It all boiled down to the last fifty-two hours, and the fourteen hours immediately after the zero hour.

The vehicle question had been satisfactorily explained, but with no final answer until Heilgrid and the Czar returned and gave me the answer I needed. Then, they would be taking equipment and supplies to the trucks. I had another situation to find out about. Banger's progress on the initiator for the timer on the transmitter. I started down the stairs and ran into Banger who was coming up.

"Hey, Boss! What's new?"

I answered, "Not much, Banger. What's new with you?"

He smiled, "I'm working on the initiator sequence for the transmitter. I've had to use two springs in order to get the pressure that was required, but it's almost done. It works very well if you can hold extra tension on the spring mechanism that initiates the start of the timer mechanism. I've got the whole thing worked out. I'm just putting it together, but I decided to come up, go to the bathroom, and catch a smoke, and some coffee, then back to work. What's the matter boss?"

I knew my brow must be furrowed. "Nothing, Banger. I'm just a little intense about getting this thing done before Sunday."

"Well," said Banger, "It works out on paper, but in practical application it could be somewhat different."

I asked him, "If we put this together, how will we know it's working without standing there and watching it?"

Banger looked somber as he answered, "There really isn't a way to tell."

This concerned me. "Will you be able to tell before we deploy?"

"Absolutely," he said confidently.

I told him, "Do your best, Banger. We are only fifty-two hours out, man."

He nodded, "Okay, boss. I'll make this short and then get back to work. Okay?"

I smiled, "Okay, Banger. Can I join you?"

He smiled back, "Absolutely."

With that we walked into the kitchen and I poured us each a cup of coffee. We stepped outside and saw Helvi was coming also.

"So what's up, Boots?"

I smiled at her and said, "Not too much, babe. Banger was just explaining how the trigger unit works."

Helvi asked, "Is it done?"

"No," I answered, "but it will be done in no time."

"That's good," she said as she turned to Banger, "How are you feeling Banger?"

He looked kindly at her and said, "Fine, Miss Helvi. Just fine."

The technical talk went on and then it came time to get back to work. I asked, "Can I look at the trigger, Banger?" "Me too!" quipped Helvi.

Banger answered that that would be fine. We went down the stairs. I was following Helvi, who in turn was following Banger. When we got to the bottom of the stairs, we proceeded into the lab where Banger showed us the mechanism and explained the spring problem. Helvi seemed very interested and was studying it intently, but excused herself and left the room without a comment.

We continued. Everything worked, but the snap down mercury switch. Banger said, "I can't find what I need. At least not here."

I took a deep breath and asked, "Well, what can we do?"

Banger's face was lined with determination when he answered, "I guess we will have to manually arm the system. The idea was to drop the unit in a non-conspicuous place and have it initiate the sequential timer. Well, if I've got to do it that way I have to worry about someone turning it off manually. Not that it is a fact, but I did not want to take that chance."

I felt Helvi's motion and a subtle wafting of perfume. She walked to the bench and asked, "May I see it?"

Banger said, "Well, yes," and handed the mechanism to her.

She fiddled with it for a moment, and when she was done she dropped the box on the floor. The distinct sound of the timer was loud and clear. Banger went over to her and simply asked what she did.

Helvi giggled and said, "I put a springy thing on it!"

We peered into the box and there was her springy thing. It was a round hair tie back. It had just the right amount of tension.

Banger reset it and then dropped it. We were aware of the distinct sound of the timer again. With a cover over it, it would be inaudible, but for now I was perfectly satisfied to hear the tick tick sound. I was amazed by this simple fix to the problem. I asked banger if he could make it so the hair tie would not slip off and he assured me that it was an absolute certainty.

I told him, "Make it so, Banger," and he proceeded to do just that. To make it secure. However, Helvi explained that it was an old hair tie and that she did have some new ones.

I asked her, "Would you get them, babe?"

She answered, "Yes, I will," and went to retrieve some.

I turned to Banger and said, "Banger, when it gets here, put in the new one and let's see what it does."

After Helvi returned with a new hair tie-back, it was installed and when it was deployed in the manner in which it would be put to use, there was a satisfying click and the familiar tick tick of the running timer. It was no miracle, just the ingenuity of a woman who solved the problem that Banger had been trying to solve for almost two weeks. I thought back to how many times my wife had done the same thing, but it still amazes me how sometimes a difficult problem is solved by just plain invention. I have found more times than not, that the age old adage of "necessity is the mother of invention" is true in many ways. Mankind has been blessed by the fruits of invention, as well as plagued by them.

At 17:00 hours I realized that we were ready, barring surprises. It was idle waiting. I was not ready for this feeling. I never am. I looked at Helvi and could see it dawned on her there was only a dry tune-up run tomorrow. The gear was ready. The men were ready. The plan was done and only had to be activated. The escape route was done. The escape vehicles were ready. The only thing not ready was me. It's always this way. My brain was not ready to accept the fact that it really was ready. When I went to say something to Helvi she looked at me with a smile, and put her index finger on my lips as a sign for silence. As time went on I could see the whole clan began to feel this feeling of "we're ready for zero hour and the clock is ticking." It is a satisfying feeling indeed.

Speaking to the clan I said, "Guys, I think we've arrived. This is why I do this. Start a job and then take it to completion. We're two quarters into the game, the second half starts Sunday evening at 16:00 hours, when we strap up and get ready to score. We can do this. Then, we've just got to hold on through the fourth quarter. Our defense measures are our best guarantee for this, but we can't let down for a second. So, until tomorrow morning, when we do our final run from deployment to strike, to retreat, and then escape. When that's done, there's nothing else that is required. So, just be you. Relax as much as is humanly possible. I wish we could all go out, but that would be inherently dangerous. Our turn will come in New York, and all of us are invited."

With that, it was as if nothing was up. We drank coffee. Those of us who smoked, did so. I'm glad I put fifteen cartons of my brand on board plus others, including menthols for Braveheart. As we talked and even managed to joke some, it grew late, and so, Helvi and I departed and went to the boat.

After arriving, I took a good look around. I went forward and looked, and then at each stateroom. I opened drawers and closets, looking at the clothes for Svetlana, and maybe others. Clothes for a twelve-year-old, who we only had Preacher's estimate of size, although he felt he should be close. I looked at bathrobes, pajamas, nightgowns, and all the toiletries that go with girls for twenty days. Helvi and I had been camping in the settee area. The supplies were mountainous, and it seemed easier that way. I couldn't think of anything else we would need. I looked at Helvi and she was doing the same thing. She was as bad as me. No stone left unturned.

I finally turned to Helvi and told her, "Stop, girl! We've done all we can. Would you like a cup of coffee, and a roll, and get some quiet time. I could use it for sure."

As I made coffee, I could hear Helvi clucking behind me. I placed the rolls on the serving plate and turned around to find my bunk made, and Helvi's too. I prefer the floor, so that's where she had made it. I watched her as she went to the entertainment center, and put La Bohéme on the player, and turned it on. I love this type of entertainment. I have never been to the Met in New York, but I swore to myself that someday I would go. I poured coffee and took it to the settee, and then returned for cream and sugar along with the rolls. I set them down. Helvi was on her bunk and facing me with a smile. I asked her what was up.

She said, "I've decided on my wish."

I smiled at her and asked, "You have? Well, what will it be?"

She answered, "I want you to take me to dinner at the restaurant of my choice, and I want you to take me to the opera La Bohéme. It will be playing on stage tomorrow."

I nodded, "Tomorrow. Yes. It will help us both relax and take our minds off of other things. You got it, my lady!"

We talked about La Bohéme and classical music, which to me is a subject I do not grow tired of, and it grew late. Tomorrow was a huge day for all of us. We would go over every detail and run through it all. Noticing Helvi was almost asleep, I said,

"Good-night."

She muttered, "Good-night," back.

CHAPTER TWENTY-THREE

My eyes popped open at the smell of very strong coffee in the air. There was Helvi making coffee and getting things ready.

"Helvi," I said, "I don't think I'm going to be very hungry, but give me a few minutes to shower, and I could sure use some of that coffee."

She smiled at me, "Don't worry about a shower. Have some coffee first."

I liked the idea, but, well, I would have to break a habit just this once. Little did I know what would happen to my routine with the boat full of people. I pulled my robe around me and went for the coffee.

When we sat down, I asked her if she was nervous about Sunday.

Her eyes widened and she said, "Terrified."

I took her hand and said, "Don't be. You'll be just fine and you'll do great."

"I hope so," she said softly.

I answered, "You will. Don't worry about it. Even though the odds are definitely stacked against us, we have some tricks that could even us up, but you never know for sure. You just switch off the telephone trunk lines on time, and go to the truck. There's no hurry. It's a two and one half minute walk and you will have fifteen minutes to get back. You know the routes?"

"Yes," she answered.

"Then," I continued, "if we do our job right, everything will work out the way it's supposed to. So, don't worry, little one."

She smiled at me, "I'll try not to."

I smiled broadly back at her, "You do that! You will be fine. I know it." I wish I was as sure as I was broadcasting, but you can never be sure of anything.

We sat down to eat and within minutes the mood changed to one that was much more relaxed. Helvi talked about the opera and how much fun it would be to go again. I was much less enthusiastic about the whole night. It is not like me to do anything but concentrate on what I had to do.

We got back to the house, only to find it alive with activity. It seems the clan was too stressed to relax, just like me. We sat and talked about what was to come, as there was to be only one change in the plan. I would be the second man into the building. Preacher would already be in place, in the guise of being Preacher. It was decided that I should be second, so I could calculate how things were going and to see if any undue attention was being paid to the strange men infiltrating the building.

The only thing that would be left to be done was to have me go ahead and drop the transmitter before entering the building. It was decided by the clan for me to be in second to possibly avert a catastrophe by being in a position to observe and act, if I could. This was okay, but I don't like changes after the plan was supposed to be set in stone, so to speak. However, I would agree to this if it was the will of the clan. It had worked before, why not again? The time was recalculated and set into the timer of the transmitter. Everything was set and right, and good to go. I asked if everybody was in agreement to one more practice and everyone thought it would be a good idea.

The deployment stage was the most uncertain, and the most important. If we can get in, we will get out. No matter what the cost. I took a supposed position at a table closest to the door. I could watch the deployment, albeit not quite like the building, it would do. Yes, it would do. It was flawless. They moved naturally, and paid for their turn on the third floor, and moved along just like the plan called for with the stopwatch running. The timing was judged by a call in on the mic. I went to the purported third floor to check the deployment of the spider. It went well. Forty-seven seconds, a like time to save lives.

After looking at the positioning of the laser eye detonators, I asked Banger, "What if someone were to move the matched pairs to a new location."

All he related to me was, "Boom! There's only one way to shut this off. The interruption pushbutton switch."

"Okay," I said, "so no one gets blown to hell getting this thing down after we're gone."

Banger answered, "Well, I don't know. It depends on if they have a specialist."

I really didn't care about the Mafia; however, I did most certainly care if a cop or Interpol would, or could be killed or wounded by this device. Banger assured me this package was built from plans already in Interpol's catalogue of explosive devices. That satisfied me, along with a feeling of relief as I have an intrinsic respect for those police officers who do their jobs well, along with disgust and disdain for those who don't.

What can I say about Braveheart and the Czar? They tossed their packages, each respectfully sixteen to twenty inches away from where they were supposed to land.

I had to laugh and said, "When those babies go off it will wake the dead and then knock them out from the concussion!"

The clan filed into the kitchen to sit and critique what had just taken place. After talking about everything for three hours, I called it all to a halt.

"My friends, we are as ready as we can get. We are ready. I didn't see anything that wasn't natural or normal. The time spent at the client desk and then your time up to the second floor of this house, puts you in compliance with the plan. You were actually under the timeline. Any questions?" I looked around at each person in the group. "No questions, guys? Okay. Then it's a done deal! The next time we do this, it will be the real thing."

From both sides of the table, a barely audible sound could be heard. You could hear "yes" in a long and drawn out manner.

"So fellas, the day is yours! We are done. This will resume at 14:00 hours tomorrow in preparation for actuating Operation Angel. Talk at you later tonight, guys." With that, my men went off to do what they were going to do, in their own way.

Everyone has a way they deal with stress. I normally meditate, but this was not in the cards for me. I had an obligation to take Helvi to the opera. Although, it was really not an obligation. She was a fine young woman with good morals and high ideals. Tack that onto the fact that she was easy on the eyes and a truly nice person, it would be an enjoyable evening, but not what she thinks it will be, except for her own expectations. I know she wanted me to have a relaxing evening before the mission, but I couldn't put it away completely. So it would, in reality, do very little for me other than entertainment.

Time came for Helvi and me to leave for the boat in order to prepare for our evening out. I finished showering and shaving and looked in the mirror. I saw the heavy worry lines that had become part of my face, and the mark of my life. I had earned every one of them somewhere along the road in my life. As I shook my head and came back to the now from my memories and thoughts, I realized I had things to do. First and foremost, was to take this lovely young lady to dinner and the opera. I dressed in my black suit. I became somewhat saddened that I was taking Helvi, and not my wife who had allowed me to run the world and to do things like this. She knew that in the end I would be home, at least for a short time anyways. I was standing in the salon, when out whirled Helvi. She was quite a picture perfect sight in many circles of people. To me she was Helvi, my friend and companion.

On our way to the car we noticed different people smiling and waving. It was amusing, to say the least. Dinner was a taste treat to be enjoyed in memories, and it would be. As the time grew shorter to making our appearance at the opera, I found my mind wandering, and then brought it back, so I could enjoy the opera.

We entered the performing arts center. It was definitely avant-garde, much the same as it is in all art centers. They were fast to embrace the new and delete the past. However, it was quite striking and very unusual. We took our seats and the opera began. It wasn't very long before my mind wandered off into Operation Angel. Every little detail played like a set of NFL game films the opposing coaches would study, so they could build a new game plan and strategy.

I knew why Helvi had picked this night and these things to do. She was hoping that she would take my mind off of the impending operation. At any other time it would have, but unfortunately, not tonight. I could not keep my mind on the opera or Helvi. Although I enjoyed the music, I found myself in no way receptive to relaxation or the diversion that Helvi had planned for me to receive. For me there was only duty and responsibility on my mind.

La Bohéme is a fascinating opera where love is found, and it endures until the end, when death claims the victory. You cannot help but mourn the loss of love that man must have felt. The devoid person he represented after her loss of life. This was not as I observed it on stage, but from childhood memories, and later in life when I had seen this production on stage at the Seattle Metropolitan Opera House and again in San Francisco. The stage became a fog bank that was replaced by a building of young women, and an operation to win their freedom and our survival. The opera came to a conclusion at 21:30 hours.

As we left, Helvi leaned close and asked, "Do you feel more relaxed, Boots?"

I told her, "I think so Helvi, but it is always a sad ending."

"Yes," she said, "but it is such a beautiful love story and such a tragedy. I think that it is one of my all-time favorites. Tell me about your most favorite."

I smiled, "Carmen, I think is my favorite. It is the first one I remember hearing on the radio at home on the house float that was my home in Alaska."

When we got to the car I unlocked the doors and opened the door for her as I usually did.

She said, "It is nice to have a gentleman to open doors. I think that nicety is not popular in Holland anymore."

I shook my head, "That's a shame, Helvi. Not many of my countrymen do it much anymore either. Although my son does. He believes in the old ways."

Helvi gently stated, "That must be very nice for his girlfriend."

"Yes," I said, "She seems to enjoy being treated like a lady, and it gives my son so much pleasure."

When we reached the boat it was 22:50 hours, and I was positive it would be a night of little sleep for me.

We were now under twenty-four hours before Operation Angel would become a reality. After Helvi and I had gotten on the boat and into our hideaway from the world, we made coffee. There was not a word spoken until we sat down and started to drink our coffee. It was a darkness that existed between now and when Angel happened.

Helvi began to speak. It was with a quiet faraway voice, "Boots, what if something bad happens?" I asked her, "Like what, Helvi?" She said, "Say, if someone was shot?" I replied, "It's to be expected, Helvi. Not to be worried about."

She asked softly, "What if you get shot. Or worse. What if you're killed?"

I was somewhat prepared for this to happen, I just had wondered when. "Helvi, it is the price I'm willing to pay for the freedom of these young women. It's a chance for them to be free, and to maybe live a reasonably normal life. Maybe even try to put part of their experiences behind them. I hope, if I die, maybe they will forget that too. Or at least let it fade from their minds and their lives. Every human being deserves to be free,

Helvi. Not to be owned."

She said in a murmur, "It just scares me."

I told her boldly, "There is nothing to be scared of. To die is to live, my girl!"

She smiled slightly, "You really feel that way, Boots?"

I gazed at her very seriously, "I am that way, Helvi. Life is a risk and as far as I know, nobody gets out alive." I had to laugh, thinking of all of the things I've been through. "Relax, Helvi."

Her smile more sincere, "Okay. I'll try." It was getting late. "Helvi, it's time for me to get some sleep, and you too." I stood up and leaned over and kissed her forehead. I told her, "Not to worry, little one, not to worry at all."

I went to my cabin to rest, which did not come.

CHAPTER TWENTY-FOUR

Somewhere in the night, I fell asleep and morning came with a crash and a scream. I was awake and on my feet. It was a new day, but my day. The day that is the culmination of months of training and thought that had gone into this day. I felt no particular emotion, except determination. Today I awoke with an icy coldness of who I was, and what I am about. Today was the clan's day to shine, or fail, and I had a cold feeling in my heart. I walked out of my cabin, soon to be two young ladies cabin, or at least one. I felt at ease.

I went to the galley and started to make coffee when a thought came to me. That I should listen to some music, so I put on the William Tell Overture. This was followed by Tales From the Vienna Woods and Handel's Messiah. There was no hurry to get to the house. I would have to sit and pace until it was time. At least here I could listen to music that calms me and that I enjoy. I began to listen as the melodic tones of music filtered through the air.

Without me realizing it, Helvi had come out of her cabin. She looked rested and alert. I hoped a repeat performance of last night's question and answer period was not going to crop up again. I didn't think that at this time I could be quite so pleasant about it. We never talked of certain things before a mission. It is just not done, for many reasons.

She came up to me and said, "Good morning, Boots."

"Hi, babe," I said cheerfully, "Want some coffee?"

She smiled and nodded, "Yes, please."

I handed her coffee to her and said, "Helvi, let's not go to the house until much later today, unless you want to."

She answered, "No. There isn't any reason to go until it's time."

"Good," I said, "I'm glad you said that. Would you like to take a walk with me, or would you like to listen to music or watch a movie, or something."

She spoke quite quickly, "I think a walk sounds like a great idea. What kind of day is it?"

I told her, "I think it's a beautiful day. The sky is blue with no clouds, yet it's not real warm. But, it's nice out there."

Helvi agreed right away, "Okay, so let's take a walk from one end of this part of the harbor to the other end, and then back to the boat."

I smiled at her, "That sounds good to me. Since there's little coffee shops all along the boardwalk, we can stop and eat or just

drink coffee, and talk about flying kites."

She laughed and said, "Why kites, Boots?"

Very matter of factly, I stated, "Because kites are fun to fly. I think we will hold hands like two little children and tell each other secrets and then we can laugh and play."

Helvi laughed again, "That sounds like a great plan and a fine idea, Boots. We will go after this record is finished and the coffee is done."

We went for our walk and as we walked past, people smiled and waved. It seemed we were the darlings of the harbor crowd. What the hell. Go with it, I say. It was much farther than either of us had realized, and we visited more than one coffee stand. We wasted a lot of time just talking nonsense and goofing around with each other. It almost made me feel like a kid again, and then the air was shattered by an alarm. The alarm on my watch was warning me it was time to go. The next twenty-four hours would be far more intense than a walk along the boardwalk with a pretty girl.

The time was 13:30 hours. It was time to proceed to the house and begin preparations. The preparations of the vans were complete.

Each van was perfect and had what we would need. Each van had one forty caliber pistol, equipped with a twenty round magazine inserted in the proper place with one in the firing chamber. They had twenty-one shots. They also had ten twenty round magazines, fully loaded. Along with fifteen-hundred spare rounds in speed loaders, they were sufficient. Each van also contained four Heckler and Koch seven-point-six-two by fifty-one millimeter battle rifles. Inserted, was one one-hundred round drum magazine, with one in the firing chamber. That gave it one-hundred-one rounds. There were also twenty spare one-hundred round drum magazines fully loaded, and fifteen-hundred rounds of spare ammunition on stripper clips.

For all of us, it was time to strap up. Strapping up is an art form. It is a combination of wearing the proper clothing that has been tailored and fitted to conceal what you are carrying. It starts from your shoes, and goes through the pants, undershirt, over shirt, and proper jacket for the occasion. When a man stands and knows what he has to conceal, he usually finds it is preferable to wear a tight T-shirt and a tight over shirt. After he's dressed, he fits his holster, or holsters, then his extra magazines and any other items to be concealed. There are different configurations for different items, as will be seen.

It must be said here, that in order to carry C-four explosive, although it is inert unless fused or on fire, it is pliable. We reformed the C-four that Banger and Braveheart would be carrying. With a rolling pin, we could decrease the thickness by one half, and still keep them in brick form. This would make it easier to conceal with the duck tape that would be used.

We started the process of strapping up the clan. Preacher, Banger, and Braveheart were first. After fitting their forty caliber pistol shoulder holsters on them tightly and in the proper position, so the pistol could be easily deployed, it was time to install the crossover shoulder holsters for the mac-ten forty-five caliber submachine guns. It fits somewhat like a pistol holster, although it must be adjusted to keep it tighter against the body, and slightly forward of where a normal carry position would be. When that was done, the extra magazine pouches were fitted to the straps of the forty caliber pistols. However, due to the length of the mac-ten magazines, an auxiliary strap had to be employed. That would hold them and keep them from sticking below the jacket line for concealment.

Braveheart wore a kilt, so strapping three one pound blocks of prefused and wired C-four was not a problem. Banger did not wear a kilt, but he went from a perfect figure to having a small beer belly by putting C-four bricks lengthwise to his body. It was under his over shirt. It just took time and thought. It went much the same for the rest of the clan, but the Czar strapped Heilgrid and I strapped Helvi, with Heilgrid's watchful eye and help.

It was 18:30 hours. It had taken two and a half hours to get everyone strapped up and gear together. Preacher had been done and left at 17:20 hours. Since then, there had been vox traffic from his mic, but nothing out of the ordinary. It would take ten minutes to walk over to the building front. The second one to leave was me.

It was precisely 19:10 hours when I looked at the clan and said, "Operation Angel is now active. Let the promenade begin."

I shut the door behind me, carrying my package with a whistle on my lips. I strolled to the drop point and knew Banger had just left the house on his walk. I dropped the package in a plastic dumpster which are quite prevalent in Amsterdam. I heard the satisfying click, and I knew the timer was indeed ticking to its destiny and a fiery end. It was an ingenious device.

I rounded the corner and proceeded to the door. There were no problems either during the walk to, or gaining entry into the building known as the Palace. I walked in and it was as I had remembered it from not so very long ago. I walked up to the client's desk, and we had a conversation about what I wanted. It was decided before the present action, with Preacher's help, what to say and who to pick for what I wanted. It would be the equivalent of five-hundred American dollars plus a two-thousand dollar deposit. I paid the clerk, and discreetly let him see that there was more where that came from. Now we were best of friends!

I wandered over to the bar and ordered a drink. All the while, carefully gauging what was going on around me, and who was who in the zoo. The employees were conscientious, however they seemed disjointed in the jobs they were doing. I proceeded to the table I had spotted that would be in the perfect position to watch the deployment.

I whispered into my mic, "Boots is on scene,"

I heard a quiet, "Okay, boss."

Preacher was still alive and doing his part in this operation. I looked at my watch. Banger should be coming in the door in approximately two minutes. That would mean Braveheart will be leaving in five minutes. Banger strolled through the door with a dumb tourist grin on his face. He barely turned his head, but his eyes were straining in every direction. A pro would act like this. That's why he was here. I glanced at Banger at the client's desk. He paid, and went for a drink.

I watched him through the doorway glance at his watch very carefully. By this time, Braveheart should be almost a minute from the door. That meant the Czar was six minutes from the door, and Slick was moving.

I heard over the mic from the Czar, "Van one."

Right behind him Slick saying, "Van two."

It was almost dark and my girl was on the move. She should be parked three minutes behind her sister in loading zone six. Czar was through the door and buying his ticket upstairs, however he went to the gambling room. That was exactly where he was supposed to be. Lo and behold, Slick was in the door.

Things were moving well so far, but with our presence, all of us in this building, it could happen quickly. Someone could recognize one of us. Or even if they thought they did, or just decided they didn't like someone's face. A thousand things could still go wrong. My stress level ramped up from the thought of someone taking exception to Braveheart's kilt, or Sandman because he was originally from an Arabic country. And what of my girls just sitting and worrying? Too much on a man's mind! What if there was trouble not related to us that would bring the bulk of the enforcers out of the confines of their lair? Braveheart was on the move, just looking around to see what was up.

Slick, of course, had been one minute late. He would be late to his own damn funeral! Bronco was four minutes out from the house. He would be here in six minutes. Helvi should be just starting back from the telephone trunk line where she, through the contact switch, would silence this place. It was seven minutes before the slow but steady exodus from the first floor upward to the upper stories. Five minutes to get into place and it would start. Here we go. Bronco was on through the front door and turned into the bar to get a drink, and then returned to the client desk. Banger was on the move up the stairs. If anyone was to look too close, you could just barely see something hanging below his jacket line.

Braveheart was on his way up, as is Sandman. Sandman, suddenly realizing that he is early, holds back some. I see him critically looking at a picture on a facing wall. There goes Czar, he's finally on his way. Bronco is there, with his payment stub hanging halfway out of his pocket. He's leaning against the wall. His cowboy hat is firmly in place and he's sipping his drink. Slick is on his way and he makes the bottom step. Some guy is coming down the stairway. Well, hell! He's a client. I thought, "Damn it!

Move, Slick." I began to move.

It was my turn. I would have to trust Bronco and Sandman that they could get there, and stay where they had to be. It's hard to look disinterested and stroll when you want to run, but your mind won't allow your body to do what common sense tells it to do, and do now. I can feel the blood pressure now. I tell myself, "It's Okay, Boots. Everybody will be okay. Slow and steady, my boy. Slow and steady." My head is intense. I want to blast these bastards, but it's not in the plan. Slow and steady. My thought is, "Remember to breathe, dummy. Breathing will help you." First steps. No shots. I am on my way.

Step-by-step. I'm past Slick, and then it's up to the second floor. Czar and Braveheart are trying to look innocuous. Next flight and nobody's coming, so I can hurry. As I broke the top of the stairs, there was Preacher, my old friend. I whispered, "Come on, Preacher. Let's kick their asses!"

He said, "It isn't meant to be. Banger has picked the lock. The door is open. It's time."

As Banger placed the last laser eye detonator, and pulled the wire down and was just finishing the final connection, Preacher was through the door. I heard, "Come on, ladies, come on." Here he was coming through with one, three, seven girls. The rest were in hiding.

In Preacher's hand was a very nasty looking mac-ten submachine gun and it was on full auto. I had failed to notice the two forty caliber pistols already in my hands. As Banger quietly closed the door, his stinger was out and ready.

"Where is Svetlana?" I asked, "We don't go nowhere without Svetlana."

I heard a small, meek female voice, "I am here. Please, not hurt me. Please, not to kill us."

I glanced at these young ladies and knew I had about three seconds to look at this group. It indeed was Svetlana. She was the tallest of them all, around five foot six or seven inches. She had long blond hair that wasn't as clean as it should be. There were six other younger girls, all terrified and either not willing to make a sound, or unable to.

Then I spied a much shorter female. She was no older than one of my young nieces. Maybe four feet five inches with medium black hair, and not a stitch of clothing on. I stripped off my jacket, and told Preacher to make her as decent as could be expected. Banger gave up his jacket. I noticed that these young ladies seem to hover around the little one in an obvious attempt to protect her as much as possible. It made me so mad! I had made up my mind to put down every Russian I saw.

I said, "Move 'em out, Preacher. Quickly please." I called down, via vox and told the clan, "The candle is lit boys!"

Three seconds later, the building damn near jumped off the ground. It was a very large explosion, to say the least. When I looked at Banger, his eyes just glinted. All I could think about now was escape.

"Coming down hot, boys! Herd them down the stairs and into the bus."

The girls, with Preacher leading the way, down and out to freedom. Banger was bringing up their rear.

I was busy working drag, to be the last man out. It was my responsibility. It went with the job. Here on the second floor was the

Czar with a cut over his eye. It sure as hell wasn't from hand-to-hand combat.

"Christ!" I said, "Look at that."

The explosion tore the doors off and peeled a wall, along with stacking a large pile of rubbish in the way. Stuff that had to be climbed over, or stepped over. We were burning time. Where were the cops?

"Damn!" I said, "We gotta go, guys!"

Slick and Sandman moved out into the space between the stairwell and front door. There didn't seem to be any heroes around, except my guys.

I announced, "Preacher, put your gun away now." God damn it, he did! Just in case, he was being kidnapped. Period. When we came to the landing before the first floor, I heard movement. "We've got creepers here, guys. Move those young ladies out of here. I've got the back door."

When it came over my ear bud, "We're here. Get out now, boss." I moved.

I backed and side stepped down the last seven stairs until I stood on the main floor.

"All out, guys!" I yelled. "Let's move it, like a swarm of hornets that's just noticed we smashed their nest they're on our six o'clock. Go! Go! Go!"

We rushed to the trucks. Three girls and four of the team were in Heilgrid's truck. I was the last one in the door of Helvi's truck.

I said as calmly as possible, "If you know what's good for us, babe, you will please move this truck before the cops, or the Mafia wake up and get here."

We were off. I really must check my watch. Nine minutes to the drop point at the dock.

"Helvi, the boys are meeting us to pick up their stuff, you know the vans?" Nothing. "Helvi? Helvi?"

Finally she answered, "Yes, they should already be there. There will not be any watchers tonight, Boots. They will be dealt with. There will be none where we drop off the trucks." That was good to know.

I voiced my concern to Helvi, "They may be in other places or they have already seen us, but we can't be concerned about that situation yet. We have to get gone. I mean really gone, my love. We have a wedding in Naples, remember?" She started to lighten up a bit.

"And would you just breathe, babe? It's about time. The world's record for holding your breath is six minutes and twenty-six seconds. We should enter your time of fifteen minutes and twenty-seven seconds!" That made her at least become reanimated. "Are you going to freeze up on me? Please don't give out on us now, babe."

Her breaths came steadily, "I won't do that, Boots. I'm just scared."

I felt reassured. She was back in control. "We will talk at the helm. We've got the first watch, six hours. We will have time to have a conversation then."

She answered decidedly, "Okay, Boots."

I never turned around to speak to Helvi. There were four girls behind me in the truck. "I will tell you what to do if you want to stay alive. Okay?"

A mousy, subdued voice answered. Right away and I recognized it as Svetlana's voice.

I told her, "I know you Svetlana. There will be no information now, but this is what you must do when you get out of the truck. You are to follow this lady to our boat." I didn't need any confusion right now. I continued, "If you have shoes, take them off. If not, don't worry. If you have any jewelry that might make noise, hold it in your hand. When we get to where we are going, you will be silent. I don't care if you break a leg, you will be quiet.

If you have jewelry that could cause a flash, take it off."

I heard someone ask, "Does that include my cross?"

"No," I said, "just cover it up so there's no flash or noise if you want to save it. Girls, doing these things as you are told will prolong your life, and with life there is hope, and without hope we are all lost and probably dead. So, if you cooperate it will be better for you. So, what will it be?"

Only Svetlana answered. I think she was used to speaking for this group. She was the mama figure.

"Well, what will it be?" I asked.

She answered softly with a frightened voice, "We will do as you say if you promise not to kill us. We will go to bed with you and your men, but please do not kill us."

Little did she know I wanted to throw up and I might still just do that, but after we set sail.

It was time to talk to Preacher. "Hey, Preacher! How do you read me?"

The answer came back clear. "Five by five, big brother. Did you hear what I said?"

I told him, "Yeah, tell the others it is okay."

Preacher said, "But they won't talk."

I hoped this would not be a problem. "If they won't, I will take care of it. Heilgrid? Are you up on the net, little sister?"

I heard her voice loud and strong, "Yes, I am."

I told her, "If Preacher can't get through to them, you try to talk with the oldest girl. They haven't said a word."

Heilgrid was quick to reply, "Okay, Boots."

I turned back to my charges. "Svetlana I do not want to go to bed with you, or your companions. The little one is what? Maybe twelve?"

Svetlana spoke up like she was trading a product, "She has not been used too much. You can have her however you want, but no kill us."

Damn! How can I get it through to her?

Helvi said, "Let me try, Boots."

I said, "Okay, babe. Preacher give your oldest girl the spare ear bud."

Preacher answered, "She doesn't have anything to hook the mic to."

I sighed, "Just hand it to her. Boots out."

He voiced, "Okay boss."

As I listened in, Helvi assured the girl she was not in bad hands. She finally stated, "Please help Boots to save you and your friends."

The answer was short. "Why? Where is his whorehouse?"

Helvi told her, "He doesn't have one."

The girl had to think about this statement. After about two minutes, she agreed.

I asked Helvi, "How long until the drop point?"

Helvi answered, "Three minutes, Boots."

I spoke into the mic. "Okay, guys. Start wrapping the battle rifles in some blankets with a tie on it. Pack up the other gear and extra magazines. Put the ammo in the gear cases. The girls who don't have clothes, give them blankets. And guys, be careful and be respectful to these young ladies, but be firm."

I heard, "Boots?"

I said, "Yes, Helvi?"

She said, "We are one minute out."

I turned my attention back to the girls. "Okay. If you girls want a better life and to be happy again, cooperate."

Up popped a familiar voice, "Or you'll kill us? We will cooperate."

I found many things to think about at this moment, but I had no time. It was about to get shaky and more than nerve-racking.

As we began to slow down, my stomach was tying itself into knots. We had to move sixteen human beings, two-hundred-seventy feet, without noise and without being observed. With everyone now covered in some way with darker colored blankets or jackets or whatever was available, we were ready. Helvi brought the truck to a stop.

She said, "Our people are here for the trucks, Boots."

I replied, "Okay, babe. Preacher, let's get 'em moving."

The back doors opened and what appeared to be darkened wraiths were moving very quickly down the dock.

"Okay, ladies and gentlemen. Let's do this thing. I'm bringing up drag, so get 'em on the boat. Quick. So go now. And no matter what, don't come back. I'll be there."

Our doors opened and my own group of wraiths emerged into the darkness. They seemed huddled together and moving like a unit. It was incredible. How could they know to stay so small, and move so very fast?

I looked around vigilantly. It's clear. I was standing by the driver's door to our old bus. Jass, one of the Heilgrid's friends, looked at me.

He said, "I don't believe you did it and got this far. I fear your trip out could be the last one you take. The Mafia runs the docks and the whole waterfront. I hope they don't decide to blow you out of the water."

I said sternly, "Well, don't they have to figure out what's going on? There's five ways out of this place and I would be, and am, betting one sailboat and sixteen lives on the idea that they only have a twenty percent chance to find us. Here comes Slick. I

wouldn't take him out to the airport in this van."

Jass laughed, "Neither would I."

I turned to Slick, "Slick, my brother, be careful, and we will see you at our new base."

He answered, "Okay, Boots. Thank you, my brother."

He was thanking me, and I felt the thanks should go to him!

"My honor, Slick. See you on the flip side." Slick retorted, "On the other side, Boots."

With that, the van and Slick were no longer visible. Only a memory for now, I hoped.

I turned to head for the boat. The dock was empty. I glanced to the left and then in turn to the right. There was not a soul to be found. I watched a fishing vessel as he jockeyed for the channel. I knew that I would soon be jockeying into that channel, but I doubted that the fishing vessel was carrying such precious cargo as the Valkyrie. I began to move very fast with one target in mind. The boat and relative safety in obscurity. As I stepped aboard, I noticed there was not one light visible, except the bridge lights. There was someone there and I knew it was my girl, Helvi, warming up the lugger.

I boarded the boat, opened the cabin door and locked it behind me. Just a habit, I suppose, but I did it without thinking. There was Helvi. I looked at her and saw she was as white as a piece of paper. Not only was she stark white, her hands were shaking. When I spoke, Helvi jumped as if she had just been shocked by sticking her finger in a light socket. She turned in time to vomit into a small waste can.

I said, "It's going to be fine. You'll be fine. It's okay." She said nothing.

I asked, "Is the vessel ready to go? Everything started, running, and ready?"

She answered, "Yes."

It was all I could get out of her. It was apparent that this young woman was ready for the excitement, but was not ready for the agonizing fear that she felt.

I faced Helvi and told her, "No matter. I'm going to check below, and then we're going to cast off and get the hell out of here!"

As I left, I heard Helvi vomiting again. I went below and I could see one group of confident, but nervous and frightened men. I knew how they felt. On the other end, I could see a small group of young women and girls who were terrified at their situation. They were absolutely silent. I didn't think any of them knew the gravity of the situation, or my part in it. Nor did they realize, unless they wanted the Mafia back in their lives, that I would not surrender them, or any of us to the Mafia.

I went to Preacher and asked, "Is everything okay and ready, Preacher?"

He answered, "Yeah, Boots. Let's do it."

I grabbed my watch coat and Portuguese skippers cap and said, "Okay, brother!" and headed back up the stairwell.

I went back into the bridge cabin and shut the door behind me. Helvi still looked shaken, but had become much sturdier.

I said, "Relax, Helvi. I'm going on deck to release the mooring lines and then we will get underway."

She answered, "Okay, babe."

"Ah, yes," I thought, "she sounds somewhat better," however, I noticed a washed out wastebasket very close within her reach.

I exited the bridge and went down onto the deck. I stepped off, and onto the finger pier. I cast off the bow line and turned to go to the stern. There was a couple from two piers over from the Valkyrie. They said hello. The wife was holding a bottle of Mont Blanc.

"I wanted you and Heilvia to have this. The bottle is from the same year that Lars and I were married. Carry this with you on your adventure. When Heilvia and you are married in Naples, please open this wine and when you drink a toast, remember, Lars and I have been married for fifty years. May it bring the luck of happiness and a long marriage to the two of you, like Lars and I have had."

I studied the bottle. The date on it was 1947. This single bottle of wine was worth probably fifteen-thousand dollars U. S. I felt a little bit guilty, but I also knew it was a gift of love, and I couldn't ruin it for this couple.

She continued to talk, so I had to beg their pardon and tell them we really had to be underway. There was the outgoing tide to catch. I explained that we had to get through the tidal surge gates before the turn of the tide from slack or it could take us a further six hours to reach open waters. They went on to ask about Helvi and I told them she was below. I hoped she was asleep. She had had one of those nights that sleep had evaded her. I had asked her to try to get some badly needed rest and I would take us out and get underway.

"Well," I said, "I really have to be on the ball. Tide nor time waits for no man, nor his vessel!"

We said goodbye and I cast off the stern line, with only the spring line left. I gained the deck and went amid ship to cast off the spring line. I coiled it up and proceeded to the stern in order to gain access to the bridge.

I went through the hatch and handed Helvi the wine and throttled up the lugger, and was heading out of the slip and up into the side channel. We were heading for the bight and then the channel. It was slow going, with a stress level of about two-hundred on a scale from one to ten.

We were four-hundred meters out of the slip, when an all black boat came up fast behind us. You could tell by the shape and the sound of her exhaust, this was a fast boat. It was in the sixty foot ring of the radar. A sixty foot boat that sounded like a racing boat, did not sit right in my mind. The sound was enough to convince me that if this vessel was looking for a boat with a bevy of private property onboard, we could not outrun them. We would have to fight.

I picked up the mic to the intercom, "Preacher could you come up to the bridge deck? We need to talk."

As he gained the bridge he said, "What's up, Boots?"

I told him, "We got a bogey on our six. Man, he's black, no offense, but he's got serious horsepower. Go over and crack the hatch and give a listen."

Preacher listened and said, "Man, we could have troubles!"

I answered, "I know. She's a sixty footer, according to the search radar sill identifier rings."

There was exasperation in his voice, "Damn! They could have an army!"

I responded, "Yeah, that's what I was thinking. Well, what do you think?"

He said, "I'll let the clan know, but don't ram him just yet. You just don't know who he is. Has Helvi heard of a patrol boat like this?"

I told him, "I couldn't ask her. She's in the head, probably getting sick again. It will be at least her third time."

Preacher laughed slightly and answered, "Man, stress and her don't go hand-in-hand, do they?"

"No," I answered, "Preacher, go ahead and bring the clan up to alert status. Quietly, man. Don't excite anyone yet."

I could hear Preacher take a breath in. "Got cha', boss. How's the boat handle?"

I told him, "Like a large sailboat would. Slow to respond, and just plain slow."

Preacher laughed, "What did you expect, Boots?"

I abruptly told him, "I want a riverine boat. Something that will fly low and fast!"

"I know," he answered, "but we don't have any with the kind of range we would need."

I retorted, "I know it too. I just feel like we are sitting ducks, just waiting to be shot and plucked. It reminds me of when we had to cross the Perfume River by going downstream two miles under heavy enemy fire in order to take the north side of Hue City and the citadel. You remember that, Preacher?"

That was quite an experience. The enemy let us get in the boats and pull out, then start on downriver. But, they let us know they were there. We were maybe five-eighths of a mile downstream, when they opened up on us with every weapon they could get a hold of. It wasn't pretty waiting to be shot, but it happened, nonetheless. The boat literally looked like Swiss cheese. We had a lot of wounded, but we went on, thinking this is your lucky day! One third of us were wounded when we hit the North shore. We had to establish a beachhead, so they could erect a floating bridge across. It didn't help us, but it did help the mud Marines who were on the other side of the river. But, they were there anyway.

Preacher answered, "I remember, Boots, and I know what you mean. It was a small miracle that any of us lived through the boat ride, let alone the argument. They were good, but our plan was better."

I had to smile to myself, "Yes, but in the end we accomplished what we had to."

He replied, "You're right, brother."

My thoughts went to the well-being of the girls. "Preacher, have you made any headway with the girls?"

He answered, "Not really, Boots. They think they have been taken by rivals to go to work for us. Damn! I wish things were different. They are even having a hard time with Heilgrid and Helvi. There were women involved in the original trapping of these girls."

I told him, "Okay, brother. I'll watch the bogey and have the clan be ready."

He said, "You got it, boss."

I had said all I needed to say at this time. "Okay, get out of here, man." Preacher returned below.

I thought of how these girls must feel. I had no idea, of course. I can only imagine and try to remember it was worse than anyone who hadn't had it happen to them could imagine. Damn, here I was in my own thoughts and the bogey had moved up on us.

"Okay," I thought, "if you're going to cause trouble, let's get to it. Big guy, you are beginning to irritate me and I'm already worried and not in a good mood!"

Two-hundred meters to the bight of the harbor. Seven-hundred meters to the channel. "Here he comes! Damn, he's fast and coming hard. He's on me now. What do you want, man? Well, you're not getting a free lunch."

The boat came abreast of us. He honked and continued to accelerate out to the channel. What the hell was that all about? It was then I realized that on the inside of the bight, especially at the piers, there is an anti-awake ordinance which reduces everyone's speed except at night.

Helvi came up the stairwell and onto the bridge deck. She asked if everything was okay.

I said, "So far, but I would think that we were being hunted by now. They just don't have any idea where to hunt."

The objects of their intense search were located on this vessel. At this time, at least, they had no idea of where to look except everywhere. Could they, with a little time, put us and the girls on this outbound vessel, or did Helvi and I do a good enough job of misleading everyone who had seen us together? If they had somehow discovered the truth, you could bet they would come charging after us. To me, it was a little like getting ambushed, only this was a constant ambush that just had not happened yet. By the time the black boat had come abreast of us, I was convinced that he was going to attack, and God only knows what would happen if it came true. But, luck had been with us and it had not happened not like that.

But, what about next time, or after that, until we reached international waters, or crossed over into someone else's part of the ocean, we would be targets. Nothing could change that fact. We were fifteen minutes from turning into the channel lanes. We approached the channel and prepared to turn into our lane of travel. It was much like a highway in the States. I had a lot more area to watch. I scanned the site pictures of both radars, and had somewhat of a visual on a container ship just passing. I could see an oil tanker approximately one-thousand meters on my portside. I knew I had found my slot. All I had to do was cross over and turn into the outbound traffic lane at the proper time. A ninety degree turn to port would put us in the outbound traffic on our way out of the inner harbor.

As I brought the boat into the lane, I requested that Heilgrid and Helvi come to the bridge. They came up and I explained that either one of them could handle the helm. I would then help the other one to set the spinnaker. Heilgrid took the helm, read the compass and put her eyes on the radar. She was glancing up and taking in one-hundred-eighty degrees of horizon. There was not much to see in the dark, but if you saw running lights on a boat with no radar reflector, there would be little chance of a collision. Heilgrid would do fine.

The spinnaker went up and began to catch the wind. Helvi and I realized we would also need to deploy the stabilizer sail just to keep in some sort of trim. We finished this arduous task, and I put my arm around her waist, and thanked her profusely for helping in this action. I kissed her on the forehead and told her she did just fine. A smile came across her face and we walked slowly back to the wheelhouse, a slang term for the bridge deck. I liked that term. So be it. We would call it the wheelhouse from now on.

We came into the wheelhouse and Heilgrid announced we were presently picking up speed. I checked the gauges and everything was as it should be. I relieved Heilgrid from the helm, a fancy word for the steering wheel and driver's seat, and positioned myself for a long ride. I thought it would be better that way. I flipped the captain's high-back seat into position and sat down. I adjusted the angle, tilt, and the lumbar support. I raised the left armrest, however the right armrest was in a perfect position for me. Being relieved from the helm, Heilgrid had already gone below to see if she could be of more help down with the girls.

I asked Helvi if she could get me some coffee, and a hot pot which would hold a full pot from the percolator. She said she would gladly get my coffee for me. That would give me another opportunity to check out the wheelhouse. I glanced around, and first saw next to me on my right, a forty caliber pistol with a full complement of magazines and rounds. There was also a mac-ten with magazines and rounds. Above the cabin crown was an H & K battle rifle, ready to deploy at any time that it should become needed. I found this fact to be very reassuring.

I waited for the coffee for over an hour. Of course, it had to be made, but little did I know, showers were being taken by a group of young ladies who had been shown their cabins. All they had to do was go through the clothes that preacher had guessed at the sizes of. He was pretty close. They did some trading of clothes, and they managed to get situated in the cabins in pairs. There was one separate cabin, and Svetlana had it. That way, she had her own cabin. As I sat and waited for my coffee, I became engrossed in the radar and I was stunned at the amount of boats coming and going in this port, but it didn't seem as big as Rotterdam. There were so many possible bogeys that came close, I did not notice who had brought my coffee. However, when I did look up, there was a clean and very beautiful young lady by the name of Svetlana.

When she spoke, out came the first words that did not include begging for her life and the lives of those she felt responsible for.

"Well, sir, you have gotten us out. So far."

I smiled at her, "How are you, Svetlana?"

She said curtly, "Fine. I am just fine." She walked to the top of the stairwell, ready to descend into the main cabin.

I gave her a wave and said, "Thank you, kiddo."

She said nothing. She was mad and was acting it all out. I said nothing more. After she left I spoke into the mic, "Preacher, you still got your ops ear in?"

I received an affirmation.

"Good, Preacher. Leave it in and on, as there is a reason to have instant comm. available. Are there any others wearing the system?"

Preacher answered, "Only one, Boots. Besides myself."

I told him, "Keep it in and on. I want to know what the girls are thinking. You can relay things that appear important."

Preacher was on it. "Okay, Boots."

CHAPTER TWENTY-FIVE

In some ways it was boring, until a vessel got to within a certain distance, then the nerves began. If I could not identify the vessel, or rule it out as a potential threat, I became stressed to the max. I would literally feel sick. I felt like a man running down the road, and the road was slowly narrowing to nine feet. There was a wall getting taller on each side. Soon the road was nine feet wide and the walls were twenty feet tall. Suddenly, a semi truck is coming down the road at a high rate of speed, and he could or would not slow down. Where are you going to go with nowhere to run to? So, you can't dodge the truck, and you're not going to out run the truck. You're just stuck! That's what it feels like. It's not a great feeling when you have to suspect everyone, and no one. It's a no-win situation and in many ways it can terrify a man.

When you are in this type of situation it tends to make you just a little paranoid about strange roads and unseen trucks. I was on such a road now with nowhere to go, but on this boat. There was plenty of other boat traffic. All it would take is for the Mafia to find out the truth about where their property was. They only had to hire a tugboat, that would be my guess. Then they would just run over the Valkyrie. It would be one of those inexplicable, terrible marine accidents. But the underworld would know what had happened. Along with those trapped in it.

If this was a good and just world, no one would have to do this type of work, or worry about traps or people who do insidious crimes. I looked out and saw there was a boat coming from my starboard side.

He's not fast, but it seems he's on an intercept course. Here we go again. It is 22:44 hours and we shoved off at 21:11 hours. We are presently making twelve knots. We have four more hours to reach open water, and then we will be turning seventy-four degrees to port, heading for the Texel cut and the open North Sea. Then on to English waters.

Helvi decided I needed company and had decided to come to the wheelhouse. The bridge was in deep red light in order to be able to see, and have few other boats see anything but our running lights. We tipped out Helvi's seat and had gotten it adjusted so she was comfortable. We began to talk.

"Helvi," I asked, "have you heard anything from these girls?"

She sighed, "Little bits and pieces. They believe you are a pimp, just stealing merchandise."

"So," I said, "did you try to talk to them?"

Helvi nodded, "Even Preacher tried, but they will barely speak to him. They believe he was a plant, to make them think he was trying to help them."

I finished the thought, "But in real life, he was no better than me. It is hard to understand, although I cannot blame them for thinking that."

She continued on, "They believe it's all that they are good for, and that their families and friends have written them off."

I couldn't say anything, as of yet, to whom had called me, but I wished we could have a heart to heart talk about mom things, especially with Svetlana. It would help to make her feel she hasn't been abandoned, and has more value than sexually.

Helvi looked quite puzzled. "I don't quite know what to think of girls this age that have been brutalized and mistreated in such a horrific manner. It is not an easy thing to sit there and look at a young girl of twelve years of age, and realize she was, as she puts it and is not shocked by what she says, eye-candy. She was a favorite plaything. She didn't like it. It was just a way of surviving until she could find her freedom. Svetlana goes over and comforts these girls. One by one, she hugs them and reassures them. She did tell them that you have kind eyes, and just maybe you're not so cruel. I listened to Svetlana as she was explaining to them all that you at least have kind eyes, and you know, Boots, after looking at your eyes, they are kind. You tend to broadcast what you're feeling. Just like a telly. It's unusual to find a man whose true intentions flow from their eyes."

I was glad that people could read something about me. Most times you can't tell if I'm a happy or sad. You can usually only tell if I'm mad or not.

"Helvi, do I look like a pimp, and what exactly does a pimp look like?"

She answered reluctantly, "Boots, they could be or look like anyone, so, yes, with a jaded mind you could appear to be at the least, a pimp. These girls do not have good memories that would make them believe that anyone could want them for anything other than for a plaything. They are apprehensive and cynical about their situation and their futures. They have only been out of that place for a couple of hours and when you took them out of there, you did it at gun point."

I knew this was true. These girls had a right to be cynical and apprehensive.

They viewed the world from a point of view that most civilized people can't come to terms with. The idea that young girls are victimized by circumstances beyond their control. Most people do not want to believe human beings can do this and it disturbs their idealistic view of themselves, and the world they live in.

As Helvi and I continued to talk about our "cargo," there were a few close calls, but evidently these were not aimed at us. They were simply boats trying to shove their way into the constant flow of traffic. We seemed to be maintaining a fairly constant speed, around twelve knots. This was good news. It put us out of the harbor before daylight, when many more boats would be moving around with a myriad of jobs and destinations. Although, up to this time, the big test would come at the first set of tidal flood dykes and gates. There's no stop required, however, since we had been involved in the rescue of our precious cargo, you never knew. All it would take would be for someone to suspect that all was not as it should be aboard this vessel. We were eleven minutes from this waypoint, in our bid to break free from this land.

Little did we suspect, that somebody had a friend or a relative who worked here. As we came closer, we saw there was a sign on the side of the control tower.

"Have a nice trip to Naples."

I said, "Well, I'll be damned!"

I turned to Helvi and she reached over and we hugged. We might be able to pull this off to a successful conclusion. There were now Dutch patrol boats around watching everyone and everything. Smuggling into the port was a huge problem of the outer and inner sea, it was the worst in this area.

A patrol boat began its approach. He came from the starboard side, abaft of the starboard quarter. As he slowly overtook us and moved within ten meters of our side, the radio crackled. Helvi picked up the mic and began to speak. I did not have any idea of what was being said or what was transpiring. I understood only some Dutch, but certainly not enough to be able to mutter a small phrase.

As Helvi spoke, I spoke to Preacher, "Heads up, Preacher! Officials coming up abaft of the boat. What do you want to do? I'll tell you what, you rouse the clan, have a discussion, and get back to me."

"Okay, Boots."

As the conversation continued, I grew more and more impatient to know what was going on. Helvi said something and then cleared the air and the mic.

"Boots, they're looking for a boat with a large number of kidnapped girls. They wanted to board until I told him where we were going and what we were going to do. Since they already had talked to, and checked the logs of departing vessels, they found our intent to sail. We have two witnesses that we left alone, with only my sister and the best man. I told them we couldn't afford to lose the tide. They seemed to agree, however they let me know that they might be back. I happily told them it would be an honor, and would they like coffee and sweet rolls? The commander of the vessel seemed to laugh and made an offhand remark! He felt that if they were welcome for coffee and rolls, he didn't think we were dangerous and probably not desperate characters. I told him we were desperate for our honeymoon. He just laughed and said, "God speed. See you when you get back home."

It was a relief to know I wasn't going to compound my misdemeanors with larger crimes. I radioed down to Preacher.

When he spoke, he let me know how they all felt. "Boots, were all for taking this sucker out and making a run for it. We've decided no one will get these girls back. We will not allow the Mafia, or anyone else to exploit or abuse them again. It's a drastic decision, but it's been made."

I answered, "Thanks, Preacher. I'll be down to thank the guys in a little while. It was good. After Helvi talked to them at length, they just sheared off to hassle someone else. Hell, they have been in contact with the harbor master and we checked out as legit and honest."

Preacher laughed, "Not a chance that that's true, Boots. We're only well-meaning brigands with nowhere to go, unless we find a place! I'm gone."

I said, "That's a wrap preacher," and the conversation was done and over.

We were now on our way to the last barrier that could keep us prisoners in this foreign land, with girls stolen from the Mafia who had contacts at the top of Dutch Society and politics. These men were the kind of men who had spent a great deal of money on friends and politicians to ensure that what we had just done couldn't happen. They would get a little static over their business interests. Since we had passed the first hurdle and escaped the notice of the constabulary, we again began the long march through the night with only one goal in mind. Freedom for us all.

Nothing had changed, it only grew worse. The waiting and stress was intense. My urge was to drop the sail, rev up the runner, and get the hell out of here, but common sense prevailed. We could not afford to draw attention to this boat, or us. Because the clan had already made up its mind not to surrender to anyone. It tempered those thoughts of trying to move faster than this boat was supposed to be capable of going. I had no desire to shoot it out with the Dutch police. However, I did not worry about a pitched battle with the Russian Mafia.

We were only one hour from the final dyke and gate system. We had been lucky to avoid discovery up until this time and I had no wish to invite discovery or detection. The only persons on deck had been Helvi and me. The many hours of sleeplessness was wearing not only on my body, but also my mind. It was indeed growing tired. It was the constant and omnipresent stress of avoiding discovery.

In one hour and thirty minutes, the helm would be turned over to the Czar and Heilgrid. Helvi and I could then retire for a much needed rest, if we were able to. The girls had the staterooms. Since Czar and Heilgrid had the focsile V bunks, that's where Helvi and I would retire. The rest of the boat was filled with other bodies and activities. We are now seventeen minutes out from the last barrier. I had to go on deck to lower sails because there is a six knot speed limit through the flood gates. Since we were under power and were using only mechanical propulsion, we had slowed down considerably, to eight knots. I reduced revolutions on the shaft until we were making five and a half knots. I ordered instructions down below. "No lights. No sound, please."

When we made the approach, we were squeezed to our starboard side by the tide in this area. As we started through these gates I had the worst feeling that something was waiting for us outside these protected waters. We passed through and then proceeded on our course for three quarters of a mile and turned one-hundred-sixty degrees West by Southwest heading for the Maasdiep Cut. It was a channel that went between Dan Helder, a Dutch port town, and Texel Island, twelve miles away.

As we went on deck the furled sails did not reach up and into position to catch all the wind that they could hold. We unfurled the sails in order to propel the boat back up to fourteen knots. There were adjustments to sail tension and our direction, but all and all it was a smooth transition from motorsailer to sailboat. It felt good to be out of the enclosed parts of this body of water. The worry would not end for another eighty-nine miles. At this speed, we would reach the North Sea center line in six hours. We would not cross the line into English waters unless we were forced to take refuge there from the Mafia.

We were proceeding on our course for the cut of Texel Island, when we were buzzed by a helicopter. It was of Russian design. Who it was, we will never know. What I do know, is that when it approached Helvi stepped out on the port wing deck, with me right beside her. Within very easy reach was a battle rifle with a full magazine of one-hundred explosive penetration rounds. It would take a chopper out of the sky quite nicely, without much trouble. They were lucky that they had not interfered with us. I found out a little while later, mine would not have been the only battle rifle in use. There were two more waiting to gain the deck, and open up on a purported enemy.

It was when we approached Maasdiep Cut that I began looking at the weather fax and monitoring the weather channels. It was not the Mafia we would have to worry about. An early storm had blown out of the North Sea. We would definitely have to scour the deck for loose objects and ropes. Working the deck was a joy after being in the wheelhouse for so long. Helvi and I went to the bow. We each had a side of the boat from the center to the gunnel. As we coiled and stored ropes and lashed things down, I was thinking, "I sure hope no one gets seasick." You only get over seasickness with drugs, which I had, time, or getting the boat onto dry land, which was not an option.

We finished up and went back to the bridge deck. We checked the latest weather report. It was not quite as bad as was originally forecast, but in the North Sea, gale force winds were never pleasant and sometimes just plain dangerous. The wind was predicted to blow at forty knots, and gusts to sixty knots. With seas running between five meters, up to and including ten meters. It sounds terrible. However, I've been in much worse as a 12-year-old kid on the Bering Sea.

I sent Svetlana below to get coffee into thermos containers for Helvi and me. There wouldn't be any rest for the two of us. Neither the Czar or Heilgrid had skippered in this kind of weather, and I have.

As we started the Valkyrie into the cut, there were groundswells coming into the channel from West-North-West. I had no depth worries, but it precluded using sail power going through the channel. It was too narrow, and with the swells we could get directional variants which could cause us to veer too close to one side or the other. If that happened, we had the possibility of hitting one of the riser shelves. I started the lugger and gave the helm to Helvi. I went out and down to the deck to furl sails. The only sail to stay out was the stay sail. It is a steadying sail that helps to keep the boat steady.

With all the duties of navigating and skippering the Valkyrie, I did not dwell on the official troubles that could come our way if we were caught and detained. In many ways, this weather helped us to avoid detection, but it also reduced our speed to eight knots. It would take between nine and fourteen hours to gain what we so desperately needed. Neutral waters and the ability to get the girls asylum. Then, it would be up to Slick to get them out. That was better then returning to Holland. At least the girls would get a fair deal.

We came abreast of the outside of the cut, ready to enter the North Sea. With coffee on the bridge, Helvi went below to get the cabin ready for rough seas. She had just finished up when the first of many waves lifted the boat in a sloughing motion. It was obvious that sea-sick pills needed to be handed out to almost everyone. I had set a course for Great Yarmouth, England, but with the waves coming at a ninety degree angle to the course, I decided to modify my course twenty-five degrees to port, so we were going downhill. The ride was much better. I heard a few bangs and thuds, but all in all, almost everything had been stowed away like it was supposed to be. Finally, the wind began to die out at the international dividing line. We turned to the south and headed for the Pais De Calias, or the English Channel. The waves, although large, were virtually coming from astern.

As the sea slowly returned to normal after eighteen hours, I found I could not move or think without great difficulty. It was time for Boots to sleep. The course was set and the sails were set, and we were pushing fifteen knots. Czar and Heilgrid came and took over control of the vessel. I told him, "No deviating, Czar. Change nothing." I was too tired to stay on my feet a lot longer. I did however, have two cigarettes and a sweet roll before I hit the bunk. It was a much needed and deserved rest after eighty-two hours.

CHAPTER TWENTY-SIX

I awoke six hours later just a little shaky, in desperate need of a gallon of black coffee and some deck air. I left the V berth to find a celebration of sorts happening in the main salon. We were at center point under full sail, heading down the channel. As I finally realized what had just been said, Helvi exited our bunk room, also in need of a gallon of coffee and air. I poured two mugs of coffee and checked the weather. It wasn't too bad. It wasn't raining. The wind was moderate and it wasn't very cold. And we were reasonably safe.

I looked at Helvi and said, "We did it, babe!"

She almost squealed, "I've heard!"

I said, "Here's your coffee, put on your jacket and lets head for the deck."

With a smile she answered, "You've got it!"

As I went to put on my jacket, I suddenly remembered something. A letter to Svetlana. Now, I would give it to her. She could read it knowing that she would feel better in her position, and maybe the other girls as well. When I walked out of the focsle cabin, I had the retrieved letter with me. I walked straight to Svetlana and said, "Svetlana this is for you. I think it's a note from a friend."

I slipped on my coat and hit the deck for coffee, and more coffee, along with a good stretch.

Helvi and I finished our second cup of coffee, and Helvi had refilled the cups again. I lit a cigarette.

Just then Helvi said, "Behind you."

When I turned, there was Svetlana with a look like she had no idea what to say.

"I am very sorry Mr. Boots for to talk about you bad. Not know why you not give letter to me long time ago."

I thought, "That's a hard question." I did not, in reality, want her to be able to tie me or the clan to her family, and especially to her mother. At least until there was less chance of getting caught. It could have been devastating to her mother and her family.

"Svetlana," I said, "I did not want to get your hopes up or to implicate your mother or family in this operation. If it had been unsuccessful it could have been bad for you, and for your mother."

At this point she looked so very young. With her lip trembling she asked, "My mother. She look how, Mr. Boots?"

As gently as I could I answered, "She looked tired and sad, Svetlana."

A small smile formed on her face, "She is then okay? Yes, Mr. Boots?"

I told her, "Svetlana, no one calls me Mr. If you are my friend, you will call me Boots. Just Boots, little one."

Her eyes fell to the floor, "I for to thank you. Feel bad I do about bad thoughts and sayings to other girls."

I smiled at her, "It's okay, Svetlana."

She looked up at me and said, "Friends to call me Misha. You will call me that?"

I looked in her eyes and said, "Okay, Misha. And please remember, it doesn't bother me, anything you might have said before. You could have said or called me anything, or the clan. What mattered was getting you here, and then to the States."

I saw this young girl's face brighten until it almost glowed. "I go to United States?"

I answered, "Yes, you are going to the States. Your mother is in the States."

She asked quizzically, "How you do this thing?"

As I thought, it came to me, "Leverage and pull, little Misha, that's how."

Tears began to form in her eyes, "Thank you. This I do very much."

I smiled at her, "You're welcome. Even more, you could do one more thing for me."

She answered much too quickly, "You want to sleep with me?"

I sighed. This would have to be handled gently, "You are a very attractive girl, Misha, but I don't think so. What I would like for you to do for me is to let the other girls that think badly of Preacher and the guys, would you please let them know they're good guys and not pimps or scum?"

She said haltingly, "Okay, for you to them I will speak."

I told her, "Misha, speak Russian. I speak Russian too."

As her assurance grew that I could read and understand Russian, and thought of her as worthy, she seemed to open up like a flower in June.

From what I could ascertain when I awoke, with our course set, we were an eight hour run to the top half of France. I had found Slick's cryptic message, and laid in a course for Cherbourg, France. That was our destination. It was where Slick and the official, along with our paperwork was waiting. I entered the bridge deck and I saw the Czar.

"You slept well, Boots? Da?"

I yawned and said, "I feel like I could have slept longer. I don't know why I couldn't."

Czar smirked a little, "You feel responsibility to personnel, Boots. That is why."

I just let that pass. "I want to check the gauges and position.

Okay, Czar?"

He nodded, "Is fine with me, my brother."

I began my gauge check. I noticed the knot meter was at ten knots. The lugger was off, but we should be a little faster. I looked out the windows of the wheelhouse. The sheets were up properly and the angle of attack was fine, but our wind speed was down. There was a four knot difference. I checked the chart and the compass, and then the long-range radar. We were right on course for a rendezvous with Cherbourg, France. We were twelve hours from the harbor entrance, however I was scheduled to call Slick four hours and thirty minutes before we turned our heading into Cherbourg Harbor. I asked Czar if he wanted me to take over.

He replied, "Is not necessary, Boots. Have you had anything to eat?"

I said, "Yeah, I had . . ." No. That was three and a half days ago. I remembered I was too busy and far too stressed to eat. I had eaten a handful of vitamins that Helvi had shoved at me, along with a bottle of aspirin. I even changed clothes in the wheelhouse while Helvi tended to the boat. I laughed lightly, "If it's okay with you Czar, I would like to shave, have a shower, and get some clean clothes."

Czar laughed and slapped me on the back. "You do that, Boots! It will make you a new man."

I went below decks and there was the object of my obsession. My girls.

I waved at them, "Hello young ladies. Miss Misha." It was like they all spoke in unison.

"Hello, Boots."

What a difference! From scum belly to good guy in one letter. Do you know what the hardest thing in the world is? Getting through the hugs and kisses of seven grateful girls under the age of twenty years old. Then to feel guilty because you have touched them, and didn't mean to. Although, it was nice to be hugged instead of shunned. I made my excuses and asked if anyone needed to use the head. They all looked at me strangely.

I explained that the head was what I called the bathroom.

Svetlana spoke for them all. "No, Boots. Please, go ahead."

So, I escaped and grabbed my clothes and shaving kit, and proceeded to shave and shower. All the girls conspired with Helvi to make me something to eat. It was a little overwhelming.

I assumed command from Czar and tried to trim the sails to get more speed out of the wind, but alas, it was not to be. As we approached the four hour mark, it occurred to me that I could be back in the States by day after tomorrow, which was fine with me. I would like to be home for at least a little while. I turned on the radiotelephone to warm it up. It seems that someone shut the radiotelephone off. There is an unwritten rule on a boat. If it's supposed be on, don't touch it! Leave it on! I got out the call sign and number. The radio operator was calling the skipper of the Valkyrie. I radioed in an acknowledgment.

She said, "Stand by. Go ahead, sir."

As the phone came to life, I didn't know who or what to expect.

I heard Slick's familiar voice. "Boots, Boots? Are you there? Over"

"I'm here. Over."

"Boots, there's trouble. The man who is supposed to process the boat and your passengers has been called home. Over"

"What do you expect us to do, Slick? Over." Man, this could be real trouble.

"His mother had a bad heart attack and he went home for twenty-one days. Over."

"I repeat, Slick. What are we supposed to do? I can't float out here forever, you know. Over."

"Yes, I know this Boots. I have been in contact with him. He is from my hometown. Over."

"That does not do us any good, Slick. Over."

"If you sail a little further, it will do you no harm, but much more good. Over."

"How do you figure that, Slick? I've got a lot of stuff to do and need to get busy. Over."

"I know, Boots, but this was unexpected, and it is his mother. Over."

"Okay, give me the spiel. Over."

"If you come to Marseille, I'll guarantee you anything you want. Over."

"Do I have time to think it over, or do you need an answer right now. Over."

"It will not matter. I cannot guarantee anything if you do not come to Marseille. Over."

"Okay, I'll lay in a course, Slick, but you owe me big time, brother. Over"

"I know, my friend. I'm sorry. Over."

"I'll break the news to the passengers. Don't forget to call. Over."

"I won't, Boots. It will be fine. Over."

"See you on the flipside, Slick. Over."

"On the other side, my brother. Over."

I had planned when we docked and cleared all of the official hurdles, to fly to Marseille to visit Slick and meet his lady at their villa on the Mediterranean Sea. But, with that call, I was glad that we had bought charts of that area. I had good and bad news. We had put in a mock course. We had to make a real course happen. I better talk to Preacher first.

I hit the intercom button on the shipboard radio and asked Preacher to come to the wheelhouse. When Preacher came in I had a stack of charts on the chart table.

"What's up, Boots?"

I figured the best thing was to get right to it. "There's been a change in plans, Preacher. We're going to change destinations."

He answered with a look of sudden shock, "Where in the world are we going? I thought Cherbourg was our destination. Isn't that where we were supposed to park?"

I answered, "Yes, Preacher, but for reasons beyond Slick's control, were going to Marseille, France."

He replied, "How are we getting there? By plane?"

I hoped this could be explained without incident. I shook my head. "No, Preacher, we're going by boat. Yes, you heard me right. We have to sail this boat through the English Channel to the Atlantic Ocean, and then go South past Portugal and Spain. Another left, and through the Straits of Gibraltar around the south side of Majorca. It's one of the islands that belong to Spain. From there to the North East point of Menorea, it's the sister island of Majorca, from that point into Marseille, France, where

Slick and his friends will be waiting for us to get there."

Preacher did not look happy. "I hate that idea, Boots."

I agreed, "I don't like it either, but what choice do we have? We need paperwork, for us, but most of all we need it for the girls." He knew I was right.

"I know, but it frosts me. There's Slick onshore at someone's house, and we're here!"

He was right about that.

It could have been much worse, however. "Yes, and we're still alive, and my friend, that's better than the alternative."

Preacher laughed a little, "I know, Boots. The big dirt nap!"

I had to smile in return. "You got it. You want to tell the others, or do you want me to?"

He sighed, "I'll do it. I am the preacher, and it seems that I am equally adept at breaking bad news, due to hard facts."

"Thanks, Preacher," I said. "Czar will probably get loud and rude. Tell him to shut up. He volunteered his group. Okay?"

He replied in return, "Okay, Boots."

I told him, "I think I will tell Helvi. If you see her down there, please send her up here. You tell the others, but I want to tell her what's up and in the wind personally. Thanks, Preacher."

"You're welcome, brother," he answered with a wave. He turned, then walked down the stairs and disappeared.

Five minutes later Helvi came up to me and said, "Boots, you wanted to talk to me?"

I answered, "Yes I did, little one. Would it bother you to have a bunkmate for a while longer?"

She said, "I'd like that. Why?"

I told her the story. She felt sorry for Slick's friend and his mother. "I will pray for her, Boots."

I told her, "You can do that in the focsle cabin we share. Helvi, yours and my job is to pilot this vessel roughly an additional three-thousand miles and we've got to find the right wind and proper currents in order to accomplish this."

She smiled and retorted, "We will do it, and who knows, Boots, it could be enjoyable."

I had to think about all that had happened. Great successes don't come off without a price, and up to this point it was an adequately good mission. It would have been nice to be done with it, but for some reason Slick didn't have a plan B. I will be discussing this when I get him alone.

Helvi and I worked on getting the Valkyrie headed back out. As we had already started our entry into French waters, we set course heading back for the centerline between the two countries. Back out into what I like to call "no man's land," and in this case it was water. We were heading for the Atlantic Ocean and it was no place to be stupid. It never is on any ocean. The territorial waters off of Portugal and Spain were enforced ten miles to one-hundred miles from shore. In reality, it was farther out than that, but both of those navies and coastal patrols couldn't cover one fiftieth of the area around Portugal, let alone Spanish waters with one-thousand-nine-hundred miles of coast. That's just an estimate. I was more interested in our course.

Helvi and I started looking at shipping lane charts, wind charts and estimates. Along with current flow charts, we discovered a reasonably safe passage one-hundred-twenty-five miles shore side. Northbound traffic was closest to shore, and southbound traffic was on the ocean side. It would not really be any safer than anywhere else on the ocean. There would still be the odd freighter or fishing vessel, and people like us using this inside lane. With the addition of radar, both long and short range sonar, and all the other electronics, Helvi and I could virtually move into the wheelhouse. We also had an autopilot with the ability to dodge objects. It had a bunk and a head (a small bathroom) we could still eat and shower on the main deck, but our job was navigation, piloting, and protection of this vessel. That is what would ensure the safety of our most precious cargo.

With the course set, Helvi and I went on deck. We walked and talked. We started on the bow stem hanging sails. As we worked our way back, we made sure every sail was up. We had spare sails, but nowhere to put them. Those were the spares, but there was one more. Helvi grabbed my hand and we proceeded back to the bow where she released a drogue sail and played out the line. I could just imagine what this boat looked like from a distance. No boat, just sails.

"Helvi, do you want to move your gear up here with mine? That way at least you have a bunk, and I'm going to move up here. I know the bridge deck is small and there are not many amenities up here, but you would have some privacy, except for me."

Her eyes sparkled and she said, "Yes, Boots. I hadn't thought about the bunks up here. They are small, unless we put them together." She looked thoughtfully, "There would only be one of us in it most of the time, and I will bring you your food and lots of coffee to you."

I said, "Thank you Helvi. It would be cozier, but I don't like sleeping in someone else's bed after they've been in it. Well, I am going to use it. Is that going to be okay?"

She answered, "You bathe all the time and you shave. I do not think Czar does this every day, and you use aftershave, and I like the smell."

I laughed, "Well, this belongs to us for the next fifteen days."

Helvi and I began to move our gear into the bunk area of the bridge deck. The Czar was still muttering under his breath about the change in plans.

I said, "What's the matter Czar?"

Czar scowled, "Preacher, he just tell me to shut up, or get off here and now! No one talk to me like that before!"

I told him, "I don't know what to say. Just grin and bear it, Czar. Let me ask you. Is this the worst thing that's happened to you?"

He answered, "Well, no."

I continued, "Then live with it. We all have to, so try to get along, brother."

He looked solemn, "Okay, Boots."

I had already decided to come down and talk to everyone. As I watched Helvi pack her gear and start to move it, I noticed two of the girls I did not know, jump to help her. There was a definite change happening. The girls seemed to be a little freer in their movements and thoughts. It was as Heilgrid had said, that they would begin to change. This is what came to mind. I just didn't have any idea that I would be with them long enough to see these changes. By all rights we should be tied to a pier in Cherbourg and they would already have started processing. I would have lost sight of my precious cargo by now, knowing that in the end, they would be home back with their families.

As fast as the moving started, it stopped with a bucket of water and some soap and dishrags. They were going to clean the bridge. I was, to say the least, amused and pleased at this turn of events. However, one girl said nothing and did not move. This I would find out about later. The bridge was cleaned and I watched my gear travel past me and up the center stairwell into the small bridge cabin, where two was tight, but three is a crowd. Helvi called for me to see what had been done and I was quite impressed. Every part of the cabin was clean, including the windows. I turned to thank all who had helped. I thought I would cry as I watched Francine, our twelve-year-old, hang a cross over my bunk. I thought to myself, "Damn, Boots. How could anybody do those things to such little girls?"

I looked at the girls and smiled, "I want to thank you all. I know I will keep you all in my heart," and I knew I would until the day that I died.

The bridge was now mine and for me to command. I checked all the gauges. I looked at the knot meter and saw we were traveling at twelve knots with a fair wind. If that was what we were going to be making, it would have to be enough. I checked and saw the radar screen was full of markers. Targets, as they are called everywhere, but none of them were on a threat course, yet. I would not feel even remotely safe or secure for myself, or especially the girls.

I had not considered letting anyone on deck topside, until we were in port, but that was changed now. I would have to let them on deck eventually, or they would feel trapped once again, but certainly not now. We would have to get out of the channel first, or at least past the Channel Islands. At the Channel Islands, the English Channel burgeons out to seventy-six miles and the risk of detection decreases by the miles we put behind this vessel and our distance from the land.

I hoped the Mafia and the Dutch authorities were looking in another direction. But, the Mafia's memory is long, and I was sure they would not forget easily what had happened at one of their businesses. It was time for me to go below and speak to the clan and guests.

"I would like to tell you why we have changed course and are now sailing for the Mediterranean Sea and the back door into our guest country. Due to an unforeseen medical crisis of one of the men who would process our paperwork, and believe me we will have paperwork, he has gone to Marseille and will be working from that port. So, we are now proceeding to Marseille via the Strait of Gibraltar. It should take us approximately fourteen days, and with luck it will be less. At our present speed, it will be the morning of the fourteenth day. As far as going on deck, I cannot stop you, but I hope that you will stay below for only one more day and night. If you can do that, then you will have free roam of this boat. The weather will be improving, kids, the farther south we go. It will be a good adventure for all of us." They just sat there and stared.

I realized I had been mechanical. The way I was talking to them was almost like a machine. I would not be something I was not, however I did change the way I talked. I tried desperately not to swear, which is not easy for an ex-Marine.

I looked around the room, "Does everyone understand, guys?"

I heard, "Okay skipper," and the tenseness left.

Francine began to laugh along with the others. Even though I had already started to turn for my new home, as I came to the stairs I turned and looked at the group of my old friends, and the new additions to my heart. I turned back and headed up to be alone with my own thoughts.

On the bridge, I could once again return to my job. I checked the course, made a small adjustment and went down to the deck to adjust the mainsail. I let out a little more slack to catch more pressure. When I returned to the wheelhouse, there was a steaming cup of coffee and sandwiches. There was a paper flower on the plate, and I wondered who had delivered it.

The day was an easy one. I had noticed Helvi was not in the wheelhouse as much as she had normally been. I was curious as to what she had been up to. I would find out later. She slept here. She didn't have too far to go. I held course, and to my port side I caught sight of the Channel Islands held by the Germans in World War II. I was alone with my thoughts, which to some seems strange, but it is my way to distance myself from other people and remain alone, and I liked it that way.

Evening came and I had not one visitor up to the bridge deck. They were all busy below deck. Since the hatchway was closed to the main cabin, I decided to call Helvi. She came up the stairwell and there were two things I noticed almost immediately. I smelled fresh coffee and I needed it. I had been out of coffee for two hours. When it's available, I will drink it or diet coke constantly. Then it hit me. My girl was wearing perfume. Interesting. And her hair was in a French braid.

I looked around and she asked, "What are you looking for?"

I smiled, "I was wondering if a small boat had come alongside without my knowing it."

She laughed lightly, "Why?"

I laughed back with her, "Because you look like you've been to a beauty salon."

She smiled fully, "No, I've been a willing participant at the beauty school for escaped girls."

I gasped, "You mean my girls did this?"

"Yes, they did, and they are doing Heilgrid's hair right now. Do you like it?"

Now it was my turn for a full smile. "As a matter of fact, yes. I do very much."

This suddenly reminded me I had not shaved today. I'd been too busy.

Helvi asked me, "Are you coming down for dinner, or are you staying at the helm?"

I told her, "All I'm going to get done is a shave and a shower, and clean clothes. Sometime tonight, I have to do my laundry." We had a stack washer and dryer in the machinery room.

"You can't," stated Helvi.

I asked her, "Why can't I, my girl."

She answered, "Because Svetlana and Maria already did it, but there are a few items missing, like your underwear and pajamas."

I laughed, "Well, that's because I don't wear any."

She replied back, "Okay, then you do not have to do laundry. Are you coming below for dinner?"

I said seriously, "I would like to, but the traffic from freighters and the like has almost tripled in the last thirty minutes."

She nodded, "That's okay. We will take care of it. I will take the helm until you get back from your shower."

I said, "Thanks, Helvi."

She answered, "You're welcome, Boots."

I got my clothes out of the drawer and hoped she was right about the clothes. This was my last set. I had only brought five sets.

I went down to the cabin level and noticed all of my girls were nicely attired and their hair was done. Some makeup had been used. They all looked very presentable. Indeed, you would think they were out on a pleasure trip, and not running for their lives. I showered and shaved, and afterwards began to dress. I noticed the deck shoes I had been wearing before had been replaced by my other pair. I had to wonder where they were, and who had gotten them. It had to have happened when I was in the shower, but I had heard no noise. I finished dressing and splashed aftershave on. I put my dirty clothes in my mesh laundry bag, and exited the shower. It seemed that no one had changed places, but there seemed to be more talk between passengers. It was good, they were verbalizing and they were becoming much more animated. This would prove to be a boon to this group of humans.

I got back to the wheelhouse. I put my dirty clothes bag in one drawer, and went to put my shave gear in the other. I found it with clean clothes, all neat and folded. I was impressed. I looked at Helvi and asked, "Helvi, what are these girls trying to do?"

She answered, "They are just trying to show their acceptance of you, and they are worried that you think less of them because of where you found them. I'm afraid they would do anything, and

I do mean anything, to win your acceptance and approval." Well, this was an interesting situation. I told her, "Well, I cannot bring them up here to talk to them, or could I?"

Helvi said, "It would be tight, but four could sit on the bunk."

I agreed. "Yes, I could get them in here to talk to them, and then no one else would know what I had said. They would think it was only their secret. Helvi, after dinner I'm going to try to get all these girls into the wheelhouse with me, so I can talk to them in private. What do you think?"

Helvi smiled, "I think it would be a good idea. It's private."

I asked, "Do you think they will all fit?"

She answered, "We will get them in. Don't worry. Are you coming down for dinner?"

I told her, "I don't think so."

Helvi smiled at me, "You smell good, Boots."

I had to smile back. "Thank you, but not as good as you."

She said, "I didn't think you noticed."

I answered, "Oh, I noticed, believe me."

She giggled a little. "Well, thank you."

I said, "You're very welcome, my girl."

She rose and said, "I will see you around dinnertime."

I replied, "Okay, Helvi."

With that, she was out and closed the upper hatch. Then, I heard her close the other hatch and I could hear only the sound of wind past the open portal. I thought to myself, this is very nice.

I had to change course for a very large liquid natural gas ship. The cargo they carry could be devastating if a static spark were to happen. Five-hundred-thousand gallons of this witch's brew would wipe a port city like Cherbourg completely off the map. The detonation alone would be heard in South America. I did not like being anywhere remotely close to these huge floating bombs.

Out of nowhere, Kelly came up the stairwell and moved my charts. I sat transfixed watching this girl. She had been kidnapped and had wound up in Amsterdam. She cleaned the map table, and then she laid out what looked like a tablecloth. Then Maria came up and in her hands was a tub. She emptied the tub and a table appeared with plates, two glasses and napkins, along with flatware. The last thing she pulled out was two candles. I must say it was a nice touch. Francie proceeded to bring up a bottle of wine, a pitcher of ice cold water, and a corkscrew. What the hell were these girls doing to my cabin?

Helvi came up the stairwell with a meat dish and rice. She put them on the table and I helped her to be seated. Coria came up next with a bowl of whole kernel corn and had salt-and-pepper in her pocket. When she left, the top hatch was closed, and then the bottom hatch was closed.

I asked Helvi, "What is this all about?"

She laughed, "If the prophet cannot come to the mountain, then the mountain must come to the prophet. This was planned by the girls. I did much of the cooking, but they tried hard so you would be comfortable and pleased."

I heard a slight noise, and then in came Svetlana with a thermos of coffee and two mugs. As she turned to leave, she bent down and kissed my cheek, and just said a simple thank you. Then she was gone.

I looked to Helvi for advice. "What is it with these girls? They only seem to cater to me."

She gazed at me intently, "You are their hero, Boots."

"No," I said, "you're wrong. I work for someone."

She answered, "It does not matter. You are their hero, and Preacher told them so."

I retorted, "Damn him! No matter what has been said, I've never done a heroic thing in my life and that's the end of the subject."

She shook her head, "Boots, be prepared for this until they're out of your life."

I sighed, "That's going to be never. They will always remain in my heart and I will remember each of them always."

As I poured wine for Helvi she asked if I was going to have a drink.

I said, "No, I'm not Helvi. I am responsible for this boat, and all of God's creations on board. I will not be impaired in any way, my girl."

After dinner was finished I would be remiss in not declaring that it was a very delicious meal with very good company, which makes everything better. I cleared the table and it once again became a chart table. This would definitely become a memory that I wouldn't forget. The tub became full and with everything cleaned up, I carried the tub down to galley and then walked into the main salon.

I addressed the girls. "When I'm done with the dishes, I want all of you to come up to the bridge."

I turned to go back into the galley and two of my girls rushed past me in order to do the dishes I had planned to wash. I told them it wasn't necessary.

Without turning to look at me they said, "We know we do not have to. We want to, Boots."

It was another broken chink in the coldness they must feel towards men in general. I was back sitting in the helm chair, as the girls filed up and into the cabin. Helvi got five of them on the bunk, and everyone else stood.

I said, "I've been wanting to talk to all y'all girls, but I wanted you to have time to decompress. Are you all feeling better?" There was much nodding.

I continued, "I'm glad to know you and I want to know more about each of you, so if you don't mind I would like to talk to each of you privately. No funny business young ladies, just talk. Call it a quest for knowledge and the gift each of you can give me. The gift you will give is to know you a little better. So far, we've been lucky. I wish I could have gotten everyone there to come with us, but I couldn't force anyone, except you Svetlana. The rest of you are miracles to me and I am truly a fortunate man. If any one of you have a question about anything, please ask. There will be no secrets between us." I hoped I had explained enough.

From Francie came, "Will you marry me, Boots?"

She was just twelve years old. Gently I said, "I don't think I can, little one. I'm already married."

"Oh," she said, "that's right. You and Helvi."

I told her, "No, my wife is at home. Seven-thousand miles away. She's a very beautiful and kind Russian girl."

Svetlana asked, "Why did you come for me?"

I answered, "Your cousin Daria asked me to. I don't know if you know her, but you have another cousin. Her name is Nadia. She and I are best of friends."

She asked me, "How much did they pay you to come get me?"

I shook my head, "Svetlana, I started out with just so much money in my bank account. When I get home it will be pretty close to what it is right now. We do not charge money to get kids, or young girls, or anyone else. It is not ethical for me, or anyone

that works with me to make a dime."

Maria asked, "Why you do then?"

I told her, "Maria, I do this because it pleases me, and I hope

I am doing the work God chose for me."

Maria flatly stated, "There is no God."

I asked, "How do you figure that?"

She scowled, "He didn't rescue me or stop them from taking me."

I smiled, "Well, you are rescued, dear one. He sent me now, didn't he?"

I heard, "But."

I replied quickly, "No buts. There are good people and bad people, and by now you should hopefully know the difference. I believe in what God says. We are our brother's keepers. Are there any other questions for now?"

"How will we get home?"

I answered, "A man I call brother. He goes by the name Slick, he's making all those arrangements while we're out here on our

adventure. Are there any other questions?"

The unanimous answer was, "No."

I said, "Well, just remember this, as far as I'm concerned, I am your uncle. I don't lie, I don't cheat, and I don't steal, except for kids that have been taken away by the wrong person or persons. If you need to talk, you can talk to me, or any of us. If you need something, it's onboard this boat, as you can tell, so you talk to me or Helvi, or Heilgrid."

I saw a few grimaces, so I added, "Or Preacher. And girls, he really is a man of God. He has his own church."

They began to disappear back downstairs into the main cabin. Helvi and I looked at each other and I knew I had to go to the wing deck. I needed a cigarette now, but before I could light it, I had tears streaming down my face. I wasn't crying outside, I was crying inside. Helvi came onto the wing deck behind me. She only asked if I was alright.

I said, "Not really, Helvi. How could I be? How could anybody be?" I again, stayed alone with my thoughts.

It was growing late and sleep would not come to me for awhile. I was sure of that. I just needed time to think this through some. When I grew tired, I would turn the alarms on, the short range radar up to full volume and engage the autopilot. The problem comes when you least expect it, and I expect it all the time. I don't like to be caught flat-footed, so to speak. Sleep came to me just before dawn. I logged it in the log book, but I was on standby watch, so I fell asleep in my chair. Not the most comfortable place to sleep, but adequate.

The smell woke me. "Ah, fresh coffee," I thought. I needed to brush my teeth first, or I won't be able to stand myself, or my coffee. As is customary, I checked the course and turned down the alarms. I checked the gauges and scrambled down the stairs to an open head for a quick shower. I was out the door and back up to the wheelhouse. I could shave and brush my teeth up here. There's just no shower. There's not enough room. I went down to the galley to get coffee and there was Svetlana. She had made coffee.

She looked at me and said, "I used to make the coffee at home for my mother. I'm sorry."

I was puzzled, "Sorry about what, Svetlana?"

She answered, "These are not my things."

She stood up and came to me crying. I held her in my arms and said, "It's okay, baby. It's alright." What could I say to her? How could I make it better for her? She had dreams, and they had been crushed by men who thought of her as property first, and a sex toy second.

What could I say? "Baby, it's the bad things in life that reminds us that there are good things too. None of this is your fault and you're going to be fine. You are young and absolutely gorgeous. You are also smart and courageous. In about every category, I think you're the top of the heap. Don't be like me, be middle ground Svetlana. Just believe in God and yourself, and you will be fine. Okay, now. Dry your eyes and let's just sit down and have

a cup of coffee together, and trust me you will be fine."

She sniffed and half sobbingly said, "Okay, Boots."

When her tears came to an end, I got her a cold washcloth for her to wipe her face. She was already feeling better when Francie came in. She went straight to Svetlana,

"I heard you crying. Did he make you cry, Svetlana?"

Svetlana jumped up and snapped, "Shut up! He would never make any of us cry!"

Francie looked a little skeptical. She couldn't quite buy it, but she listened as I spoke to Svetlana. As I talked to her, I felt that all I could do was to bolster her sagging confidence.

"Boots, how can anybody love me, or marry me, and let me have babies after what I have done?"

I just shook my head, "What did you do? You did nothing that you weren't forced to do. If a man can't understand that, he's not good enough for any of my girls. To hell with him! Find a good man, and you will. I swear you will." I think and hope that she believes it, because it's true. I'm sure it is.

When I looked over, I first saw that Francie had been listening. When I looked up again, I found that I had all seven of my girls listening. You know, I love these girls. It was hard not to. It seemed the rest of this day would be calmer than the past few, and I was thankful for that.

CHAPTER TWENTY-SEVEN

Since the four days that had passed since the galley incident, I had girls in the wheelhouse, and about everywhere I went. This did not appear to make anyone happy but the girls, myself, and Preacher. He thought it was good for them to listen to an old codger like me. I thought, "Well, maybe he's right." However, it seemed the others were not quite as happy for my success with the girls. I once again had climbed the steps to my home. Helvi was standing there, arms crossed, and less than pleased about something, so I asked her why?

Helvi said sharply, "You only have time for the girls and I do not think that it is an altogether good thing."

I asked her, "For who Helvi? Me, the girls, or you?"

She retorted, "For everyone. You don't spend time with me. You aren't spending any time with the clan, and they are grumbling."

I shot back, "And you are too."

She replied, "Yes."

I held my tongue, for a minute. I took a deep breath and tried to sound kind. "Helvi, please understand I'm not trying to ignore anyone, but if the girls come to me I will not turn them away. Any more than I would if you came to me, and Helvi, the operative word is come. I seek no one, but if I am sought out, I try to turn no one away. I will talk to Preacher and the rest of the clan. They are my business, and I will straighten everything out. I will have to talk to you later, Helvi, if you are here that is."

I immediately sought out Preacher. I asked him to get the clan together and meet me on the fore deck on the bow of the boat.

He told me, "No problem, Boots."

First, I went to the galley, and got some coffee and then went to the bow of the boat, onto the fore deck. When I got there, I saw that everyone had been assembled. "Well that didn't take long," I thought to myself. I sauntered up to them and then stopped. I looked around at all of them. I said, "So, I hear you guys feel left

out, and that I'm not around too much. Is that true?"

They answered, "Yeah, kind of, Boots."

"Well," I told them, "Then you go sit up in that cabin day after day. It wasn't the original plan. I was supposed to have some help. You guys didn't come up there. Hell, no! You sat down in the salon and watched canned TV, and talked, and who the hell else knows what! Who came to the wheelhouse? No one but the girls, and boys, let me tell you, you're older than them, and I thought maybe wiser. How come none of you either have come to me while I navigate this boat, or have made an effort to help these girls feel better about what happened to them, and convince them that they are still valuable as humans? Have you made them feel that there isn't a big W for whore tattooed on their forehead? I'm ashamed of you, my brothers. I am ashamed and disappointed with the whole damn bunch of you! I thought you were more caring than that. If any of you want to talk to me, you know where I'll be, but remember this, if one of those girls is there first, they are first. If the boat needs tending, it's first, and I'm last. You sorry bunch of . . ." That was where I stopped.

I was just outside the door when preacher put his hand on my shoulder.

"Well, Boots, you haven't changed. You're still Boots, and you act like him. You're right. Maybe it is us that needs take a hard look at ourselves. I agree. It's awful easy to sit and let someone else run the boat, do the maintenance, work the deck, and try to make these girls feel better about themselves."

I interrupted him, "I thought you were a real preacher type? From what I've seen and heard, you can talk the talk, but with these girls,

Preacher, you can't walk the walk. Did you think your job was over when you left the palace? Man, do your god damned job, Preacher! Help them and their souls, because I assure you, sir, they are in pain! All I can do is try to help. I didn't go to a god damned school to learn it. What? At your church you don't have souls in torture, or is it that they are just whores? Or, better yet, they are not black whores, and if you fire on me, so help me God, Preacher, I'll give you a thrashing, you my friend, will never forget! So, all y'all go think about what I just said, and if you can't find the truth of it, the clan is dead! We will bury it!" I turned and without a further word, I went to do the job that no one else wanted to do.

I sat down, but was so worked up, that I figured something would soon force me to get up. I got up and turned to go down the steps, and there was Helvi.

"Boots, I'm sorry. I should have been so much more involved in helping you, and especially the girls."

I snapped, "You are damned right! You should have been! All y'all should have been able to see the sheet instead of the mattress! What you did, Helvi, was superficial at most, and that's always sad. Still, if you meant what you said, and mean your apology, I accept it gladly, but don't lurk around behind my starboard side. If you want something, or need to know something, you don't slink around looking for leverage. Okay?"

Quietly, she answered, "Okay."

I started out the door, "If you will excuse me, I need some coffee and I don't want the girls to know how thoroughly angry and disgusted I am, so I'll get my own coffee."

Helvi headed for the door saying, "No, Boots, I will get it. I am so sorry."

I said nothing and wouldn't be saying much to anyone, but the girls for a couple of days. I wanted to know more about them anyways.

CHAPTER TWENTY-EIGHT

It has been an interesting time. I have learned a lot from each one of the girls, except Anna. She was the last girl I talked to and she just looked down and didn't talk back. I'm afraid I had to know why and kept asking until I fear we were both sick of the question. In the end, I gave up. It wasn't too long after that, Francie came up to the bridge. I asked her why Anna didn't talk.

She seemed a little surprised. "Didn't anyone else tell you, Boots? She can't speak. Her voice box was ruined as a small child, so when she talks, it sounds horrid!"

"Is that all? Can she read?" I asked.

Francie said excitedly, "Yes, she can and she can even spell!" I was sure that if she could read and spell, she could write. So, when Francie grew bored with me and went to leave, I asked her to tell Anna that I would like to see her again, please, but there would be no questions.

When she walked in, I handed her a note. It simply said, "Good morning and how do you feel today?"

A huge smile broke across her face. Suddenly, this sad girl turned into a much happier young lady. She wrote her answer, "I am sorry I cannot speak. Am ashamed very much. Good morning, Boots. I am well, and much happier now. I can write-talk to you. I love you. You save me."

I wrote back, "Thank you, Anna. How did you lose your power of speech?"

Slowly she wrote out, "I been nine years old and got very sick. Could hardly hear and no could speak. Parents not think Anna good child. Give to orphanage people, and you save me. Thank you, Boots. From bottom of heart. Now, maybe I have not for a place to live, to go back to. I go back to live at orphanage."

I shook my head and wrote quickly, "I don't think so. I wrote your Mama and Papa. They could not find you. You were gone. They want to find you and are coming to France to see you. If they should decide they don't want you, I will take you and make you my daughter."

She looked deeply into my eyes, I believe all the way to my soul, and wrote, "No can tell if parents want Anna, but happy I am if you take me away. Maybe parents good. If not, you take Anna."

I read the note, and as I quickly as I could, wrote back, "In a Moscow minute!"

She just jumped up and hugged me tight, and I hugged her back. It was an overwhelming feeling, and an emotional day for me.

There was much to write in my journal while I sat in my skipper's chair. Helvi came back in and went straight to bed without a word. I pulled the drapes on the day bunk shut. The night wore on until 02:00 hours. I awoke at 05:22 hours, in my chair. I slowly stretched and stood. Quietly, I turned and went down to the galley for coffee. When I brought it up, Helvi was checking course and gauges.

Helvi said, "Everything checked perfect as usual, Boots."

I replied, "You got one great boat, Helvi."

Helvi smiled, "Thank you."

I told her, "You're very welcome. I assure you it is truly a fine vessel, for her age. How old is she?"

She answered, "She was built in 1910. She's eighty-seven years old."

I said, "She looks just like new."

She laughed a little, "I had her completely gone through and fixed last year."

I answered, "It doesn't matter, Helvi. She's a fine sailboat."

Suddenly she said, "God, Boots! It's my turn."

I smiled, "That would be nice, at least for a couple of hours. I'm beat down."

She replied, "It's okay, Boots, I don't really mind. I love this boat."

I could see why. It had been built for her grandfather before World War I. If this boat could talk! Wow! What stories she could tell.

I crawled into the bunk with that thought on my mind, and the faint smell of Helvi's perfume. It seemed as if I had just closed my eyes, when my night of sleep was through. Morning had once again come with a scream, and an immediate return to consciousness. This was normal for me, but not for most people. I struggled to completely wake up and get dressed. I did not hurry. I stepped out from behind the curtain and was hit with the aroma of fresh coffee.

"Helvi, my girl. You knew, didn't you?"

She smiled brightly, "I've grown accustomed to your waking, and here's your coffee."

I replied, "Thank you, my girl."

She nodded and said, "You're welcome."

I glanced at my watch. It was 06:30 hours in the morning. The air seemed close, so I opened the wing hatches and then the roof vent. It began to clear, or was it just my head? I'll never know.

It was a beautiful morning on the sea, and I was pleased with the company on this boat. I looked out off the port beam. I saw another sailboat on much the same course as the Valkyrie. She was faster, albeit she probably was not as comfortable. I heard the stirrings of life below deck, and knew that today was another good day.

I glanced out over the vessel. There were already two girls on deck, happy that they could do so, I'm sure. I called and waved to them. Svetlana and Francie waved and smiled back.

What can be said of Svetlana more than I have already said? I found her to be a remarkable young woman. For all of her troubles, she shows very little pain, and her outlook towards the future seems to be much brighter to me. She was looking forward to a reunion with her mother in New York, USA. Gregor has a lot of pull and friends. The transition for Svetlana should go off without a hitch.

After the fifth day out, Slick called to let me know all of the girls families were going to be in Marseille.

He told me, "After all, the paperwork will be done. It will take about three hours for everyone, plus the ship. Do not, my friend, forget to get rid of the garbage!"

I replied, "No problem, Slick."

He asked, "Where are you?"

I told him, "About half way there. Between one-hundred-fifty to two-hundred-twenty-five miles off and North of La Goruna, Spain."

Slick sounded pleased, "Well, you are making fair time. Thank you for getting the girls names and home towns, Boots. That was all I needed on this end to make it happen."

I laughed, "Well, my friend, you needed them, and these girls need people to love them."

"That's for sure!" he replied, "It's pretty much in the bag, Boots. Only one more family to get here. They leave tomorrow."

Everything was back on course.

There were a few more things that I was curious about. I asked him, "Hey, Slick. Any news from Holland?"

"Yeah," he said, "It seems there was a gas leak, or something, and a subsequent explosion at some entertainment house, but there were no reports of deaths."

I smiled to myself, "That's good that no one was killed. Have to watch those gas leaks, or whatever! I was just wondering what was going on at home."

Slick answered, "Well, sure you would, Boots. When do you expect to dock?"

I replied, "In the morning, in nine or ten days, if nothing unforeseen happens."

He was quick to reply, "We will be waiting. Everything is in order and part of the wedding party is already here."

I told him, "Can't wait, Slick."

He said, "That's a positive vote for both of us, Boots. See you on the flipside."

I responded, "On the other side, brother," and the connection was broken.

There was a time that I was alone in the wheelhouse when little Francie came in. She seemed a little sad and distant, so I asked her why.

With tears welling in her eyes, she said, "Boots, I don't know if I can go home. It was my fault."

I asked, "What was your fault, little one?"

One large tear rolled down her cheek. "I went to where my mother told me not to, I went into the city alone. That was where it happened. Where I got lost for so long, and was taken away. I think my mother will hate me for disobeying, and my father will be ashamed."

I was just a little taken aback by Francie's thoughts. "Little one," I said, "I don't think anyone will hate you. And, if you were my daughter I would not be ashamed of you. I would be glad to have you home where you belong, and I would love you and take care of you. Your mother and father love you, and have been scared for you. It will be fine, little one. I promise, by the

blood of my ancestors. I promise, you'll be fine."

She sniffed a little, "Thank you, Boots."

I replied softly, "You're welcome, baby. Now get to bed. It's late young lady."

She hopped up and answered with a smile, "Okay, Boots. Goodnight."

I said, "Goodnight, little one." I watched her leave, still the little girl, and I felt my own tear fall for her.

It was much the same with every girl, except Anna. She was almost defiant. In some ways, she could not be blamed. According to her story, she was either sold or given to an orphanage, and when the time was right she was sold to the Mafia. So, to say the least, she was extremely apprehensive about the outlook for her future. I had made her a promise, and I would keep it. If nothing else, I would take this extraordinary girl home with me and she would become my daughter. It made me wonder what went through people's minds when they undertook to change facts by getting rid of the truth of a less than perfect child, even if it was well intentioned. It is a sad state of affairs for parents to trade a child in on a better future for themselves, with less trouble and hassle.

Things onboard this vessel had begun to calm down some, but only in the way that all the occupants of the Valkyrie seemed to be one big happy family. There seemed to be far more understanding of the girl's situation. The clan was interacting somewhat with the girls, and they responded with much enthusiasm. It was fun watching the girls play and just reach out to seek recognition and approval. Time passed, and I began to see a vast change not only in my girls, but in the way my guys responded. I watched these somewhat introverted and vindictive girls, become more outgoing and less suspicious of everyone. It was for me, extremely pleasant and satisfying, to say the least.

We were seventy-three hours out of Marseille. It was Monday. The time was 08:20 hours and we are seventy-six miles from the Straits of Gibraltar. The weather is incredible. I can see why people like the weather in this part of the region. It is warm and clear, at least at this time of year. I was moving across the many shipping lanes. I was careful, of course, but it looked like New York or Los Angeles at traffic hour. As I turned to port on my heading towards the straits, I saw the girls were on deck. While I watched, I thought of how many eyes there could be out there.

I had to make a decision to either risk the watchers, and maybe fight, or ask the girls to go below and remain there until the waters widened out. At its narrowest point, the charts indicated that from shoreline to shoreline it's approximately seven miles wide. However, the traffic channel is far narrower. It is three point six miles. All shipping in and out of the Mediterranean Sea are lifelines into a huge amount of seaports from Spain to Turkey. I considered all of the factors and decided that the girls on deck could be an attraction, but there was nothing here to tie this boat, or us to any part of the world. They could stay on deck. It was a risk, but after what we had already accomplished, and the risks we had already taken, it didn't seem to matter. Until they stop criminal activities, there will be those of us willing to use it to our advantage.

Six point nine hours and we should be abreast of Gibraltar and into the Mediterranean. Well, once again into the breach, dear friends, and we would win through, or they would regret the day they met the clan! The sails were reset and adjusted so our tacking would present a minimum of risk. If it was not feasible, we would revert to the lugger and a few sails. That way we could at least maintain eight to eleven knots. But, the winds were kind and we sailed on into the straits and into the night. It was an accomplishment to get this far, but much remained to be done, and there were many more miles to be sailed.

The hours slowly passed without notice. Every one of them as a star on our way to reunite these girls with their families. I had taken to being just a little reclusive after the big blow out, and yet I never felt like that with the girls. Someone had to be more interested in them than just rescuing them. Since I'm not a shrink, but having worked with quite a few of them in my recovery cases that I've been involved with, I knew they would need reassurance that they were normal and valuable to themselves and to others. They could do that by just being themselves and not worrying about their past, although I'm sure the memories would remain for their lifetimes. Mine still haunt me. It should not override the fact that they were valuable human beings. If I can reinforce that, I will have helped to start them on their long road home, besides the free ride.

Seventy-six miles seemed to come and go very quickly. It seemed like morning was just a minute ago. In fact, 15:50 hours was the time, and we would be fully into the Mediterranean. We would be changing course to steer clear of Algeria and since we needed to be approximately one-hundred-fifty miles off the coast, it would put us in a perfect position to turn to port almost one-hundred degrees on our last leg into Marseille. I planned to call Slick when we were abeam of Majorca, Spain to see what was up. As I said, it was an interesting spectacle to watch the slow change of formerly imprisoned humans stretch their wings. When we went into the Mediterranean the mood seemed to change. I couldn't put my finger on what it was, but it was there, nonetheless. It bothered me to a degree. There seemed to be a veil falling over every one.

Most of the time I remained in the wheelhouse, and no one else really wanted to be there. I had asked, but no volunteers, except for

Helvi. Even she was apparently changing. I began to listen to the whispers throughout the boat and it became louder, the truth of the matter. When we were coming close to Majorea was the clan wanting to be done with it, and the girls had a great trepidation of returning to their families.

The only one that was more introspective about this was Anna. She began to spend time in the wheelhouse. We wrote questions and answers back and forth between us. She asked if I

believed her story to which I replied, "Yes. To a point."

She wrote, "What do you mean?"

I wrote back, "Your parents were trying to get you an education."

She scowled and wrote, "Well, I did not get one there!"

I continued, "I know. Where your parents sent you was supposed to be a boarding school. Your parents did not discover

you were not there for seven months."

She scribbled, "Must have made them happy."

I sighed and wrote, "I do not think so. You were listed on the international registry for missing children in Russia. This seems to be happening a lot. I know people from America that have adopted children from Russia. The magic number seems to be thirty-thousand American dollars and all court costs and bribes." I felt somehow I had to make her understand her parents did not know how Anna would end up.

Anna frowned and wrote, "That does not seem to be a very good thing for the children."

I wrote, "I don't think it is, but sometimes people have kids they can't help or feed, and believe they are better off in an orphanage. There are those who do not want their children. On the other hand, there are people with money who want to buy children. Big collective farmers in Russia and Eastern Europe buy children to work and treat them like livestock. When the children die from overwork and being underfed, the farmers just buy more."

"How could anyone think like that, Boots?"

I shook my head, "I don't know, baby. You know what happens to most of the children? They are bought at a nominal price, or stolen. They are used like you were, or as personal sex slaves, until their owners grow tired of their toy and dispose of it, only to buy another."

Anna looked sad. "Yes. I know of this. Two women across the hall from us. It happened to them. They have no one, so they stay. I would like to change that Boots, somehow."

She still had compassion for others. I wrote slowly and carefully, "If you want to, you can do anything. I live by two rules. Number one, failure is not an option. Number two, death before dishonor. I'm not saying to die. I just do not believe in negative ideals. If you want to do it, do it. You can. No question other than that needs to be asked. I believed I could get Svetlana away from the Mafia and I did, but much to my pleasure I got you, and the others with her. It wasn't more satisfying, it was just a greater victory over the inhumanity that is the cause behind this evil crime. Remember, Anna, some people view me as a criminal, and it does not bother me. If I am a criminal for fighting this crime, well, so be it. I use their crimes against them and I'm good with that." I felt she needed to know this.

Her eyes widened as she wrote, "Are you ever afraid?"

I answered, "I don't think so. I am not sure. I have never thought about it much. I probably won't think about it."

As she transcribed, I looked at this young lady wondering, just wondering. Finally, I read her note.

"I was almost too afraid to come with you, but Francie and Svetlana said it was a chance to escape from where we were and maybe from you."

I thought for a moment. I answered, "If I meant you any harm, I wouldn't have come for you, but I can understand why you would be afraid."

She smiled and wrote, "Thank you, Boots, for talking to me."

I smiled back and replied, "I talk to all human beings. It is people I hate. People are not always human, little one."

With that exchange, she got down off the second's chair, kissed me on the cheek, and ran out the door. I knew what was partially wrong on the boat. It was the apprehension of these young ladies. Why they were in that state was unknown to me, but I was sure it would become apparent. For some reason I felt it too, and couldn't explain it.

The night wore on. It was past the time when everyone else would be sound asleep, or close to it. The radar screen was entirely too full for me to get any rest, yet if I turned on the alarm it would sound endlessly, so why bother. It was getting late with no let up on the radar, but I would find myself only catnapping. As the morning of day thirteen came up, with its customary scream, I suddenly realized I was still strapped into the skipper's seat. The straps were to keep the helmsmen from being thrown out of the chair in very bad weather. I unbuckled and turned around. There was Helvi asleep on the bunk, and she wasn't alone. There were three girls in that bunk with her. How they all fit I will never know! It was just a mass of arms and legs. I had to leave before my laughing woke them up.

CHAPTER TWENTY-NINE

It was 04:00 hours in the morning, and far too early for a general reveille, although I did, I'm sure, smell fresh coffee. I walked into the galley and there was Svetlana, Francie, and Anna. They were all drinking coffee and talking.

When I drew close I said, "A penny for your thoughts, ladies."

Svetlana spoke abruptly, "How far away are we from Marseille?"

I glanced at my watch and tried to think. "In two hours we will be making our port cut to Marseille and in twenty-five hours we should be in Marseille. That means at approximately 09:00 hours tomorrow, ladies, just twenty-nine hours from now. I will be calling Slick in four hours. Why?"

Francie said, "Boots, we want to go home but were afraid. Everyone knows what has happened to us and what we had to do."

I replied, "Only your family knows, kids."

Francie piped up, "We know, Boots, but it feels weird and scary. They are going to try to change us back into little girls."

Here was the veil. The crux of what has happened to my girls. They didn't know how to be young girls anymore, for very obvious reasons.

I took a deep breath and began to speak. "I don't think ladies with no thought of what you've all been through, but if you like, I can talk to them and explain. The problem is that they have no reason to listen to me. As you will probably find out when you are back with your family, my name will never be mentioned again. I will become as hated as the men who had you. You see, girls, I represent the bad part of your past. I remind families that what happened to you was real. Most people do not want anyone or anything around them that reminds them it was real. Most people don't want the truth. They want to be lied to. But, along with this comes your right to obliterate it from your minds also. No one wants to know, so you will not tell them, and in turn, you will forget me, I hope." I needed them to know it was alright.

I continued, so I could get it all out. "Yes, girls. I hope you forget me, and if you are lucky you might even hate the thought of me. Please understand that it is all right to do that. I accept that with a modicum of humility. All I need to know is that I got you back and that you will be the best humans you can be. I know this to be true. I will talk to your parents and explain that, but when I hug you and say goodbye, that's what it means. I will remember each of you with happiness in my heart and hope that you're doing well, but I will never know because you will go on with your lives. So, don't worry about going back. You will do just fine. I have faith in my kids, all of them, and you are my kids."

As our coffee meeting broke up, I glanced at my watch. I had been down here for over an hour and I needed to get back to the wheelhouse. I grabbed another mug of coffee and a headed to the bridge. When I got there I found Mariah at the helm.

I got to the bridge deck and she looked at me and announced, "Everything is all right, Boots."

I was amazed. "How did you know what to do, Mariah?"

She smiled, "My father has a fishing boat. Not so beautiful as this one, but I run his boat with him."

I thought, "Well, will wonders never cease!" I told her, "Thank you very much, Mariah. I had not meant to be gone this long."

She gave me a sidelong look. "I hear you talking to the girls.

I am one of your kids, yes?"

I softly told her, "Yes, dear, you are. I will remember you until the day I go to the next world."

She smiled, "I think that is very good for me. Maybe God also forgive me, for what happened to me."

I asked her, "Why would he have to? Did you go on purpose?"

She looked down at her feet, "No. I go to dance and wake up there."

"So," I said directly, "I don't think you have to worry about God blaming you. How do you think your father will act?" She said, "I hope he is happy, but I am now whore." "Why would that be?" I asked her.

She retorted, "Because of what I do!"

I told her, "That does not make you a whore, Mariah. Is a soldier a murderer if he is told to kill people in war?"

She answered, "No, he is a very brave soldier."

That is where I cut in, "And I think you are a very brave girl!"

She replied, "I believe my father will not think like that. I don't know, Boots, but I will find out when I get home."

I had made up my mind to talk to all of these girls. We would be docking in less than thirty hours, so I would do that this afternoon, just before 15:00 hours. About eighteen hours before we should be docking. I hoped.

I took over the helm from my seventeen-year-old assistant and scooted her down below to take care of herself, and to eat. She had just gone down the stairs with a smile. God! They were such kids! I checked the course and made a slight adjustment to it. I began to hum to myself. Not any song, just humming. When I realized I was humming it suddenly became apparent that pleasure can come to us in many ways. Mine was being happy about what I do. Many of my extended family believes I have wanderlust, and they couldn't be more incorrect. I don't desire nor feel a need to travel. Actually, it is not one of my most favorite things to do. But, if you give me a kid or someone in need of me or what I can do, I'm there!

There have only been four times I've received pay for anything. It got dumped into what I do. My wife understands it and stands for it, but it hasn't been easy on her, I'm sure. But, it's true. I get pleasure from the things I do. There's no rush, or anything like that. It just makes me happy, and my humming got louder.

I looked into the radar and saw a very interesting picture of too many ships and boats in this place. We were not in danger, but I would have to be constantly vigilant to make sure. With the wheelhouse empty, I turned on the regular radio and was listening to classic rock music from the sixty's and seventy's. Francie came up and asked me where that music came from.

I told her, "I'm not sure, but I grew up with this music."

She giggled and said, "It's that old, Boots?"

I smiled broadly, "Yes, dear. It's that old. You know, back when dinosaurs were alive."

She squinted and said, "You're not that old, Boots!"

I told her, "On the contrary, my dear. I am older than even the dinosaurs!"

She laughed her rather musical laugh and then went somewhere.

I was just sitting there, when the radiotelephone came to life. The land station was calling Valkyrie. I turned the music down and answered.

Slick came on the air, loud and clear. "Boots, my brother. How goes the battle?"

I answered, "Fine, I think, but Slick, how many in the wedding party?"

He said loudly, "It's a full house, except the well wishers from New York. They send their condolences, but await your return to the states with your new bride."

I replied, "That was nice of them."

He asked, "When do you expect to arrive?"

I told him, "We should be in the harbor at about 08:40 hours, Slick. Is my slip ready?"

He answered, "It will be."

I asked, "And how will I find it?"

He boldly stated, "You will have no trouble, my friend. It is well marked with red, white, blue, and pink balloons and

streamers. The name on the dock is Exodus."

I laughed, "How apropos, Slick."

He laughed, "I thought so too."

Seriously, I asked him, "Slick, have you been with the people in the party?"

He said, "Yes, Boots, I have."

"What are their moods like? My bride is very apprehensive about everyone who might misjudge her."

He replied, "I don't think she needs to worry. They are very levelheaded and do not seem to be overly judgmental, nor do they expect too much, but much happiness. Assure your bride that she will be welcomed without question." I felt relief. "Okay, Slick. Anything else?"

He kind of snickered, "Yes, Boots. You might be surprised at who is attending the welcoming, my friend." That was something to think about.

"You got it, Slick. See you on the flipside."

He replied, "On the other side, my brother." And he was clear and gone off the air, but I had received the information that I needed.

I was glad that Slick had called. He always seemed to know the appropriate time to get involved in my life. We had worked together many times in the past, and I will look forward to working with Slick in the future. I have always figured, you can never have too many people you can count on, and also call friend and brother. We were so close that at different times we had shared pints of each other's blood, and we had both been glad to give it. One of us was there when the chips were down for the other.

It was 15:25 hours. I wanted to talk to the girls before arrival, which was only eighteen hours to port and docking. I called them all together and sat them down in the salon area. I just looked at them. I was forming a mental picture to keep. After all, I do have a photographic memory.

As I locked this picture in my memory forever, I said, "Girls, I do not know if I will be able to, or have time to tell you, each and every one of you, how proud I am that I had the opportunity to help in rescuing all of you and how much I've come to love each and every one of you. You, my kids, are exceptional in every way. I will never be able to let you know just how much I admire each of you. I wanted to tell you how each one of you gave me just a small piece of your soul, and in turn, there's a piece of my soul in each of you. You are my kids now, so I expect you to act like it. Remember, I will always love you." They were silent, but I could see tears welling in their eyes.

I looked around, and then continued. "Today I talked to Slick. He assured me, after talking to all of your families, that the only thing of any importance to them is that you get home. Mariah, you worried. Don't. Your papa doesn't care about anything but getting you home. None of them care, ladies. So, relax. Svetlana, your Mama will pick you up from the airport. I will be flying with you to assure your arrival. I want you girls to feel free to come see me if you need to. Any time until eight in the morning. After that, I'll be busy navigating into the harbor. Anybody want to talk? No? You all seemed to be a little shocked. Don't be, it's going to be fine. I will see you later, my girls."

With that, I went to the bridge and then to the wing deck. There, I cried at losing my kids, and cried because it looked like I would indeed get them where they belonged. At home and safe once again.

I came back into the wheelhouse, there was Svetlana sitting one seat over from mine. I regained my seat and looked at the radar.

Finally, she spoke, "Boots?"

I glanced over at her, "Yeah, baby?"

She asked, "Will I like America?"

I laughed slightly, "I think we've talked about this, Svetlana."

She giggled coyly, "Yes, but I like to hear about it."

I gave her a big smile, "Well, let me tell you, I think you will like America, because I'm sure America will love you. I see wonderful things in your future. I've told you you're beautiful, and along with that beauty you have a truly beautiful heart. That's a hard combination to beat, at least where I come from. I don't know if it will make a difference to you, but I would think every self-respecting American young man will want to buy you dinner and marry you. But, always remember it is your choice. Only you can submit any part of you that you're willing to give. You do not have to sleep with anyone unless you want to and it is certain that men will love and cherish you, so it will be up to you as to how you act." I hoped she would understand how special she was.

She smiled sweetly and said, "Thank you, Boots. You seem to know what to say when it's needed."

I took her hand and said, "Svetlana, let me tell you this, you are almost a full year younger than either of my own children. In fact, you are just of the age, you could be one of my children. So, I feel especially close to you. Maybe it's because I am close with Nadia and Daria, and when I met your mother, I knew somehow you were special. I was very right about you and it makes me feel happy inside to help you and your friends. I am honored and feel privileged to do this work."

She looked at me with admiration in her eyes, "I love you, Boots."

I told her gently, "I love you too, baby."

With that, she jumped up and gave me a quick hug. She gave me a kiss on the cheek and said, "I'll see you later, Boots."

I replied, "Okay, baby."

As she drifted down and away from me, I thought, I am happy. I looked up and then at the radar. I looked at my watch and hit the loran readout. I figured it was my turning time. It was eleven minutes until I pulled a port turn for one-hundred-two degrees and we would be on the downhill leg. The short one. We were going downhill. Ten, nine, eight, seven, six, five, turn. The turn started and finished. The boat had done well. Now, we were only twelve hours and fifteen minutes out of the harbor.

It was a very uneventful night, other than the girls getting just the right clothes out for meeting each of the excited parents. The clothes were picked and showers were taken. They all had to have their hair done, but like they said, makeup and fingernail polish could be done in the morning. In some ways, it was a lot like sending my daughters to the senior prom. I wished now I had gotten them nicer clothes, but I had no idea at the onset that it would be such an event. But, then again, I had no idea that I would wind up with seven girls instead of one, either!

As it grew later and things began to quiet down, Preacher came up. It was only the third time since we had been waterborne that he had come to the wheelhouse. When he came through the door, I asked him, "What's up, Preacher?"

He shifted from one leg to the other nervously. "Not much, Boots. I came here to tell you I am sorry for not being more responsive to the girls needs. It had nothing to do with their color, but you were right, about there not being any ladies of the night at our church. They don't stay. No one will tolerate them, including me."

I retorted sharply, "Well, Preacher, these girls were not hookers or whores by their own volition. As far as your church not liking or allowing them access to the church body because of their past, it is sanctimonious and unchristian behavior. Remember who it was that helped a harlot to her feet, forgave her, and told her to go and sin no more. He offered to let anyone kill her if that person had done no wrong. She was spared and forgiven. She became a loyal follower of the man who saved her and was his constant companion, as well as his mother's. So, my friend, as I say to doctors, physician heal thyself! I tell you, Preacher, save yourself!"

His face tightened and he lowered his head and apologized again. A few minutes later I heard him apologizing to my girls.

With that little tiff settled once and for all, the boat was getting silent. The only noise came from the galley area. I glanced at the radar and I saw no targets. We were out of the normal lanes of traffic, heading in towards Marseille. I would only have to watch for the ferry from Barcelona to Genoa Italy. With a few free minutes I felt I could take a break.

I went down the stairs and into the galley. Helvi was there drinking coffee. I said happily, "A penny for your thoughts, babe, and is there more coffee?"

She smiled and said, "Plenty of coffee here," and she poured me a cup.

I only saw sleeping people around us.

She said, "Let's go to the wheelhouse."

I replied, "Suits me."

She was first up the stairs and I followed her on up to our private cabin that was never quite empty. Not even late at night, as Helvi slept up there also.

I wondered what she had on her mind.

Hesitantly, she spoke, "Boots?"

I answered, "Yes, Helvi."

She began again, "We have brought this boat all the way here and it's been fun, but who will sail her home?"

I asked, "Do you want to take her back right away?"

Helvi's eyes widened, "Oh no! We're going to spend six months to a year here."

I smiled, "Why don't you just sail her home?"

She shook her head, "I don't know if I can."

I laughed, "I am sure you can if you want to, if you don't, I'll talk to Slick. He will give you a number to call and he will arrange for a skipper to take her home."

She looked at me hopefully, "Do you think you can do it?"

I thought of where I might be in six months to a year. "I don't know, Helvi. When you're ready, call. If I'm available, I'll do it for you, but I can't say for sure if I will even be home, so I don't know. I guess we'll cross that bridge when it comes up. Okay?"

She smiled, "Okay, Boots."

I smiled at Helvi. "Well, Helvi. You've been on an operation. What do you think? Want to do it again?"

She took a deep breath in, and exhaled slowly, "I don't think so, Boots. There's too much to think about and a lot to do and you don't make any money."

I cut in, "And it's no way to find a husband, have kids, and get rich. Is that about it?"

She replied softly, "Yeah, that's about it."

I nodded and understood, "I thought so. Lots of people have good intentions, Helvi, but this type of work isn't what it seems to be. It's different when you're into it. Don't worry about not wanting to do it full time. There's a misconception to this job. When you first get involved, you think of it as noble, heroic, and I guess it is. In some ways. But, it takes dedication to do these things, because you have to live the ideals that you're working from." I felt it was important for her to know that I realized this was not the life for everyone.

I continued even though I felt Helvi was uncomfortable with the subject. "It's not glorious. It's not a job that you do to be famous for, or make money at. To most people it would mean including their moral obligations to each other, and to the ideal of doing what's right, just because it's right. That is a lot to ask. People do things because it is a way to make money, rather than because it's the right thing to do. Like I said, it's not a job most people would want to invest their time in, or dedicate their life to. I can't blame them, but then there are people like me, who think about those things they could have if they had money. It is far less important to them than the ability and dedication to do what is right. They do it along with their families. Who do without the best of things and make do with those things that can be afforded at the time, because a job needs to be done. Honestly, Helvi, it's all right."

She really had nothing to say. She just said, "I will see you later, Boots," and pulled the curtains shut for privacy.

I set the proximity alarms on the radar and clicked the autopilot on. I made sure it was set on dodge. I could recline in my chair and try to get some sleep. The morning came once again with a scream at 05:20 hours. "Damn!" I thought. I looked around and saw no vessels. I looked in the radar and there was no traffic. I checked the loran and got a reading. I referenced it to the chart. I was roughly twelve miles past the ferry to Genoa, Italy. We were indeed forty-four miles out. It was getting close and I was pleased.

I turned to see if Helvi had company, but saw she wasn't in the bunk. I headed on down and into the galley. There was no one there, but the boat was full of sleeping bodies where they were supposed to be. I decided to make some coffee. I got the pot and grounds, put it on the burner, and sat to wait for it to perk. It wasn't long until my nose was pleasantly being teased by the aroma of the fresh brew, and I could hardly wait to pour it down my throat. After it was done and had sat, I filled two mugs and took them up to the wheelhouse. I got comfortable and began to drink my coffee. Before long, Helvi came up.

She looked at me sternly and said, "You have my mug and it is full of coffee."

I kind of smiled and asked, "What did you want in it?"

She replied flatly, "Coffee."

I responded, "Well?"

She said, "Well, I'm having coffee with Heilgrid."

I answered, "Okay." I couldn't help but think, "If her sensibilities have been challenged, so be it. Have a good time." She said nothing more. She took her cup and left.

I went to shave and shower and put some nice clothes on. Not fancy. I just looked like a captain ought to look. By the time I was through and dressed and back in my chair with more coffee in hand, we had traveled approximately twelve miles. I was just sitting there enjoying my coffee when the radiotelephone came alive calling the Valkyrie. When I answered I found out it was Slick.

"Good morning, boss."

I answered, "Good morning. What can I do for you today, Slick?"

Happily he cried, "Bring that boat to port, Boots! How far out are you?"

I replied, "Approximately thirty miles, Slick."

He chuckled, "Damn, Boots! You do this every time. You pick your time and you make it!"

I laughed, "I don't know about that, but thank you, Slick. How far out do we dump the garbage?"

Turning serious, he stated, "Less the little stuff, five miles Boots. I'll see you at five miles out. So don't blow us out of the water, Boots."

I answered, "Cool Slick. How will you be marked?"

He said, "Large streamers. One red, one blue, and three whites. When you see it, make sure you dump the garbage, okay?"

I answered, "Okay, Slick. Anything else?"

Hesitantly, he said, "Yes and no, but it's not important."

When Slick held back it was usually not good. Well, one way or another I needed to know. "Tell me anyway, Slick."

He started slowly, "Boots, I don't know how to tell you, but these families are going to have a small gathering. Everyone's invited but you."

I was pretty quick to answer, "I figured that, Slick. It happens almost every time just like this. Don't tell anyone else, brother, but at least have a drink with me."

I heard him sigh, "That's no problem, Boots. You're not too upset?"

I did not want him to know that sometimes, it did bother me.

"No, not at all," I said.

He answered, "Well, I'll let the families know."

I asked him, "Slick, take care of Svetlana for me. Will you?"

He said, "That's not a problem, Boots."

His words came as a relief to me. "Thanks, Slick."

He answered, "You're welcome, Boots."

I told him, "See you on the flipside, Slick."

He replied, "On the other side, my brother." And the call ended.

"Well," I thought, "they want to start forgetting right away. Well, hell! That's fine. If that's what they want, that's what they'll get. It was probably better that way anyway. Yup, that's it." I decided to call Slick back. When the call went through I asked, "Where's everyone staying until their flights, Slick?"

He answered, "Everybody, families, girls they are all in the same hotel. It's very nice."

I asked him, "Will you get me another place to stay?"

He answered, "Boots, I thought you knew?"

I questioned, "What Slick?"

Laughing, he said, "My brother, you and Svetlana are staying at my château."

I was a little taken aback. "No, I had no idea Slick."

He continued, "When the parties over, I will bring Svetlana to you. Don't worry, I will not be alone, as you will not be alone."

That was Slick, always on the lookout for a friend. "Okay, Slick. See you on the flipside."

He answered, "On the other side, brother."

Well, that was settled. It's not that I hold ill feelings toward the families. They are right. The sooner I'm gone the better it is for them, as well as me. I had to change gears here and now.

Time wore on and I found myself getting excited about being on terra firma again, and getting rid of these sea legs. We were five and a half miles out of port, when a blip came on the radar screen. I called the clan in the boat and told them it was time to put out the garbage. "The battle rifles go. All accounted for magazines, ammunition, everything over the side but the forty calibers, boys. And make sure you only keep three magazines each. Everything else, over the side." As it went over, we marked off the garbage checklist.

We were three-hundred yards from the maneuvering French harbor master's boat. I dropped the sails and furled them. The boat drew up alongside. The harbor master, customs, and immigration came aboard, and so did Slick. Those men I recognized, but one other man came with them.

As Slick walked to me, he held out his hand and smiled, "My friend, you have done it once again. Let us start the motor and head on into port and the docks. You look quite well, and not too much the worse for the heavy wear, my brother. How do you feel?"

I shook his hand firmly and stated, "Pretty damn good, Slick. Pretty damn good."

Slick leaned over slightly and in a barely audible whisper said, "Wait till I can talk to you in a more private place without ears. These men are here at the request of a high official of France. By the time we get to the dock, my brother, this boat and everyone on board will have gotten here legal like, with all the proper stamps and papers for you and your personnel, and personal weapons. These are not allowed in France unless you have a permit, which, my brother, I took care of on the second day I was home."

I told him, "I thank you, my brother. And for all of this, I owe you my life. For all you are doing."

He smiled broadly, "You, my brother, are worth it all. For these seven lives you brought home. I will introduce you to my friend when he is done."

As I heard the lugger start up, I understood this was Slick's town and we were his personal guests. This man was truly my friend.

In a true whirlwind of activity it appeared, at least by my watch, to have taken approximately one and one half hours to have Valkyrie tied neatly in her slip. One of Slick's own. He had moved one of his boats to another marina. There on the dock was a name placard that said, "Exodus" and hanging over the Valkyrie's own name were temporary name plates saying "Exodus", just as Slick had promised. As usual, he was true to the letter of his word. While the paper processing continued, Slick handed me a license for handguns with a title of courier. It was signed off for two, forty caliber Smith & Wesson pistols and six magazines. I was not shocked, but amazed. Slick had said he was retired, but I had to wonder. After this came to light, it had taken an additional one hour and fifty-eight minutes to finish with visas and passports for the entire ship's company. I could not tell how it was done, but it was an assembly line approach. It was innovative and fast. Something one must get used to, with Slick in charge.

After good-byes were said and hugs given, the girls were taken to the cars, where they were joined by security forces and personal security. I watched as they disappeared into the distance. They would be traveling twenty-five minutes from here, to a very nice hotel on the bay in Toulon.

Sensing my discomfort, Slick told me, "It is not far from my home, but not to worry, Boots. Some of my friends are there to make sure the girls are secure."

That I could believe. Especially, if they were anything like the personnel that went with them in the cars as they left. I could believe that they were probably French Foreign Legion personnel. I didn't know for sure, and did not insult Slick by asking.

After about thirty minutes, Slick stood, looked at me, and reached out his hand to Svetlana. "Miss Svetlana, would you please come this way?"

When she didn't move, I stood and just said, "Come on, Toots. Let's go."

She stood, and we strolled up the gangplank to his car. We were not alone. There was a huge contingent of very serious looking fellows, who did not look like they would easily let anyone rain on this groups parade getting into Slick's Mercedes.

Before Svetlana, Slick, and I entered his car, Slick directed us over to another car. A black limousine with one man inside. I could see this because the door was open. He was not alone by any means. There was also a contingent of very tough and professional looking men surrounding his car. When we had approached within ten feet, the lone man stepped out of the backseat of the limousine. We stopped approximately five feet from this gentleman and Slick approached him. As Slick got very close to this man, I watched his hand come up. Likewise, this man's hand came up also. As they shook hands, I figured this was the man who Slick had said he wanted me to meet. The nameless man waved me forward towards him. When I was as close to him as Slick was, the introductions began.

Slick said, "Sir, this is the man you wanted to meet. His name is Boots."

He extended his hand, "Hello, Boots."

Shaking hands with him, I answered, "Hello, sir."

Slick smiled, "Boots, I would like to introduce you to the first assistant director of the French secret service."

I replied, "It is an honor, sir."

He smiled, "The feeling is much the same, Boots. Your exploits, my friend, are legendary!"

I laughed, "I hope not sir!"

Looking quite serious he said, "Well, they are! Trust me, it is in the right places here in France, Boots."

I felt truly honored, "Thank you, sir."

With that he bid us farewell and entered his car. It seemed like only seconds before he was gone. I had to wonder why this man wanted to meet me. I asked, "What gives with the big guy, Slick?"

He answered, "Boots, he is my former boss. When I retired from the service, the man you met was just above me. I've known him on a professional, as well as a personal level for many years. Since I've known you, I have told him of your exploits for years. At least since we started working together."

I was less than enthusiastic about his indiscretions in revealing what I do. However, this man worried me less than most. In his job, secrets were his business. I laughed, "Damn, Slick! You are connected way up on the food chain, my brother!"

His tone solemn, "He is the one who made it possible for the clan to work through France when needed. But, you have to understand, Boots, it is unofficial in an official way."

I just had to shake my head, "It's good to know the king, Slick, and you're the king."

We all got into Slick's Mercedes. As the driver whisked us away, I realized I had no idea where Slick lived. We left Marseilles and went along the coastal area going towards Toulon. Approximately one kilometer before Toulon, we turned right going towards the Mediterranean Sea. There it was, in the distance. A restored French château on a bluff overlooking the Mediterranean.

It was a gorgeous home, and as we approached the château, Slick made the comment that it was always a work in progress. His companion, Claudette, who as Slick said, "had been around long enough, that he was going to marry her!"

He said, "She is always changing things, Boots. Adding and moving. Sometimes, I think, is enough, and then she sees something, somewhere, that she wants to add to our home."

I laughed, "That's pretty normal, my brother. It happens at my home also," and we all laughed.

The car pulled up the long driveway. I found it to be a quite magnificent French château. Well done, and tastefully restored with many improvements, and many going on. We went in and were greeted by a quite beautiful French woman. The introductions were completed. I had met the lovely Claudette! I found out she had been with Slick for twenty years. Somehow, I did not find this to be far-fetched. There wasn't much tomcat in Slick, or me. We loved what awaited us at home.

Claudette showed me to my room, as she had previously done for Svetlana. She swept into the room. It was amazing and nice to see. She showed me everything, including the bath and the closet.

She said, "Here is your suit, Boots. Slick had it made for you."

I thought to myself, "Damn him. I hate suits and on this operation I've had to wear too many as it is, and now, oh, whatever."

I smiled at her, bowed, and said, "Thank you so much, Lady Claudette."

She smiled sweetly, curtsied, and answered, "You are quite welcome, sir Boots."

As I escorted this woman back down to the first floor, there was Slick, coffee in hand. "Here, my friend, you will have your coffee on my terrace."

We went out to the terrace. It was a startling view, to say the least. A view made even better with the company of my good friends.

There was a hint of concern in Slick's face when he stated, "It is a shame, my brother, you will not be at the hotel tonight. However, I do have a note from Francie's parents. I do not think they agreed with any of this business."

I heard a feminine voice behind us, "What business is this?"

I turned at the same time as Slick did, there standing in a startlingly beautiful, rosy red, summer dress was Svetlana.

I replied, "Nothing, little one."

She crossed her arms and said with a pout, "This I do not believe, Boots. You said you didn't lie, now what business is this?"

I turned and looked at Slick. He explained it all while Svetlana sat silent and stiff. After Slick explained everything, without a word she stood and left.

Slick turned back to me and asked, "What was that all about, Boots."

I told him, "It's really rather normal for parents to start cutting ties as fast as possible. I do not like it either, my brother."

He shook his head and stated, "To leave you out is not good form. Very bad. And that one has a temper, my friend." I told him I believed he was correct.

Slick put his hand on my shoulder and said, "As I was saying, Boots, if you would like, Claudette would like to have a special dinner for you. I will only be here for dinner, but, as you already know, I will be leaving later for a while. I will take Svetlana to this party, and the reunification of parents and young ladies. I think it will now turn out much different than the parents had planned." I knew in my heart it was true, and it was my fault for being there, and having our conversation overheard.

I tried to talk to Svetlana, but she would say very little. She was getting ready for a phone call from the states. Claudette had arranged for Sasha to call Svetlana, and time was very near for that call. When I left, she said nothing. The call came through and I could tell it made her very happy, and of course, she cried. It made all around her a little weepy, and I had to leave and find a less emotional environment.

As I was prone to do, I found the kitchen. Claudette was busy chopping and baking, and in general I thought too busy to talk. While I was getting coffee, something flashed in my head. A memory. Claudette was chattering away about something. I sat down and listened to her talking. There was an accent evident in her speech.

I summoned from my memory the language of my great grandfather's, and my family, and as I did, I uttered the phrase, "This kitchen smells like my mother's kitchen," in Baroque, a language of the Pyrenees.

She stopped and wide-eyed, she stared at me. She asked where I had learned that language.

I told her, "I learned it at my great-grandfather's knee and from the rest of my family."

She looked shocked. "But you live in America."

I laughed, "Yes, I do, but my family has been in America long before the Mayflower had been built."

She wiped her hands and said, "This is not possible. You speak Baroque. No one not from my home can speak this."

I smiled at her and stated, "It was there, that my family came from so many years ago, Claudette."

She rushed around to me and she hugged me. "It is not often, Boots, I hear the sound of our language."

I hugged her back, "It is true, Claudette, this language is not common, and to find someone from my birthright is rare indeed, and in truth it makes me feel very good."

She smiled and asked, "There are people in Louisiana who are called Cajun, Boots. Do you know of these people?"

I nodded, "Yes, it's in the line of my family."

She nodded energetically back, "It is the legend of the leaving! When Baroque knights left with their families to find peace once again in a new land."

I knew this story well. "Yes, I've heard this story from my great-grandfather, my grandfather, and from my father. It is one that I taught my children."

She smiled knowingly, "That is good, Boots, and it is good to find each other in far-flung places."

I inhaled deeply through my nose and upon smelling a delicious aroma, I asked, "What are you making Claudette?"

Running over to cover the pots, she smiled coyly and said, "I'm not telling you now, especially now. Does Slick know you're

Baroque?"

I said, "I don't know. I don't think it's ever come up."

Claudette answered, "He is not Baroque, and the people, they won't accept him."

I nodded, knowing how clannish Baroque families could be. "It is much the same with me, except my wife was accepted by my mother. That caused all of them to accept her. She is Russian."

She stated softly, "That would be very hard, but the Baroque hate the French, and the Basque, and the Spanish."

I touched her arm gently and said, "This I know Claudette, but let's not talk about hate right now."

She shook her head, "No, we should not talk about hate. Do not tell Slick. I will tell. It will be a big surprise for him. It will make him laugh."

Just then, Slick walked in. "I should have guessed where I would find you. In the kitchen where the coffee is."

I changed the subject immediately and asked, "How is Svetlana, Slick?"

He answered slowly, "She will be fine. She had a long talk with her mama. I think she is excited to be going home." Claudette looked quizzically at both of us. "You are both oafs! Of course she is excited. Why would she not be? She is free and going to the land of her dreams."

Well, she was right. What else can you say? Nothing. It made me feel happy inside.

I knew dinner was approaching, so I excused myself and went to my room. There, I proceeded to shave and shower. When I came out, my suit had been laid out for me. I dressed and came down the staircase and was greeted by a handsome French country gentleman. Suddenly, in floated Claudette, with Svetlana coming along directly behind her. My jaw must have been quite unattached, as Svetlana swirled into the room. She must have felt very good about herself and how she looked. She looked incredible! She could be the belle of any debutant party.

Slick seated Claudette, and likewise I seated Svetlana. The table looked quite impressive, all done with silver, candlesticks, and china plates. Slick made the comment that Claudette had changed her mind and cooked a meal in her old fashioned way. He told us, "She's expecting someone from her people."

As he said that Claudette stood raising her glass and said, "To my fellow outcast. From the land of our forefathers. I bid you welcome, clan brother."

Slick had no idea what was happening. I stood and raised my glass and stated, "From the blood in my veins, I have been accepted by my clan sister, and I recognize her right to my life, as hers belongs to me, and we belong to our people."

Slick almost fell out of his chair. "Why did you not tell me before, my brother?" he said.

I laughed, "It just never came up, Slick, but from my point of view, I don't want to talk about it now. This is not the time to talk of these things. This is Svetlana's time, my friends, let's talk about that."

It was a superb meal, topped off by Svetlana and Slick leaving for the party, although I fear it did not go quite as the parents had planned. They had planned a separation party. To me it was a normal thing. To those involved, I'm afraid they took a different view. Slick brought Svetlana into the hall. As he told it, all of the girls began talking, but it was Francie who started it.

"Where's Boots?" she asked. She turned to look at the other parents and not her own.

Svetlana spoke up very loud and very clear, "He was not invited by anyone in this room, and he's the one who should be here." With that, a look of rage came over her, and as she said goodbye to the other girls and told them in a voice that could have started an ice age, "Ask your parents why he's not here. I love you all and I'm going to do what Boots expects all of us do. Have a good life and be good women and put the past in our pockets and use it to pad our behinds, as Boots said. I will pray for you all. I must now leave you to be with Boots. He will be taking me home tomorrow. Goodbye and may God bless and watch over you all."

Slick said, with that she turned to him and said, "I am ready to go now, Mr. Slick. Would you be so kind as to take me home?" With that, they left.

When they came back to the Château and I heard this story, I was upset with myself for letting Svetlana overhear Slicks and my discussion on the terrace. I went to her on the terrace where I found her in tears. As I tucked this little girl under my arm, much as I had done to my wife, to Nadia, and to Daria. I said, "Oh, my little one. Life is not fair is it? Or it doesn't seem so. But, it is not all that bad either. I'm sorry your last night with your friends was ruined by me."

She started to speak and I put one finger against her lips to shush her, "Not to say a word, little one, until I'm done. It is not a bad thing, you know. It is natural for mothers and fathers not to want anyone around that reminds them of the truth, especially when the truth is bad. We have, I think, talked about this before, so do not blame them. They are only trying to forget and justify what they do, but remember, little Misha, I had the joy of coming to your rescue and of bringing you home, and for me that's enough."

Sobbing she replied, "Boots, no one stood for you, but us girls."

"I know," I said, "the clan is a dying thing, little one. They no longer seek the right, but the riches. It is sometimes so, and Helvi and Heilgrid do not care enough to do it either. It is okay. Dry your eyes, my soft hearted child. It will be fine. Tomorrow is a brand new start. For you, it will be the beginning of a great new adventure."

She sniffled and dabbed at her eyes. "And what about you, Boots?"

I smiled and said, "Ah, my little one, there are other lost lambs in this world that I must go and find and then return them home to where they need to be. The thanks is not in the party, Misha, but in the returning. So, are you better now? For I speak the truth of it."

From behind me I could hear Claudette, "He is a descendent of the great knights of our people, Svetlana. He is a seeker of the truth, the light, and the way. His is to struggle against the evil of this world, and he chooses to do his work by combating those who would do evil. He fights those who would buy, sell, and steal humans. It is his way. Do not be sad, but be happy that he does this. It is his calling and his duty." Never a truer statement was made. It was my way of life.

Svetlana seemed to calm down at hearing Claudette say those words. "Then now, little one, dry your eyes and do not be sad. It is a good thing," and with that Svetlana turned and hugged me. She then ran off.

Claudette came near to me saying, "It is so cut and dried for you, my brother. What you just did for that girl will always remain in my heart. You are a good man, Boots, and for that I will always love you and keep you in my heart."

I smiled and replied, "It always bothers me to be thanked, or for people to think I'm different. I think everyone should follow their true path."

Right then it came to me, the words from my father who had long ago passed, "It's the little miracles, Boots. It's the little ones that add up." I had to agree with my father.

With a deep sigh, I asked, "Claudette, is there any café, my sister?"

She smiled and answered, "For you always, my brother."

CHAPTER THIRTY

Once again, my night had begun with too much coffee, along with too many cigarettes. In time, morning came with the familiar scream. I went through my routine and then found Svetlana. Knowing the answer, I asked her, "Are you getting excited, Svetlana?"

She squealed, "Oh, yes. I can hardly wait!"

I smiled at her and said, "Well, we'll be flying from Marseilles to Paris, and an hour and a half later, we will be on our way."

As I bid Claudette farewell, she said, "I will never forget you, Boots."

I laughed and hugged her back, and said, "Of course you won't! I'll be back to talk of old legends. When men were men."

She smiled her beautiful smile, "And I will be looking forward to your arrival, my brother."

I told her, "And I will be looking forward to my return, my sister." Then, we were on our way.

All of a sudden Svetlana seemed afraid. Slick saw this, and asked, "What is the matter?"

In a worried voice, she asked, "What if they won't accept my papers."

Boldly, Slick said, "These are bona fide papers, my dear. With not only the French seal, but your papers from America are stamped with their great seal. They are not false papers, Svetlana. They are yours for real."

She calmed down to a bubbling cauldron. Slick and I smiled to each other.

He told me, "Your things will be shipped to your home, my brother, along with presents for your wife, and your family."

I shook his hand warmly, "Thank you, Slick."

Almost embarrassed, he answered, "It is of little concern, my brother."

At 07:30 hours I bid my friend goodbye. The journey almost at an end, but for me only to begin again somewhere new.

Svetlana and I went through customs. We had nothing to declare and our papers were stamped. Without question, the signature on her papers was nothing to challenge. When immigration stamped Svetlana's and my papers, she let out a small barely audible sigh.

As is usually done, he asked, "I hope your stay was satisfactory?"

He handed me my papers and I said, "Yes, it has been most rewarding."

If he only knew how rewarding it had been for me! We went down the jet way to the hatchway of our freedom bird. When we were inside, we turned and went to the rear of the plane where it was customary for me to ensconce myself, for reasons already stated. The plane began its taxi. Svetlana was staring out the window with a childlike amazement. We picked up speed, and in my own mind I said, "Rotate." When the plane reached its cruising altitude, we were flying towards Paris, where we were to fly back to New York, on the Concorde.

Svetlana did not know this, but what is one more surprise? The flight was flawless, as was the landing. Like always, I deplaned last with Svetlana's hand in mine. We were in the international terminal, so there were no more customs or immigration stops here, but two men came up with very official secret police identifications. They presented them to us at the complement of the French government to ensure our safety. There was a name mentioned, however, only I would know Slick's real name. This little, big-hearted French man had not forgotten one step anywhere along the way, and I was very grateful. We were escorted into the La Presidente restaurant where we sat, and ate a light snack, followed by coffee for me, and tea for my lady, Svetlana.

The call came to board. She had no idea it was the Concorde until we boarded the plane. It was not my first time on this bird, but it was nerve-racking nonetheless, for some reason. It would be my last. I did not enjoy flying in this plane, but it is nice to leave Paris and land in New York in time for a mid-afternoon lunch. I thanked our advisors, and they shook hands with me.

It came out of nowhere, "See you on the flipside."

"On the other side, my brother," I said automatically. "I'll be damned," I thought.

As I turned and Svetlana and I boarded this unusually high-speed craft, she was startled by the idea that she would be in the land of her dreams in four hours. We were shown our seats. I could see Svetlana's nerves were on maximum overdrive, and I had to help her get the seatbelt on. She was vibrating. I finished buckling her belt. I leaned over and kissed her on the forehead and told her, "You will be home in four hours, little one, so you just sit back and try to relax. I haven't lied to you once. I withheld the truth once, but only once. This is a great ride."

The engines were started. A great vibration began, as usual. It was not a bad vibration, but one of pure, raw power. We began the taxiing out maneuver, and then we were cleared for takeoff. The digital mach speed indicator readout was on, but it was registering zero, and then it began. That scream from the engines of the plane, begging to roll. A feeling of infinite speed and power wanting to just get gone. At one-hundred and seventy-five knots, I said, "Rotate." The nose of the plane came up, and the Concorde began to claw for the heavens. There is no feeling on earth like this.

The plane gained altitude. There was little let up in our fight to gain the thin atmosphere where this bird flew, far above the regular planes. Planes far below us were flying at eight miles above the Earth. We were at eleven miles up, moving at a level of speed only obtained by fighter aircraft. At Mach two point five, we were traveling at an earthshaking eighteen-hundred miles per hour or more. When I told Svetlana, her eyes bulged at the thought.

I asked, "What is it, little one? What now is bothering you?"

Almost breathless, she replied, "It's happening, Boots. My dream is coming true."

I looked into her still innocent face, "I hope you are not disappointed, little one. You know the old saying, be careful what you wish for, you might get it."

She shook her head, "Boots it cannot be worse than Russia, and could never be as bad as where I was before you saved me."

I smiled and said gently, "No, it's not that bad, little one. That I promise. Not yet anyways."

After a while, I glanced at my watch. I chuckled.

Svetlana asked, "What is so funny?"

I answered, "I wonder where the kitchen is on this bird. Lunch should be served shortly," and it was. I had ordered a steak for Svetlana and a salad for me. Along with our meals I ordered a gallon of coffee and milk for the little one, and to me she was. As all people become. At least those that I go to find, they become my family. Safely returned, and carefully saved in my journals, and the photos in my mind. Some were not happy endings. They just aren't, as much as I want them to be. They're not.

Time passed and I started to feel the usual signs we were descending.

With a panic, Svetlana turned to me, "What is wrong with the plane, Boots? We're falling!"

I patted her hand and assured her, "No little one. Soon you will see the shore of the land you have longed for. Your mama is there, and so is the rest of your family. It's home, baby, you're almost home."

Just then the shore she had traveled this horrendous journey trying to get to came into view. Well, she could now see it, and she cried. This happened much to the annoyance of some of the other passengers. I told them to go stuff it. They had no idea and no right to say anything. They had no clue as to how blessed they had been in their lives! Unlike this girl, who had suffered such a brutal assault trying to attain, not just for herself, but for her mother, America.

While the plane descended, I comforted this lost girl who had been found. We descended lower. We were on our final run and coming in for a landing. Svetlana had a death grip on my left hand that I'm afraid could not be duplicated by anyone. As the nose of the plane cantilevered down and the attitude of the jet became like a big glider, it was only moments before landing. Ah. There. That impact. That said, it was good to be on the ground, now I can rest. It's funny, what things run through your mind. It had been ninety days plus since my journey had began, and here I was with what I left to go get and bring back. It is after all, another day in the world. And it will continue for a while yet.

The plane taxied to the jet way. The other passengers debarked, but I waited to be last and Svetlana was second. We passed through the hatchway. I breathed deep and filled my lungs. It was a breath of free air, once again. I looked at my charge and helped her to get her customs papers in order.

She stepped up to the immigration man, who joyfully and quite loudly stated, "An immigrant! Welcome to America, young lady, and I'm proud to welcome you to your new home." He

winked at her and said, "It's the best part of my job."

While Svetlana waited for me, he asked who I was.

I told him, "I happened to be in France when her papers came through. I'm just a friend of the family with the great fortune to ride home to America with the daughter of my friend."

He smiled. "Welcome home, sir."

With those words spoken, I walked with Svetlana to the portal and told her, "Well, go ahead, little one. It's your dream coming true. Get going. Your mom is just outside, about seventy-five feet down that runway. Don't worry about me. Go."

She turned and ran. It was the last few feet of a journey that had started with a dream and had almost ended in tragedy, except for one sticking point in the way. A true staunch supporter of truth and freedom. Me.

It was not to be quite so easy for me to disappear from the operation named for this girl. As she greeted her mother and the rest of her family, Daria walked back to get me. A man in tears of pride for his country.

Where this girl had dreamed of being, and a man who was raised to do the right thing. Boots. It's the little miracles. It's the little miracles that add up. I quit crying and walked the long walk down the ramp way with Daria.

I was greeted like a member of the family, along with a conquering hero which made me very uncomfortable. I did notice the absence of one key player. Gregor was nowhere to be found or seen. As this crowd of family and friends greeted and hugged Svetlana, they quite literally were beating me up pretty well. If they were not pummeling my back, they were hugging me and kissing my cheeks. Daria led me to a car, with a huge smile and a firm grasp on my left arm.

When we got into the car, Daria began to cry. I asked, "What's wrong Daria?"

Through her tears she answered, "I'm just so happy. Happy you did not get killed."

I smiled, "Well, me too!"

She looked into my eyes, "But, you brought Svetlana home. I'm so proud of you, Boots!"

Then I received a dozen more cheek kisses. As we drove to Gregor's home, I don't believe that Daria could have gotten any closer to me without a skin graft!

We pulled into the drive at the citadel. There seemed to be a very large number of people outside of Gregor's house. Adding the ones from the airport with these made quite an impressive crowd.

I asked, "Who are all of these people, Daria?"

She said, "They are mostly friends, Boots, but many are family."

When the car in front of us pulled ahead and stopped, there was Alexi and Boris escorting guests into the house. Svetlana and Sasha exited the car in front of us.

We pulled up and Alexi looked at me, smiled, and stuck out his hand, "Welcome home, sir, and congratulations."

I shook his hand warmly, "Thank you, Alexi."

I helped Daria out of the car. She never lost her grip for a moment.

We went through the door after Svetlana and Sasha, and I immediately saw Gregor with his arms open and tears in his eyes. He was overjoyed to say the least. In fact, a little too much overjoyed for being just an uncle. Out of nowhere, the picture Sasha had shown me of her husband and Svetlana came to mind. Although, it hit me that there was a difference. Then it jumped out at me from nowhere. This was not just Svetlana's uncle. He was Sasha's husbands and Svetlana's fathers, brother, and his twin! Since Svetlana's father was a very happy and outgoing man, Gregor must have inherited the dark twin traits. That of being stoic and far less demonstrative. Damn! The truth had been there all along. I had just plain missed it. I had missed the evidence. I guess I could not see the tree for the forest in this case.

The beginning of the party was just starting. It seemed that everyone would mingle and listen to ensemble music until dinner was served. After dinner was to be a prayer time. Then we could do whatever we wanted. Dance, snacks, or drinking.

Daria pulled me aside and explained to me that I was in bad need of a shave, shower, "and Boots, please put on some nice clothes. Like your tux."

I could promise you this, there was no way I was putting on a monkey suit tonight! For any reason! I told Daria what I planned to do. I was going to wear my black suit and shirt, along with my cowboy boots and my black cowboy hat. Daria looked disappointed, but Svetlana came over and commented that she thought it was perfect. Without further adieu, I retired for a little while to my room.

I have to admit upon thinking about it, everyone did seem to be in nice suits for men, along with the women wearing gowns and their finery. As I dressed, there was a knock on my door. I asked, "Who is it."

I heard a young female voice say, "It is Svetlana, Boots." I yelled back, "I'm almost ready, darlin', but you can come in.

I'm decent."

Svetlana swept into my room. "Boots, you look beautiful."

I smiled and replied, "And you're a dreamboat in that gown, my dear. I think Daria will be jealous of you."

She smiled back and said, "No. She sent me to get you. Uncle Gregor said it is only fitting that you escort me into the dining room."

As I gazed at this young lady who was part of my life, I said, "My lady. May I escort you to the dining hall for our evening repast?"

Svetlana blushed a little because of my bow, but she curtsied and said, "It would be an honor, sir."

We took the elevator to the second floor and then proceeded down the steps into an empty hallway heading for the newly decorated dining room. As we entered the archway facing the hall, there was a huge sound made by the clapping hands in the room. I wanted to crawl into a deep hole and cover it over. I do not like public demonstration, especially if it has to do with me. There were six steps to the main floor. Gregor was on Svetlana's side and Sasha was on my side. We gained the bottom step onto the floor. Gregor of course, stuck out his arm for Svetlana to hold onto. Likewise, I offered my arm to Sasha.

We proceeded to the head of the table, with Gregor seating Sasha to his left around the table end. Likewise, I seated Svetlana on Gregor's right. Gregor sat in the middle quite alone. I was to sit to Svetlana's right side and then Daria in turn to my right. There was a young woman of Svetlana's age sitting to Sasha's left. Likewise, a man that seemed to be older sitting to her left. As the seven of us sat down the others seemed to know where they were supposed to sit. I had not been to a formal dinner like this for a long time. It must have occurred to Gregor that I would feel like a goldfish in a pint jar being filmed, however he took no notice of my discomfort.

Dinner had started at 19:00 hours. It was now 21:45 hours, with dinner coming to a close. There was activity behind Gregor. There was a ten by sixteen foot platform with three steps around it. There was also a lectern in the center of this platform. While the plates were being cleared away, there was some discussion going on between Gregor and a man who was setting up the platform.

Gregor stood, "Ladies and gentlemen, I must leave for a few moments. There are some things I must take care of before the next part of the welcome home for our Svetlana, and the man who made it possible."

As the dishes were cleared off, new wine glasses were placed in front of each person. Since the tables were set up in a U pattern, with Gregor's table at the head and two tables were joined on each end. Somewhat like a U to be sure. I was sure that it would take quite some time to clear the table and place the glasses, however I was wrong. It had only taken fifteen minutes to clean up, with the glasses set, four carts with wine appeared at each table. These wine bottles had already been opened in order to let them breathe. While the waiters stood by their carts, Gregor returned.

Gregor did not sit, but picked up a small knife and rapped his goblet. "Ladies and gentlemen." A few moments later he rapped on his glass again and spoke much louder. "Ladies and gentlemen, if I may have your attention. It now comes time for our good father to speak to us."

As I watched the very priest that I had uttered those infamous words in front of, to whom I had made a spectacle of myself. As he approached the dais, he had a bible in one hand and another in his left hand. He stepped up onto the platform and walked to the lectern. He put the books onto the reader plate and leafed through one and then the other.

He spoke, "Would you all please stand? Let us pray."

As the priest read the prayer, he turned to his right and Gregor came out in what looked like a uniform jacket with a sash on it. After the prayer, two likewise attired men came up to the table where I was seated. They asked if I would come with them. I looked at Daria and she had a coy smile on her face, likewise Svetlana and Sasha. As I stood, they took up positions on either side of me, and then escorted me up the center aisle. When we reached the platform I was asked to stop. I must admit I was mystified by what was happening. There had been no warning of this. I was at a total loss.

The priest began another prayer. When it was finished Gregor came over to me and asked me to follow him and do as he asked. I was still quite in the dark about what was going on. He led me to a certain spot just to the left of the lectern. There was a heavy thick rug there. As I stood there Gregor just said, "Do as the priest says, my friend." Looking at the priest he was speaking of Saint Gregory the Great. Although, I did not have much knowledge of this saint. The priest came and stood in front of me. "Kneel, my son."

As I knelt, all I said was, "Bless me father."

With those words, Gregor brought a sword forth to hand to the priest and as the priest said, "Hero of the weak, protector of the faith," He then touched both sides of my shoulders with the sword. "Let it be known, that this man has been found to be worthy. Rise, Sir Knight."

This I could not understand. This was only done in the middle ages.

"You my son, have now received a knighthood in the order of Saint Gregory the Great. You received this for your courage and faith. For your steadfast resistance to evil. For letting nothing of man stand in your way as you do God's work. It is said, my son, suffer unto me the little children for they are the lambs of God. And you, my son, are a Good Sheppard." He blessed me, and made the sign of the cross on my forehead and likewise my chest. He said, "Turn and be recognized." As I turned, there was an uproar from the crowd.

Around my neck was the ribbon with the medallion of Saint Gregory. I had naught to say. I was dumbstruck, to say the least. Add that to bewildered, then you can guess how I felt. All I wanted to do was leave and not be seen. However, the best I could do was to be escorted away from this spot by Daria and Svetlana. As I write about this, it seems like a dream, until I pick up the medallion.

With the ceremony completed, there was a general exodus from the room, although I sat completely transfixed staring at the table. There seemed to be a tug on my arms, not only from my right, but also from my left. As I rather blearily looked into Daria's eyes I began to snap out of it.

"Boots! Are you alright? Come on. You have to go with Uncle Gregor for a little while."

I answered, "What for now, Daria?"

She whispered, "You have to get your new jacket on."

Agreeing I said, "Oh. Okay."

Walking away from Daria and Svetlana with Gregor, I heard Svetlana ask Daria, "Is he going to be okay?"

Daria answered, "Yes, he will be fine. He's just not used to being thanked by many people other than his family."

Svetlana nodded, "I know that to be true. He told me what would happen while we were on the boat."

Daria said softly, "He's always right, Misha."

That was what I had heard before I passed through the door. I put on my tunic and I must admit that it was pretty ornate and striking. Let's face it, for me it was a trip at the very least. For the next five hours it was talking and dancing, along with handshakes, congratulations, and chapped cheeks from kisses by well intentioned women of all ages. It should be mentioned that the first dance was to be mine and Sasha's, with Gregor and Svetlana. It is what started this shindig! For me, well the last dance of the night was the best. It was my waltz with Svetlana and then Daria, my two little ones. As I retired for the night, I could not sleep as the others did. I wandered the halls and rooms of this great house looking for the answers that always seemed to be elusive to me.

Coming into the kitchen in a semi daze looking for coffee, I found a shoulder to rest my troubles on. My good Alexi. The salt of the Earth and my kind of people. Those I can relate to. When he saw me, he rose and bowed.

I sighed, "Stop Alexi. Please. I've had enough of this."

As he looked up, he smiled, "I am proud of you, Boots. I mean, sir."

I smiled at him, "I'm not sure what I am Alexi. I need a good cup of coffee and some Russian music. Not the symphony either! I need Russian peasant music. I'm just a peasant, Alexi.

No matter what, I am a peasant. I like it that way. It makes it easy not to be confused."

Alexi nodded, "I agree, sir."

I felt relief, "Thank you, Alexi."

After getting to my room, I took my alarm clock and turned it off and then put it in my closet. After a quick shower, I got ready for bed. When I pulled back my covers, I found a note. I got into bed, but before going to sleep I read it. It was signed, "Your servant for life and your best friend, Svetlana." I locked it into my briefcase, in its own compartment and I drifted off to sleep.

With morning came the scream. I glanced at my watch and found it was late, by my standards. It was 05:14 hours. Today, the part of the clan that could come would be coming in for their day in the sun. I was sure that it would be quite a party for them. For me, I could not go through another night like that.

It was much reminiscent to the day I was at my base in the States after I had returned from Vietnam. When at morning formation I received two medals for heroism in combat. They gave me a ninety-six hour pass. I was glad. I wanted no recognition for getting them. I was self-conscious about the backslapping and congratulations for receiving them. I had no intention of reliving the moments when I had earned them, or mentioning the dead that I could not save. I have never nor will I consider myself a hero or someone special. I am just a guy who does what's right.

I knew the last of the clan would be here by 16:00 hours. My flight would leave La Guardia at 18:20 hours heading west. Homebound at last! I knew my precious wife and my Nadia would be waiting in Seattle. Lee had already left two days ago for Nadia's. There would only be time for giving thanks to my friends and fond farewells to all. I had already picked up another rescue case, and time was burning, and the flame needed to be put out.

When I boarded my flight it was with many mixed emotions for all those of whom I had helped to bring home. But in severing my ties with two Russian ladies who would remain in my heart until time itself ended, it must be said here and now, without the work and help of the clan none of this would have been possible. They believe in an ideal and they believe in me, but at the forefront and most importantly none of us could live with the idea or thought of a little Russian girl being trapped by her dream.

The End

www.ingramcontent.com/pod-product-compliance
Lightning Source LLC
Chambersburg PA
CBHW051133120626
46547CB00012B/791